CONSTITUTIONAL LIMITS ON COERCIVE INTERROGATION

CONSTITUTIONAL LIMITS ON COERCIVE INTERROGATION

Amos N. Guiora

OXFORD
UNIVERSITY PRESS

OXFORD
UNIVERSITY PRESS

Oxford University Press, Inc., publishes works that further Oxford University's objective of excellence
in research, scholarship, and education.

Oxford New York
Auckland   Cape Town   Dar es Salaam   Hong Kong   Karachi   Kuala Lumpur   Madrid   Melbourne
Mexico City   Nairobi   New Delhi   Shanghai   Taipei   Toronto

With offices in
Argentina   Austria   Brazil   Chile   Czech Republic   France   Greece   Guatemala   Hungary   Italy
Japan   Poland   Portugal   Singapore   South Korea   Switzerland   Thailand   Turkey   Ukraine
Vietnam

Published by Oxford University Press, Inc., 198 Madison Avenue, New York, New York 10016
www.oup.com

Oxford is a registered trademark of Oxford University Press

Library of Congress Cataloging-in-Publication Data
Guiora, Amos N., 1957–
    Constitutional limits on coercive interrogation / by Amos N. Guiora.
      p. cm.
    Includes bibliographical references and index.
    ISBN-13: 978-0-19-534031-0 (alk. paper) 1. Police questioning—United States—History. 2. Criminal
investigation—United States. 3. Due process of law—United States. 4. Military interrogation—United
States. 5. Torture (International law) 6. Detention of persons—United States. 7. Prisoners of war—Legal
status, laws. etc.—United States. 8. War on Terrorism, 2001—Law and legislation—United States. I. Title.
    KF9625.G85 2008
    345.73′052—dc22

                                                                                              2008003516

1 2 3 4 5 6 7 8 9

Printed in the United States of America on acid-free paper

You may order this or any other Oxford University Press publication by
visiting the Oxford University Press website at www.oup.com

One cannot go through life without mentors. I have been very fortunate to have three such powerful figures in various stages of my life: my father, AZG, who has been a constant source of unending wisdom and knowledge; Professor Lewis Katz who both as my teacher when I was a law student at Case Western Reserve and later as my colleague at Case became what my family refers to as my "virtual father"; and Professor Gerald Korngold who as dean at Case graciously and generously opened the doors of academia for me.

CONTENTS

Preface   *ix*
Acknowledgments   *xiii*

1. Introduction   *1*

2. Introducing the Hybrid Paradigm and the Historical
    Analogy   *9*

3. Application of the Hybrid Paradigm   *33*

4. Interrogations in the History of American Criminal Law:
    Adding Historical Perspective from an Examination of
    African American Interrogations in the Deep South   *45*

5. Interrogation Standards of the Fifth and Fourteenth
    Amendments Applied to Both Citizens and Noncitizens   *65*

6. Coercive Interrogation, Threats, and Cumulative
    Mistreatment   *83*

7. Torture   *105*

8. Interrogation Methods and the Eighth Amendment   *129*

9. International Law Pertaining to Torture and
    Interrogation   *141*

10. Concluding Recommendations   *149*

Index   *163*

PREFACE

How we interrogate "post-9/11" detainees is the fundamental question in balancing the inherent tension of national security considerations against individual civil and political rights. More significantly, the interrogation measures we adopt define who we are as a society. Do we violate the rights of those we have detained? Do the ends always justify the means in trying to obtain information we think a detainee may have?

More than six years after 9/11, we are still discussing these questions. As some commentators have noted, it is surprising—if not astonishing—that the interrogation debate is still ongoing. In truth, we are still in the baby steps of the debate.

The confirmation hearings for Attorney General Mukasey highlighted this issue. Rather than unequivocally stating that waterboarding is torture, Judge Mukasey chose to skirt around the issue. The past six years have displayed mental gymnastics that have generated a nod and a wink approach to counterterrorism interrogations. The pictures from Abu Ghraib were not an aberration; rather they both reflected and were the result of a pervasive atmosphere created by the White House.

Despite the heated atmosphere of the current American political dialogue, we must step back and examine where we are with respect to operational counterterrorism. This is particularly true regarding interrogations. This book seeks to address that very gap. The gap exists with respect to the legal and policy aspects of counterterrorism and the public's perception and understanding of the issue.

The issue of interrogation is misunderstood, misrepresented, and often the object of political spin. The topic is too important to be left to misinformation and disinformation. It is time to address the issue rationally, concretely, and concisely.

In attempting to do so, I looked back into American history. As the pages that follow describe, the experience of African Americans in the detention settings (the backwoods, the back of the sheriff's car, or the jail cell) of the Deep South yesteryear offers an effective historical analogy regarding the roughly 25,000 detainees the United States is holding worldwide. Although historical analogies are not free of controversy, they are effective in explaining current affairs.

The historical analogy is also helpful in explaining the core focus of this book—the constitutional limits of interrogation. In addressing the limits of interrogation, my fundamental premise is that detainees have rights: not *mere* rights, but rather constitutional protections and privileges. The protections to be extended emanate from the Sixth, Eighth, and Fourteenth Amendments.

Does that suggest that the detainees deserve the same rights as American citizens? No, but this premise does argue that the consistent denial of protections to the detainees is both unconscionable and illegal. The constitutional argument proposed in this book is based on the fact that the United States has held these individuals in various detention centers worldwide. Although not held *in* the United States, they are held *by* the United States. They are subject to interrogation by U.S. military and civilian personnel. If brought to trial, they would be tried by courts of U.S. jurisdiction.

In the historical analogy, the Supreme Court's belated granting of constitutional protections to African Americans was enormously important in an effort to protect what was then an otherwise unprotected class. Some of those very protections need to be extended to today's otherwise unprotected class.

To impact the public debate, a book cannot be only theoretical. It must propose practical recommendations. I offer two such recommendations. First, define the detainees as neither criminals nor soldiers. To resolve this quandary, I advocate the adoption of what I call the *hybrid paradigm*, which seeks to resolve the status of detainees, their rights, how they can be interrogated, and how they can ultimately be brought to trial. The hybrid paradigm suggests extending to a detainee certain rights predicated on criminal and international law. It also offers a concrete recommendation under what conditions and where post-9/11 detainees can be tried.

The second recommendation addresses the limits of interrogation. The coercive interrogation regime proposed in these pages reflects a balance between the two critical rights that are the essence of counterterrorism conducted by civil, democratic society subject to the rule of law. The coercive interrogation regime is neither *torture lite*; nor is it the traditional interrogation associated with the criminal law paradigm. Rather, it suggests interrogation methods—subject to strict scrutiny and control—in accordance with the hybrid paradigm.

My twenty-year career in the Israel Defense Force Judge Advocate General Corps included postings as a prosecutor in the West Bank Military Court prosecuting Palestinians suspected of crimes ranging from rock-throwing to murdering Israel Defense Force (IDF) soldiers, Israeli civilians, or Palestinians suspected of collaborating with Israel; as a judge in the Gaza Strip Military Court hearing cases against Palestinians accused of the above crimes, and lastly as the Legal Advisor to the Gaza Strip where, among other responsibilities, I had command responsibility for the military prosecutor. During the course of this career, I gained intimate working knowledge of interrogations, interrogators, and interrogatees.

My twenty years of legal, policy, and operational counterterrorism have shown me the paramount importance of the interrogation setting. The legal, judicial, and operational paradigms applied to interrogations define the essence of civil, democratic society. It is the ultimate manifestation of the moral compass. A society that crosses a line in the sand with respect to what can and cannot be done in the name of national security will lose its moral upper hand. It can also suffer operationally—both tactically and strategically.

Although the questions addressed here are difficult, a liberal democratic society must confront them. Otherwise, the slippery slope beckons us, and once on this slippery slope, it is all but impossible to turn around. Approaching the edge of the slippery slope is also dangerous. There is no doubt that society—public and leadership alike—must protect itself from many legitimate threats, both internal and external. How society protects itself and what limits it, described as "self-imposed restraints," is a question of enormous importance that the government and public must address.

AMOS N. GUIORA

ACKNOWLEDGMENTS

In writing this book, I have been very fortunate to have surrounded myself with an extraordinarily loyal group of friends and colleagues. The book's genesis was in an earlier project that resulted in the publication of an article, "Interrogating the Detainees: Extending a Hand or a Boot." To my great fortune, I was able to cajole and convince three individuals, whose efforts were critical to the writing of the article, to devote their time and energy to this book. In addition, I asked three friends and colleagues to read and comment on the manuscript.

Brian Field and Erin Page, both Case Law graduates, worked with me for the past several years, and both graciously agreed to continue with this book project after graduation. Their efforts both as researchers and editors (for the article and book alike) were of enormous importance. Although both have day jobs, their commitment to making this project happen was critical to its completion. For that, I owe Brian and Erin an enormous thank you. I am fortunate to have such loyal students agree to work with me *after* their graduation. Brian's efforts with the book truly made him the ball carrier, and for that I am forever grateful.

Professor Martha Minow of Harvard Law School was the initiator and nurturer of the article project; with respect to this book, she read the manuscript in its various stages. As a mentor and friend, Professor Minow's comments significantly contributed to the final product.

Dan Barr, a partner with Perkins Cole Brown & Bain, U.S. Army Col. (Ret.) Dennis Tomcik, and Ted Wasky, the Special Agent in Charge of the Federal Bureau of Investigation (FBI)'s office in Cleveland before he retired—three friends and colleagues volunteered themselves (at my request) to read and comment on the manuscript. I asked them to do so because they have different professional expertise, all relevant to the issues the book seeks to address. I am deeply indebted to them for their time, effort, and candor. Special thanks to Dan's secretary at Perkins Cole, Sharon Neilson, for wonderful logistical support.

Needless to say the comments—substantive and editorial—made the book better. Ultimately, all faults and errors are mine alone.

The completion of this project was greatly facilitated by a generous summer stipend from the S. J. Quinney College of Law, the University of Utah. Many thanks to my good friend, Dean Hiram Chodosh for his vision and support in awarding me the stipend. Dean Chodosh's gracious and generous welcome when I joined the S. J. Quinney faculty this fall greatly facilitated completion of this project and has created an environment that will enormously contribute to future scholarship.

Many thanks to my editor, Chris Collins, for suggesting the project, facilitating the approval process, and then giving me the space to work on the book.

AMOS N. GUIORA

CHAPTER 1

Introduction

As the theme of this book is the coercive interrogation of suspected terrorists, it is important to engage in a broad discussion concerning terrorism. That discussion must begin with a definition of terrorism.[1] The working definition for this book will be: "terrorism is a deliberate attack intended to kill, injure, or cause property damage to innocent civilians and/or the deliberate psychological intimidation of the innocent civilian population by a terrorist organization for the sake of advancing a social, political, or religious cause."

In developing and analyzing counterterrorism strategies, of which interrogation is a critical component, decision makers and the public must come to grips with the following reality: the so-called and misnamed War on Terrorism cannot be won.[2] At best, terrorism can be marginalized or minimized with "good days and bad days," suggesting that some terrorist attacks will be successful—others unsuccessful. It is impossible to *kill them all*. Furthermore, in the context of the rule of law, suspected terrorists have rights. How many rights will be a theme discussed in this book;

---

[1] There is much debate concerning the definition of terrorism, more than 109 have been identified.

[2] Misnamed because under international law, "war" can only be conducted between states, and terrorists, even if state supported, are not states.

1

what is critical to remember is that an individual subjected to interrogation is still only a suspect.

Intelligence gathering, of which interrogation is a critical aspect, can be described as a jigsaw puzzle, which requires the assembling of bits and pieces of disparate, enormously complex, information. It is greatly complicated by the danger of possible attack hanging over the intelligence community. Lawful coercive interrogation, as I propose in this book, can significantly contribute to the prevention of a planned attack and the conviction of an individual involved in terrorism. It cannot, however, prevent all terrorist attacks.

Torture, which has been offered by some as an antidote for terrorism, is illegal, immoral, and does not lead to actionable intelligence. In addition, the blurring of lines between the permissible and impermissible as others have advocated, does a fundamental disservice to the general public, political leaders, and the interrogators themselves.

Coercive interrogation, as this book proposes, is the implementation of lawful interrogation methods, intended to enable the state to most effectively protect itself against the twin threats of terrorism and an unfettered executive. An unfettered executive will advocate a *by all means necessary* interrogation regime—devoid of constitutional protections, Congressional oversight, and judicial review. Conversely, a regime premised on the rule of law understands the constitutional—and moral— requirement of the limits of interrogation. Coercive interrogation achieves the following: it enables a lawful balancing of the legitimate rights of the individual with the equally legitimate national security rights of the state. As such, it protects suspect and society alike.

As I will articulate in this book, the Supreme Court's holding in *Hamdan v. Rumsfeld*[3] is the modern day version of *Youngstown Sheet & Tube Co. v. Sawyer*,[4] in seeking to limit executive privilege and power in war time. Although the Court's history of active judicial review in times of armed conflict has left much to be desired, this book is written with an eye toward the day that U.S. Supreme Court justices will adopt the Israeli model of active judicial review. That model is premised on a court actively engaged in reviewing the actions of the executive. Furthermore, the U.S. Congress, in the aftermath of 9/11, largely neglected its constitutionally

---

[3] 542 U.S. 507 (2006).
[4] 343 U.S. 579 (1952).

mandated responsibility of checks and balances by failing to engage in oversight of the executive.

The lack of active judicial review and congressional unwillingness to fulfill its Constitutional responsibility significantly contributed to the failure to develop an interrogation regime premised on limitations. The pictures from Abu Ghraib, the rendition of detainees to U.S. allies that torture, and the policy of torture authorized by the Bush administration, highlight the need to address the issue of interrogation. As terrorism is not going anywhere, now is the time to begin this conversation in a mature and practical fashion.

Who Is the Intended Audience?

This book is written for a cross section of audiences, including policy-makers, the general public, scholars, the media, and interrogators themselves. To ensure reaching out to such disparate audiences, the book is not legal heavy. Nevertheless, as the book's fundamental premise is the granting of constitutional rights and protections to a largely unprotected class, a discussion of the U.S. Constitution is necessary. Further, in a discussion defining the limits of coercive interrogation predicated on the experiences of African Americans in the Deep South, it is necessary to engage in a careful analysis of how the U.S. Supreme Court analyzed and discussed those interrogations. To that end, a discussion concentrating on American judicial history is necessary.

Furthermore, no discussion regarding interrogation in the current historical paradigm would be replete were an analysis of international law and torture not included. Although neither are this book's focus, they are relevant to the conversation that the public must have with itself and with its leaders. To that end, relevant international conventions addressing the rights of the detainees will be discussed. To most effectively present concrete, practical recommendations for articulating a lawful coercive interrogation regime, it will also be necessary to discuss specific interrogation measures.

Although some audiences might have less familiarity than others with the specific issues addressed in each chapter, the book's multidisciplinary approach gives no one audience an advantage over another. The goal is to present this complicated and important issue in a comprehensive and practical fashion.

In addition to the goal of engaging multiple audiences, I also write this book seeking to protect the interrogator from careless national leaders. My tools in doing so are the U.S. Constitution and American history.

After examining post-9/11 discussion and debate regarding interrogations, I am left with the feeling that addressing "what can be done" has been largely untouched. Rather, scholarship and commentary alike have discussed torture *ad nauseam*, rather than concentrating on practical recommendations of how we can conduct interrogations.

To that end, this book articulates the do-able, rather than undo-able, limits of interrogation. The middle ground that is the practical objective of this book has been largely unaddressed for the focus has been on the far "sexier" topic of torture.

The War on Terrorism

In the immediate aftermath of 9/11 President Bush declared "war on terrorism" and boldly (if not arrogantly) proclaimed "bring 'em on." Although the President subsequently suggested that the phrase was ill-chosen, the sentiments undoubtedly reflected a visceral reaction shared by many. Nevertheless, the phrase is highly problematic. I suggests a Wild West approach to an issue requiring sophistication, patience, and an intimate understanding of the limits of power.

A leader's temptation to respond to an act of terrorism is understandable; whether it is effective, viable, and reasonable is a different matter. In discussing terrorism, it is important to differentiate between single-act terrorism and the daily grind type of terrorism.

The events of 9/11 reflect single-act terrorism, whereas the constant bombings in Iraq or Israel reflect daily terrorism. The former is predicated more on symbolic efforts, whereas the latter is based more on life's reality. That is not to deny the tragedy of the loss of innocent life that Tuesday morning nor the damage to America's psyche and the resulting changes in how Americans live their daily lives. Nevertheless, and without diminishing its significance, 9/11 is inherently different from the *constant* dangers faced by Marines patrolling Iraq.

As suggested by others, we are "stuck" with terrorism. To that end, we must engage in candid lessons-learned analysis, facilitating discussion of what we have done well and what needs to improve. What the military refers to as *after-action reports* are critical to understanding how we can most effectively protect ourselves in the context of balancing competing interests and concerns. This is imperative as terrorists are not going to fade away; rather, their success in Iraq has emboldened them to the point that the question is not if another terrorist attack will occur, but when. Although the United States has spent enormous monetary and political capital, many of the fundamental questions regarding terrorism have gone largely unanswered, or at best unsatisfactorily addressed. Perhaps the presidential campaign of 2008 will give this issue the urgency it demands.

To begin addressing the limits of interrogation, the following ten questions must be discussed and hopefully resolved:

1. How does the United States define terrorism? (In addition to the 109 definitions previously alluded to, the Federal Bureau of Investigation [FBI], Department of State, and Department of Defense cannot agree on a definition.)
2. Are those captured (hereinafter referred to as *detainees*) in Afghanistan or Iraq (and perhaps elsewhere) to be granted full criminal rights?
3. Are the detainees to be defined as prisoners of war (POWs) and therefore accorded full Geneva Convention protections or at the least, partial protections, and if so, how "partial"?
4. Will the detainees continue to be tried at Guantanamo Bay by Presidentially mandated military commissions or is an alternative to be developed?
5. Will U.S. constitutional protections and privileges be extended to the detainees and if so, which ones?
6. In determining resource allocation, how is *effectiveness* defined?
7. In undertaking the cost-benefit analysis of operational counterterrorism, how are threats to be determined, defined, and categorized?
8. How is risk assessment to be defined?
9. Does the public understand that, as Justice Brandeis said, "a policeman can't stand at every corner" and therefore terrorist attacks will succeed, and innocent civilians will continue to die?
10. What limits on individual civil rights will be tolerated in balancing the equally legitimate rights of the individual with the national security rights of the state?

Added to that long list of queries is the fundamental question that will concern us: What are the limits of interrogation? Before proceeding, it is important to explain why six years after 9/11 we need a new approach. Precisely because of the importance of the unresolved questions posed above, it is imperative to adopt a new approach to counterterrorism. The immediate response of the Bush administration to 9/11 was panic. The examples are well known: the detention of 5,000 individuals suspected of being Arab Americans; the establishment of military commissions at the expense of running roughshod over the opposition of Judge Advocate Generals of the four services without consulting Congress; the hurried creation of the Department of Homeland Security and Transportation Safety Authority; insistence by Vice President Cheney that Saddam Hussein was linked to 9/11. The responses reflect an administration thoroughly unprepared, therefore lashing out at real and perceived enemies from within and without the United States with equal vengeance.

The Bush administration acted not only with vengeance but with a dangerous view of executive power and disregard for the protections of civil liberties. The very nature of the conflict has not been satisfactorily defined, a failure that is extraordinarily dangerous. The nebulousness that precludes defining the limits of power is particularly problematic in the interrogation context.

More than six years after 9/11, the question is, what has this led to? Are Americans safer? Has Al Qaeda been significantly impacted by American operational actions? Has American counterterrorism proven effective? Has the administration properly balanced the competing rights addressed above? Have the enormously complex dilemmas inherent to how civil, democratic society conducts counterterrorism been addressed?

Despite the significant amount of scholarship and political commentary available regarding this seminal question, the issues have been skirted. The series of memos commonly referred to as the Bybee memos written in the aftermath of 9/11 engaged in nothing more than mental gymnastics.[5]

---

[5] These memos attempt to circumvent laws prohibiting torture through the use of mental gymnastics, stating that:

"For purely mental pain or suffering to amount to torture, it must result in significant psychological harm of significant duration, e.g., lasting for months or even years."

"[E]ven if the defendant knows that severe pain will result from his actions, if causing such harm is not his objective, he lacks the requisite specific intent even though the defendant did not act in good faith. Instead, a defendant is guilty of torture only if he acts with the express purpose of inflicting severe pain or suffering on a person within his custody or physical control."

Those memos—irresponsible in advocating violation of American and international law—authorized torture to be conducted either directly or indirectly by U.S. military personnel, Central Intelligence Agency (CIA) employees, or contractors. They did a fundamental disservice to those most in need of clear instructions—the interrogators themselves.

Although in violation of international law, the policy directive endorsed by the White House and the subsequent series of memos directly authorized by then Secretary of Defense Donald Rumsfeld, were immoral and of highly questionable value. Conversely, the instructual response of the political left that detainees should not be subject to an interrogation paradigm distinct from traditional criminal law similarly reflects an unwillingness to engage in honest and candid debate regarding the limits of interrogation. In addition, it reflects intellectual dishonesty and political immaturity in refusing to carefully—not politically—debate how to define those responsible for 9/11.

No discussion of counterterrorism would be complete without addressing the balancing between the competing tensions—civil rights and national security. Without engaging directly in this discussion, we will ultimately fail to articulate limits to interrogations. Furthermore, we will, as a society, be guilty of subscribing to the much repeated cliché: "what happens in Vegas, stays in Vegas." To that extent, we must engage in careful discussion regarding the rights and status of the detainees.

CHAPTER 2

Introducing the Hybrid Paradigm and the Historical Analogy

An individual accused of involvement in terrorism must be brought to some form of trial, but the American criminal law process is inapplicable to the current conflict.[6] To guarantee the suspect *certain* rights and privileges, the hybrid paradigm would provide the following: (1) lawful coercive interrogation of a suspect granted Miranda[7] protections; (2) remand hearings before a court designed to prevent indefinite detention; (3) the right to counsel of the suspect's own choosing; (4) admissibility of intelligence information into trial; (5) bench trials before specially trained judges; (6) conviction based in part (but not more than 50%) on intelligence information; (7) sentencing guidelines; (8) and right to appeal to an independent judiciary. The hybrid paradigm also calls for the Foreign Intelligence Surveillance Act (FISA) Court[8] to become a domestic terror court premised on a Congressional amendment to Article III of the Constitution.

---

[6] Amos N. Guiora, *Quirin to Hamdan: Creating a Hybrid Paradigm for Detaining Terrorists*, 19 FLA. J. INT'L L. 2 Winter, 2008.

[7] "You have the right to remain silent. Anything you say can and will be used against you in a court of law. You have the right to an attorney. If you cannot afford an attorney, one will be provided for you at interrogation time and at court". Miranda v. Arizona, 384 U.S. 436 (1966).

[8] 50 U.S.C. 1801–1811.

The hybrid paradigm seeks to develop a judicial regime predicated on the requirement to balance competing interests. It is all but impossible to achieve a perfect balance in any context, particularly when innocent civilians are randomly targeted for death and injury. However, that is when society must demand that the executive branch, along with congressional and judicial oversight, balance competing concerns. American history is replete with profound and disturbing examples of the consequences of an unfettered executive responding to attacks on America (the internment of 140,000 Japanese Americans, the Supreme Court's acquiescence in *Korematsu v. United States*[9] and the Palmer Raids[10] in the aftermath of World War I are prime examples).

The hybrid model is critical to the discussion of the limits of interrogation. The hybrid paradigm is premised on the following assumptions:

1. Terrorists are not criminals as understood in the American criminal law paradigm.
2. Terrorists are not POWs according to the Geneva Convention definition.
3. Terrorists must be granted a trial.
4. Counterterrorism is dependent on intelligence information based on human sources [human intelligence (HUMINT)]. Sources are at enormous risk from members of their community who will inevitably define them as collaborators with the enemy and, if possible, commit unspeakable crimes to deter potential collaborators.
5. Traditional jury trials are inappropriate for trying terrorists.
6. Administrative detention of detainees where neither the individual nor his or her attorney is privy to confidential, classified intelligence information justifying detention is the least preferred form of detention.
7. The State must have the tools and means to protect its citizens.
8. Detainees must be guaranteed independent judicial review.
9. Suspect terrorists must be granted certain constitutional rights concerning their interrogation.
10. Indefinite detention is unconstitutional.

---

[9] 323 U.S. 214 (1944).
[10] The Palmer Raids were a series of controversial raids by the U.S. Department of Justice from 1919 to 1921.

Hybrid Paradigm's Practical Advantages

Although a variety of terms have been used over the past six years in conjunction with terrorists including *enemy combatants*, *illegal combatants*, *unlawful combatants*, and *illegal belligerents*, the hybrid paradigm clearly articulates the detainee's status and rights to be granted. Further, in an effort to engage the reader in a practical discussion regarding the limits of interrogation, the constitutional rights articulated in the Fifth and Fourteenth Amendments will be analyzed with respect to the detainee paradigm. In addition, the limits of interrogation will also be discussed in the context of the Eighth Amendment's prohibition on cruel and unusual punishment.

Granting Fifth and Fourteenth Amendments protection to detainees ensures that the right against self-incrimination and guarantee of due process will be extended, even though these individuals are suspected of having committed terrorist acts against Americans. It is precisely the enormous powers of an executive reacting (perhaps wildly, if not blindly) to such an attack that validate the hybrid paradigm. The hybrid paradigm protects both the state and the detainee while ensuring the latter be granted *certain* rights. As our discussion of history will show, the result of not guaranteeing the rights of an otherwise vulnerable and unprotected class is tragic.

The American Deep South

Although I do not suggest that the backwoods of Alabama in the 1930s are identical to Abu Ghraib in 2007, there are disturbing similarities that one ignores at the risk of approaching the *slippery slope*. In both paradigms, injury was wrought on individuals by representatives of the state, the harmed individual possessed minimal outside recourse, the distinction between innocent and guilty was considered superfluous, and individuals in positions of responsibility willfully turned a blind eye to the atrocities.

Intellectual honesty and historical accuracy requires that the reader understand that profound differences exist between the Deep South of eighty years ago and Abu Ghraib. African Americans were subjected to race-predicated interrogations rather than interrogations seeking information. The sheriff whipping the detainee in the car was not seeking information relevant to a crime, but was to inflict maximum pain on an African American solely because of race. Such interrogations were nothing but a masquerade intended to provide the community and its officials with an opportunity to harm an individual who, in all probability, was innocent of any crime. Whether the individual was innocent or guilty, a fair trial was not awaiting him. Nevertheless, and despite the dissimilarity between information-based and race-based interrogations, the similarities are significant enough to justify the historical analogy proposed. Hand in hand with the constitutional protections of the Fifth, Eighth, and Fourteenth Amendments, this book seeks to establish practical limits on interrogation that will prevent the horrible injustice of the past from once again rearing its ugly head.

Defining Terrorism

We must distinguish between various categories of terrorists. Not every detainee can be subjected to the same methods because not every detainee is suspected of presenting the same danger to the state. Although the President declared "War on Terrorism," it would be a stretch to suggest that every detainee held in Abu Ghraib, Guantanamo Bay, and Bagram is an enemy. Similarly, then Secretary of Defense Rumsfeld's unequivocal declaration that those in Guantanamo Bay are the worst of the worst represents classic executive overreaction that endangers detainees and society alike. Or does it?

The U.S. military adopted the approach of "round up the usual suspects" after invading Afghanistan and Iraq. Rather than developing a mechanism where suspects would be screened prior to detention and transported to one of the detention centers, the U.S. military relied on insufficient intelligence and arrested thousands of individuals. In addition, there was no process to satisfactorily assess the specific threat each individual presented to the national security of the United States. Neither was there a process to assess whether the individual presented a *continuing* threat. In other words, two critical decisions, initial detention and continued detention, were largely made without criteria or process.

Although some of those initially detained and subjected to interrogation were members of Al Qaeda and could supply much needed intelligence information regarding the organization, it is equally true that many of those detained were neither Al Qaeda affiliated nor in possession of relevant information. The mass-arrest approach and the administration's assumption of the detainees' guilt was continuously articulated by former Secretary of Defense Rumsfeld. Appearing on *Meet the Press*, Rumsfeld stated that the detainees in Guantanamo are all "bin Laden's bodyguards ... suicide bombers ... terrorists ... these are bad people. These are not good people."[11] While visiting Guantanamo, Rumsfeld remarked that even if a military tribunal were to order the release of a detainee, the individual would not be released. Rumsfeld's comments notwithstanding, individuals have been released.

In seeking to articulate the limits of interrogation, it is crucial to analyze the significance of the so-called War on Terrorism and to define who the real enemy is that the United States is fighting. Who is the *real*—rather than *perceived*—enemy? How is *the* enemy to be defined? Who can be interrogated? What intelligence information does the interrogator possess with respect to the particular detainee, his or her background, clan, and level of involvement with respect to past or future acts of terrorism? The question is whether the interrogator is properly equipped for the interrogation of a particular detainee or employs an "all terrorists are the same" approach. Given the international law requirement to distinguish between combatants and noncombatants and the practical need to allocate valuable resources in a highly discriminating fashion, a proper inquiry into each individual detainee is an absolute requirement. Furthermore, if the interrogator does not know pertinent details regarding the individual, the quality of information will be greatly reduced.

Terrorism is the world of dark shadows and back alleys. The terrorist is not readily identifiable to the soldier on a street corner in Mosul, Kabul, or Ramallah. In identifying, or seeking to identify, the enemy, we inherently impose our cultural values and act accordingly. To wit, Yaser Esam Hamdi was detained in Afghanistan solely because American forces observed that he was carrying a weapon. This example is critical to understanding the complexity of interrogations. Individuals who presented no significant threat were detained and subjected to interrogations *as if* they presented such a threat. The inherent lack of distinction illustrated by detentions such as Hamdi's not only results in the misallocation of valuable resources, but also creates an environment where excess is all but guaranteed.

---

[11] *See* transcript from *Meet the Press* (June 26, 2005), http://www.msnbc.msn.com/id/8332675/.

International law requires that a soldier be trained to distinguish between a combatant and an innocent civilian. This has enormous implications in the interrogation setting.[12] The failure to distinguish between civilians and combatants leads to a unified (i.e., indiscriminatory) approach that is both ineffective and violative of human rights.

In using the phrase "War on Terrorism," President Bush grouped all suspected terrorists into one broad category. However, what distinguishes counterterrorism from traditional warfare is that engagement is not between soldiers of different states but between soldiers and civilian combatants who fall into four broad categories: doers, senders, financiers, and facilitators. Effective counterterrorism requires not only categorical classification but also an ability to distinguish detainees on an individual basis.

By grouping all suspected terrorists into one category, the President all but guaranteed that each detainee would undergo similar interrogation experiences void of basic protections as they were all, purportedly, the "worst of the worst." Although some of the detainees may have been involved in terrorist planning and activity, others may not have been involved. Few objective observers would suggest that carrying a gun in Afghanistan (Hamdi) is cause for indefinite detention in Guantanamo Bay.

Because of the failure to adequately develop *boots on the ground* intelligence, the soldier and interrogator alike often do not know who is standing opposite them.[13] This approach of grasping in the dark ensures mistreatment, violations of basic rights, violations of international law, torture, and ultimately insufficient and incorrect intelligence information. This is a direct result of either detaining the wrong individuals or because the detainee simply wants the interrogator off his back.

Detainees, Intelligence Gathering, and the "War on Terrorism"

Who are these individuals who have, in some cases, been held for more than five years either directly or indirectly by the United States? How is it that thousands made their way to one of the detention cells controlled by the United States?

---

[12] Amos N. Guiora, *Teaching Morality in Armed Conflict: The Israel Defense Forces Model*, 18 No. 1–2 JEWISH POL. STUD. Rev., 3 (Spring 2006).

[13] This disturbing reality was made clear to me in numerous conversations with U.S. military personnel.

On September 11, 2001, the United States was forced into the world of terrorism. The United States government responded in the halls of Congress, the White House, the courts, and militarily. Shortly after the 9/11 attacks, a coalition formed by the United States demanded that the Taliban turn over Osama bin Laden.[14] Upon the Taliban's refusal, the U.S.-led coalition determined to use military force to overthrow the Taliban consistent with President Bush's September 12, 2001, pronouncement that the United States no longer distinguishes between the perpetrators of the terrorist attacks and those who harbor them.[15] The Taliban government was overthrown in less than two months by a coalition of the international community and the Afghan Northern Alliance. This conflict, and the ensuing search for members of Al Qaeda throughout South Asia, forced the administration to address the question of how to deal with captured terror suspects.

On November 13, 2001, the President issued an Executive Order establishing military commissions to try individuals suspected of terrorism activity captured by the United States. The military commissions were to be conducted unilaterally by the United States military under a more lenient procedural system than in domestic courts.[16] As time went on, and in response to widespread criticism, the administration added procedural safeguards.[17]

The administration argued that the detainees provided much needed intelligence regarding Al Qaeda's operational plans. Counterterrorism is dependent on intelligence information, and without relevant and timely intelligence, a state cannot conduct effective counterterrorism. If operators (boots on the ground) do not have reliable and corroborated intelligence, they will be unable to successfully take the fight to the enemy. Developing reliable human sources (HUMINT) requires the following: (1) a keen understanding of the local culture, (2) linguistic sophistication (understanding a language is insufficient as language is far more complex than the spoken word only), (3) understanding the region's history,

---

[14] For a chronological timeline of the war in Afghanistan, see *Afghanistan Timeline*, at http://www.mapreport.com/countries/afghanistan.html (last viewed Aug. 3, 2006).

[15] Detention, Treatment, and Trial of Certain Non-Citizens in the War Against Terrorism, Military Order of Nov. 13, 2001, 66 Fed. Reg. 222 § 2 (Nov. 16, 2001).

[16] *Id.*

[17] *See* Military Commission Order No. 1 (Dep't of Defense Mar. 21, 2002), *http://www.defenselink.mil/news/Mar2002/d20020321ord.pdf.*

(4) understanding (if relevant) particular clan cultures, and (5) understanding the geopolitics of the region.

As the National Commission on Terrorist Attacks Upon the United States (9/11 Commission) made clear, the intelligence community's numerous failures were a significant part of the government's inability to prevent the attacks. The Commission's recommendation to unify "strategic intelligence and operational planning"[18] highlights this point. The intelligence community intercepted many pre-9/11 related communications but was unable to translate them. This was a direct result of the interceptors' inability to understand the language they were hearing. Accordingly, they could not provide analysts with the raw data.

Receiving information from a source requires winnowing the chaff from the wheat, otherwise every piece of information received will be viewed with the same gravity and seriousness. Understanding the source's motivation is a primary aspect of intelligence gathering and analysis: Does the individual bear a personal, family, or clan-based grudge with the identified person? Does the source have a history of mendacity? Is the identified person capable of involvement in the activity suggested by the source? Does the source have a financial incentive in providing information? Can the intelligence received be corroborated?

In addition to information received from sources, commanders also receive information from individuals caught in the attack. Information received ultimately is intended in large part to serve the following purposes: to prevent a terrorist attack, to identify individuals involved in previous attacks, to detain an individual, and to interrogate the detainee. The decision to detain an individual for interrogation purposes is, therefore, largely predicated on information received from a human source that can be bolstered by information premised on intercepted communications [Signal Intelligence (SIGINT)].

As has been widely discussed elsewhere,[19] when the United States arrived in Afghanistan its intelligence gathering ability was highly limited, if not ineffectual. This resulted in a highly problematic mix of individuals being brought into interrogations, some directly tied to terrorism, some peripherally connected, and some none whatsoever. As a group, they did

---

[18] National Commission on Terrorist Attacks Upon the United States, Sect. 13.2.

[19] *See generally*, Douglas Jehl & Thom Shanker, *Congress is Reviewing Pentagon on Intelligence Activities*, N.Y. TIMES, Feb. 4, 2005, at A4; Paul Krugman, *The Uncivil War*, N.Y. TIMES, Nov. 25, 2003, at A27; and *Is America Safer Now?*, L.A. TIMES, Apr. 9, 2004, at 12, California Metro section.

not represent the worst of the worst. The lack of distinction, even if not race based, suggests the appropriateness of the historical analogy this book proposes.

Developing categories of dangers posed by particular individuals is paramount to avoiding "rounding up the usual suspects" and ensuring that individuals are not denied basic rights. Developing rights-based categories is critical to ensuring effective interrogations, otherwise not only are violations of rights all but guaranteed, the information received from detainees will, in all probability, not be "actionable."[20] Properly categorizing the detainees significantly contributes to developing an appropriate rights regime.

This is not the first time in American history that we have attempted to define nontraditional detainees. Although previous instances have not been successful, it is important to examine them to help both define detainees today and to establish the appropriate judicial regime.

During the Civil War, Lambden Milligan was arrested on the charges of conspiracy against the government, giving aid to enemies of the United States, inciting insurrection, disloyal practices, and violation of the laws of war.[21] Rather than bringing Milligan to trial in the regular established Article III courts, the decision was made by Brevet Major General Hovey, military commandant of the District of Indiana, to try him before a military commission in Indianapolis. The Supreme Court held that bringing Milligan before a military tribunal violated both his Sixth Amendment right to a trial before an impartial jury and his Fifth Amendment right to a grand jury. Further, as regularly constituted courts were available, the Court held the establishment of the military tribunal violated Milligan's basic constitutional rights:

> Military commissions organized during the late civil war, in a State not invaded and not engaged in rebellion, in which the Federal courts were open, and in the proper and unobstructed exercise of their judicial functions, had no jurisdiction to try, convict, or sentence for any criminal offence, a citizen who was neither a resident of a rebellious State, nor a prisoner of war, nor a person in the

---

[20] "Actionable intelligence" is information that can be acted on operationally by commanders and interrogators; intelligence that is not actionable does not contribute to operational counterterrorism and if acted on can result in the misallocation of scarce resources.

[21] Ex parte Milligan, 71 U.S. 2, 6 (1866).

military or naval service. And Congress could not invest them with any such power.[22]

During World War II, German saboteurs were captured on the East Coast and Florida. On reaching the United States, the German soldiers buried their uniforms in the sand. Therefore, according to the Geneva Conventions, they were no longer soldiers, which requires the wearing of uniforms and bearing arms to be a considered a soldier. Although controversy exists regarding the details of their capture[23], the five Germans were brought before a military tribunal established by President Roosevelt for the specific purpose of hearing their case. Although one of the five, Herbert Hans Haupht, was born in the United States to German parents, the United States argued that he relinquished his American citizenship when he joined the German army. The Supreme Court heard the soldiers' appeal regarding the legality of the commission, *Ex Parte Quirin*. In a brief opinion, the Court held that the commission was lawful and added they "have no occasion now to define with meticulous care the ultimate boundaries of the jurisdiction of military tribunals to try persons according to the law of war."[24]

In addressing the Germans' arguments, the Supreme Court in *Ex parte Quirin* used three different terms in one paragraph to reference the captured Germans.[25] This lack of semantic rigor contributed to the Court's failure to offer a strict definition of the saboteurs. The inability to apply a single term suggests that the Court was unwilling, or unable, to define the enemy. As the multitude of terms indicates, the *Quirin* decision, on which the Bush administration based its November 2001, Executive Order,[26] does not provide a proper definition of "enemy combatant." Rather, much like Justice Potter Stewart's approach to pornography, "I know it when I see it,"[27] both the Government and the Court have

---

[22] *Id.*
[23] Amos N. Guiora, *Quirin to Hamdan: Creating a Hybrid Paradigm for Detaining Terrorists*, 19 FLA. J. INT'L L. 2 Winter, 2008; LOUIS FISHER, NAZI SABOTEURS ON TRAIL 136–137 (University Press of Kanasas 2005) (2003).
[24] *Ex parte Quirin*, 317 U.S. 1, 45–46 (1942).
[25] *Ex parte Quirin*, 317 U.S. 1, 30–31 (1942) ("enemy combatant," "illegal combatant," and "unlawful combatant" are used in the same paragraph).
[26] Detention, Treatment, and Trial of Certain Non-Citizens in the War Against Terrorism, Military Order of Nov. 13, 2001, 66 Fed. Reg. 222 (Nov. 16, 2001).
[27] Jacobellis v. Ohio, 378 U.S. 184, 197 (1964) (Stewart, J., concurring).

chosen not to engage in active discourse or close examination of specifically who an enemy combatant is.

The *Quirin* Court applied an enemy combatant definition to individuals who had actually been soldiers. The German saboteurs in *Quirin* lost their status as soldiers when they purposefully discarded their uniforms, unlike terrorists, who do not belong to a regular army.[28] The appellants' actions (removing their uniforms), however, enabled the Court to correctly determine that they were not acting as soldiers at the time of their capture and thus not entitled to prisoner of war status.

The Executive Order issued by President Bush was predicated on *Quirin* (one of the Supreme Courts' weaker moments with respect to both content and style) and premised on an ideological philosophy that sought to minimize the rights of detainees to a bare minimum. The initial response was clearly reflected in the approach forcefully advocated by Jay Bybee and John Yoo. Subsequent efforts—including the Military Commissions Act—are similarly lacking in delineating clear rules.

The Supreme Court most recently addressed the issue of the military commissions and enemy combatants in *Hamdan*. The Court stated that:

> The commission's procedures ... provide ... that an accused and his civilian counsel may be excluded from, and precluded from, ever learning what evidence was presented during any part of the proceeding ... the presiding officer decides to "close." Grounds for closure include the protection of classified information, the physical safety of participants and witnesses, the protection of intelligence and law enforcement sources, methods, or activities, and "other national security interests." Appointed military defense counsel must be privy to these closed sessions, but may, at the presiding officer's discretion, be forbidden to reveal to the client what took place therein. Another striking feature is that the rules governing Hamdan's commission permit the admission of any evidence that, in the presiding officer's opinion, would have probative value to a reasonable person. Moreover, the accused and his civilian counsel may be denied access to classified and other "protected information," so long as the presiding officer concludes that the

---

[28] Geneva Convention Relative to the Treatment of Prisoners of War Art. 4(A)(2), Aug. 12, 1949, 6 U.S.T 3316, 75 U.N.T.S. 135.

evidence is "probative" and that its admission without the accused's knowledge would not result in the denial of a full and fair trial.[29]

In further analyzing the procedures for the military commissions, the Court held that: "Even assuming that Hamdan is a dangerous individual who would cause great harm or death to innocent civilians given the opportunity, the Executive nevertheless must comply with the prevailing rule of law in undertaking to try him and subject him to criminal punishment."[30]

If the administration were to take up efforts to address the Court's holding, it would be important that this be done clearly and concretely. The importance of narrowly defining terrorism-related crimes cannot be sufficiently emphasized. One of the great dangers that civil, democratic society faces is the panic response previously referenced. The most effective manner in which such responses can be avoided—or at least minimize their impact—is to strictly define culpable actions. Otherwise, the criminal code will be a catchall. The danger from the perspective of the interrogation setting is that interrogators will engage in fishing expeditions devoid of specificity. In an environment encouraging "by all means necessary," possible violations are all but certain.

As an example of the need for specificity, the term *actively engaged* is to be defined as follows: participating in the planning of an attack, providing harbor to those committing the attack, ensuring the availability of financial resources, providing significant logistical support, or actually performing the act. These four parts form the essence of terrorism. In rejecting the government's argument regarding Hamdi's right to challenge his detention, the Supreme Court held as follows:

> We therefore hold that a citizen-detainee seeking to challenge his classification as an enemy combatant must receive notice of the factual basis for his classification, and a fair opportunity to rebut the Government's factual assertions before a neutral decisionmaker. "For more than a century the central meaning of procedural due process has been clear: 'Parties whose rights are to be affected are entitled to be heard; and in order that they may enjoy that right they must first be notified.' It is equally fundamental that the right to notice and an opportunity to be heard 'must be granted at a

---

[29] *Hamdan at* 2786–2787.
[30] *Hamdan,* at 2798.

meaningful time and in a meaningful manner.'" These essential constitutional promises may not be eroded.

At the same time, the exigencies of the circumstances may demand that, aside from these core elements, enemy combatant proceedings may be tailored to alleviate their uncommon potential to burden the Executive at a time of ongoing military conflict. Hearsay, for example, may need to be accepted as the most reliable available evidence from the Government in such a proceeding. Likewise, the Constitution would not be offended by a presumption in favor of the Government's evidence, so long as that presumption remained a rebuttable one and fair opportunity for rebuttal were provided.[31]

However, what has been most problematic is that, rather than define the issue, the executive and judicial branches today, with congressional acquiescence, have simply continued the tradition of not consistently defining the combatant.

Bringing the Discussion Up to Date

Shortly after the Executive Order establishing the Military Commissions was issued, the U.S. Senate's Armed Services and Judiciary Committees held a series of hearings.[32] Administration witnesses justified the establishment of the military commissions by arguing that to effectively fight terrorism, an alternate judicial regime was required. According to the Bush administration, Article III courts were inappropriate and incapable for trying terrorists and those who provided them safe harbor.

In relying on *Quirin*, the Bush administration established a unique judicial regime for the express purpose of trying detainees. It was premised on two foundations: (1) that the detainees were not prisoners of war and therefore could be brought to trial, and (2) that the detainees

---

[31] Hamdi v. Rumsfeld, 124 S. Ct. 2633 (2004).

[32] U.S. Senate Committee on Armed Services, Dec. 12, 2001, To Receive Testimony on the Department of Defense's Implementation of the President's Military Order on Detention, Treatment, and Trial by Military Commission of Certain Non-Citizens in the War on Terrorism, http://armed-services.senate.gov/hearings/2001/c011212.htm. U.S. Senate Committee on the Judiciary, *DOJ Oversight: Preserving Our Freedoms While Defending Against Terrorism*, Nov. 28, 2001, *available at* http://judiciary.senate.gov/hearing.cfm?id=126 (last visited Oct. 19, 2006); Dec. 4, 2001, *available at* http://judiciary.senate.gov/hearing.cfm?id=129 (last visited Oct. 19, 2006); Dec. 6, 2001, *available at* http://judiciary.senate.gov/hearing.cfm?id=121 (last visited Oct. 19, 2006).

were not entitled to traditional Article III protections afforded to defendants in the criminal law paradigm. According to administration officials who testified before the Congress, the fundamental purpose of the Executive Order was to bring "justice to persons charged with offenses under the laws of armed conflict"[33] and to "target a narrow class of individuals—terrorists."[34] In response to widespread criticism[35] that the order insufficiently guaranteed to detainees any rights or protections, the Department of Defense issued ten instructions intended to facilitate the order's implementation. The ten instructions addressed a wide variety of issues:

- Instruction 1: Military Commission instructions
- Instruction 2: Crimes and elements for trial by the Military Commission
- Instruction 3: Responsibilities of the chief prosecutor, prosecutors, and assistant prosecutors
- Instruction 4: Responsibilities of the chief defense counsel, detailed defense counsel, and civilian defense counsel
- Instruction 5: Qualification of civilian defense counsel
- Instruction 6: Reporting relationships for Military Commission personnel
- Instruction 7: Sentencing
- Instruction 8: Administrative procedures
- Instruction 9: Review of Military Commission proceedings
- Instruction 10: Certain evidentiary determinations[36]

Criticism, which came quickly, centered on the lack of an independent judiciary, the lack of an appeals process, the lack of a sentencing

---

[33] Testimony of The Honorable Michael Chertoff, Assistant Attorney General, Criminal Division, U.S. Dept. of Justice, Nov. 28, 2001, *DOJ Oversight: Preserving Our Freedoms While Defending Against Terrorism, available at* http://judiciary.senate.gov/testimony.cfm?id=126&wit_id=66 (last visited Oct. 19, 2006).

[34] Testimony of The Honorable John Ashcroft, Attorney General, U.S. Dept. of Justice, U.S. Senate Committee on the Judiciary, Dec. 6, 2001, *DOJ Oversight: Preserving Our Freedoms While Defending Against Terrorism, available at* http://judiciary.senate.gov/testimony.cfm?id=121&wit_id=42 (last visited Oct. 19, 2006).

[35] William Safire, *Kangaroo Courts,* N.Y. TIMES, Nov. 26, 2001, at A17; Robin Toner, *A Nation Challenged: The Terrorism Fight,* N.Y. TIMES, Nov. 18, 2001, at 1A; Statement of The Honorable Patrick Leahy, U.S. Senator (Vermont), Nov. 28, 2001, *DOJ Oversight: Preserving Our Freedoms While Defending Against Terrorism, available at* http://judiciary.senate.gov/testimony.cfm?id=126&wit_id=66 (last visited Oct. 19, 2006).

[36] U.S. Department of Defense, Military Commissions, Military Commission Instructions, *available at* http://www.defenselink.mil/news/Aug2004/commissions_instructions.html (last visited Oct. 19, 2006).

regime known to the detainee, the process by which counsel is assigned, the broad rules of evidence, and the ability of the prosecutor to submit classified evidence to the court that the defendant would not be entitled to review.

Determining the appropriate forum for trying suspected terrorists requires addressing the correct or appropriate term to be used for those engaged in terrorism and what rights they are to be granted.

> Have the attacks of September 11 resulted in a shift from meta-phorical war/actual crime control to actual armed conflict? The suggestion that international terrorists pose a criminal threat is met with impatience in some quarters, as if it somehow diminishes the magnitude of the events of September 11. Terrorist crimes arguably differ from other transnational crimes, in that they are politically motivated and pose a threat to national security. However, in dem-ocratic societies, crimes against national security—espionage, for example—are not generally handled by military commissions. The Military Order of November 13 appears to rest on a perception that the current terrorist emergency is legally of a warlike character, and not simply a danger to national security or suitable grounds for military involvement in law enforcement.[37]

One possible solution is the adoption of the criminal law paradigm. The criminal law process guarantees the accused, and subsequently the defendant, the following protections: (1) a presumption of innocence until proven guilty, (2) evidence is submitted to an open court of law, (3) the right to confront witnesses,[38] (4) the right to remain silent,[39] (5) right to appeal to an independent judiciary,[40] and the (6) right to trial by a jury of peers.[41] Perhaps, the fundamental right granted by the crimi-nal law process is the defendant's right to confront his accusers enabling cross-examination in open court.

However, as counterterrorism is premised on intelligence information,[42] this right cannot be fully extended in a manner identical to the traditional

---

[37] Joan Fitzpatrick, *Military Commissions: Jurisdiction of Military Commissions and the Ambiguous War on Terrorism*, 96 A.J.I.L. 345, Apr., 2002.
[38] U.S. CONST. amend. VI.
[39] U.S. CONST. amend. V.
[40] U.S. CONST. art. III (creating an independent judiciary).
[41] U.S. CONST. amend. VI.
[42] Intelligence gathering largely emanates from two sources; HUMINT, which is human intelligence and SIGINT, which is signal intelligence. HUMINT depends on individuals

criminal law paradigm as the prosecution would be obligated to make intelligence sources available for cross-examination. As has been documented, the risk is life-threatening should sources be obligated to testify.[43]

Adopting a paradigm that does not guarantee the defendant the right to confront witnesses, enables the prosecution to base a case in part on unconfirmable—if not unverifiable—intelligence information. This is an enormous risk from the perspective of protecting the defendant's rights. As an example, albeit one that was criticized by the Supreme Court in *Hamdi v. Rumsfeld*,[44] the United States attempted to introduce intelligence information via the Mobbs Declaration.[45]

> On remand, the Government filed a response and a motion to dismiss the petition. It attached to its response a declaration from one Michael Mobbs (hereinafter "Mobbs Declaration"), who identified himself as Special Advisor to the Under Secretary of Defense for Policy. Mobbs indicated that in this position, he has been "substantially involved with matters related to the detention of enemy combatants in the current war against the al Qaeda terrorists and those who support and harbor them (including the Taliban)." He expressed his "familiar[ity]" with Department of Defense and United States military policies and procedures applicable to the detention, control, and transfer of al Qaeda and Taliban personnel, and declared that "[biased upon my review of relevant records and reports, I am also familiar with the facts and circumstances related to the capture of … Hamdi and his detention by U. S. military forces."

---

willing to act as sources for a variety of reasons. For a fuller description of this, *see* Amos Guiora, *Targeted Killing as Active Self-Defense*, 36 CASE W. RES. J. INT'L L. 319 (2004).

[43] *See* Thomas C. Homburger, Vice Chair of the Anti-Defamation League's National Commission, Statement of Anti-Defamation League and American Jewish Congress B'nai B'rith International, Hadassah, and the Jewish Council for Public Affairs to the House Committee on the Judiciary (May 23, 2000), http://www.fas.org/sgp/congress/2000/homburger.html.

[44] Hamdi v. Rumsfeld, 124 S. Ct. 2633 (2004).

[45] The Mobbs Declaration is a statement supplied by a DOD official, summarizing the intelligence information known to the authorities regarding the activities of a particular defendant. The material is used in detention hearings. In Israel, the classified information presented to the judge regarding a defendant was previously referred to as "negative security material" and reflected the known intelligence based on HUMINT and SIGINT alike. The material was used for a variety of criminal law and administrative sanctions. The primary issue is the reliability of the source(s) and whether the material is corroborated.

Mobbs then set forth what remains the sole evidentiary support that the Government has provided to the courts for Hamdi's detention. The declaration states that Hamdi "traveled to Afghanistan" in July or August 2001, and that he thereafter "affiliated with a Taliban military unit and received weapons training." It asserts that Hamdi "remained with his Taliban unit following the attacks of September 11" and that, during the time when Northern Alliance forces were "engaged in battle with the Taliban," "Hamdi's Taliban unit surrendered" to those forces, after which he "surrender[ed] his Kalishnikov assault rifle" to them. The Mobbs Declaration also states that, because al Qaeda and the Taliban "were and are hostile forces engaged in armed conflict with the armed forces of the United States," "individuals associated with" those groups "were and continue to be enemy combatants." Mobbs states that Hamdi was labeled an enemy combatant "[b]ased upon his interviews and in light of his association with the Taliban." According to the declaration, a series of "U.S. military screening team[s]" determined that Hamdi met "the criteria for enemy combatants," and "a subsequent interview of Hamdi has confirmed that he surrendered and gave his firearm to Northern Alliance forces, which supports his classification as an enemy combatant."[46]

Another possible source of categories and rights is the POW paradigm set forth in the Geneva Convention. In a series of memos, the Bush administration clearly argued that those detained in the "War on Terrorism" were not guaranteed Geneva Convention rights.[47] Although the memos were subsequently "corrected,"[48] the initial response is instructive in analyzing how the administration defined terrorist status. In arguing that the individuals were not subject to Geneva Convention protections, the administration determined that they were not soldiers.

---

[46] David Dyzenhaus, Aurthur Ripstein, and Sophia Reibetanz Moreau, LAW AND MORALITY: READINGS IN LEGAL PHILOSOPHY, 764–765 (University of Toronto Press, 3rd Ed., 2007).

[47] Memorandum from Jay Bybee, Assistant Attorney General, to Alberto Gonzales, Counsel to the President (Aug. 1, 2002), in MARK DANNER, TORTURE AND TRUTH: AMERICA, ABU GHRAIB, AND THE WAR ON TERROR (New York Review of Books 2004); and see Amos N. Guiora & Erin M. Page, The Unholy Trinity: Intelligence, Interrogation and Torture, 37 CASE W. RES. J. INT'L L. 427 (2006).

[48] See, Memorandum from Jerald Phifer, to Commander, Department of Defense Joint Task Force 170, in MARK DANNER, TORTURE AND TRUTH 168 (New York Review of Books 2004); Memorandum from Donald Rumsfeld, Secretary of Defense, to Commander USSOUTHCOM (Jan. 15, 2003), in MARK DANNER, TORTURE AND TRUTH, 183 (New York Review of Books 2004).

Thus, the administration determined that the detainees were to be denied basic international-law rights with the exception of receiving food, water, shelter, and basic medical care. What rights were they denied? According to the administration, the detainees could be subject to torture,[49] indefinite detention,[50] and denied independent judicial review.[51]

If the Geneva Conventions[52] are to be applied, captured soldiers are to be returned to their home state on the cessation of hostilities. Unlike war as traditionally understood between states, whose culmination is marked by an agreement between the warring states, the present situation has no universally agreed beginning. An agreement marking its conclusion is not foreseeable. The lack of a foreseeable, agreed-on end to the conflict directly affects the detainees' present and future status. As those detained will not be released in the foreseeable future, the question of their status directly impacts the rights granted to them.

Unlike criminals, whose date of release is determined either by judge or jury in their presence, enemy combatants as defined by the Bush administration are to be held literally in a "black hole." Indefinite detention, then, is a linchpin in defining the rights—or more accurately, lack of rights—of an enemy combatant.

In highlighting the lack of detainee definition, the November 2001 Executive Order,[53] fails to even attempt a definition of "enemy combatants."[54] According to Section 2 of the Executive Order,[55] the following individuals will be brought before the military commissions:

(a) The term "individual subject to this order" shall mean any individual who is not a United States citizen with respect to whom I determine from time to time in writing that:

---

[49] *See* Amos N. Guiora & Erin M. Page, *The Unholy Trinity: Intelligence, Interrogation and Torture*, 37 CASE W. RES. J. INT'L L. 427 (2006).

[50] Brief for the Respondents, Hamdi v. Rumsfeld, 124 S. Ct. 2633 (2004).

[51] Detention, Treatment, and Trial of Certain Non-Citizens in the War Against Terrorism, Military Order of Nov. 13, 2001, 66 Fed. Reg. 222 § 4 (Nov. 16, 2001).

[52] Geneva Convention Relative to the Treatment of Prisoners of War. art. 118, Aug. 12, 1949, 6 U.S.T 3316, 75 U.N.T.S. 135.

[53] Detention, Treatment, and Trial of Certain Non-Citizens in the War Against Terrorism, Military Order of Nov. 13, 2001, 66 Fed. Reg. 222 § 2 (Nov. 16, 2001). *See also* Chapter 6.

[54] In fact, the Military Order of Nov. 13, 2001, does not even use the term *enemy combatant* at all. Rather, it describes in general terms *individual subject to this order*.

[55] Detention, Treatment, and Trial of Certain Non-Citizens in the War Against Terrorism, Military Order of Nov. 13, 2001, 66 Fed. Reg. 222 § 2 (Nov. 16, 2001).

(1) there is reason to believe that such individual, at the relevant times,

  (i) is or was a member of the organization known as al Qaida;

  (ii) has engaged in, aided or abetted, or conspired to commit, acts of international terrorism, or acts in preparation therefore, that have caused, threaten to cause, or have as their aim to cause, injury to or adverse effects on the United States, its citizens, national security, foreign policy, or economy;

  (iii) has knowingly harbored one or more individuals described in subparagraphs (i) or (ii) of subsection 2(a)(1) of this order.[56]

According to the above, an enemy combatant, and thus a detainee, can be defined as any individual, who in any way, shape, or form came in contact with any member of Al Qaeda during any period of time with the intent of causing harm *in the* broadest definition of harm to the United States. Enemy combatant, as defined in the Executive Order, is an individual who need not have been involved in an act of terrorism in the present. Rather, it is sufficient to have only provided assistance, even if minimal. Furthermore, the degree required is not defined, thereby leaving significant grounds for liberal interpretation on the part of the executive in determining whether an individual is an enemy combatant.

When the Bush administration established the military commissions, the intention was to provide a forum whereby enemy combatants suspected of violating the Executive Order would be detained, interrogated, and tried. Since 2001, more than 660 individuals[57] captured in Afghanistan were transferred to Guantanamo Bay. These individuals, accused of being enemy combatants were considered by the U.S. government

---

[56] *Id.*
[57] Guantanamo Bay Detainees, http://www.globalsecurity.org/military/facility/guantanamo-bay_detainees.htm (this is the highest number of detainees held at one time at Guantanamo Bay, but the numbers fluctuate as more people are detained, and some are released).

to be the "enemy." The numbers speak for themselves; of the 598 individuals initially detained,[58] 267 have been released.[59]

Justice O'Connor's troubling words in *Hamdi* that "the Constitution would not be offended by a presumption in favor of the Government's evidence, so long as that presumption remained a rebuttable one and fair opportunity for rebuttal were provided,"[60] reflects a perspective that suggests a slippery slope regarding rights denied to the defendant. A critical issue in the detention of enemy combatants is determining what threat the individual poses to the nation's security. One of the disturbing conclusions emanating from Guantanamo Bay is that some individuals were detained without cause. Furthermore, individuals were transported to Guantanamo although neither intelligence nor evidence was available regarding their involvement in terrorism, as required by the Executive Order.[61]

What must be now established is when might an individual be designated an enemy combatant, detained, and potentially remanded. Justice Stevens dissent in *Padilla*[62] addresses this issue:

> Whether respondent is entitled to immediate release is a question that reasonable jurists may answer in different ways. There is, however, only one possible answer to the question whether he is entitled to a hearing on the justification for his detention.
>
> At stake in this case is nothing less than the essence of a free society. Even more important than the method of selecting the people's rulers and their successors is the character of the constraints imposed on the Executive by the rule of law. Unconstrained Executive detention for the purpose of investigating and preventing subversive activity is the hallmark of the Star Chamber. Access to counsel for the purpose of protecting the citizen from official mistakes and mistreatment is the hallmark of due process.
>
> Executive detention of subversive citizens, like detention of enemy soldiers to keep them off the battlefield, may sometimes be

---

[58] Guantanamo Bay Detainees, http://www.globalsecurity.org/military/facility/guantanamo-bay_detainees.htm (this is the number of original detainees from Aug. 5, 2002, but since then there have been additional transfers to Guantanamo Bay. By Nov. 24, 2003, the number of detainees was approximately 660 but has declined since then.)

[59] Press Release, U.S. Dept. of Defense, Detainee Release Announced (Feb. 9, 2006), http://www.defenselink.mil/releases/2006/nr20060209–12461.html.

[60] Hamdi v. Rumsfeld, 124 S. Ct. 2633, 2649 (2004).

[61] *See* Carol D. Leonnig, *Panel Ignored Evidence on Detainee*, WASH. POST, Mar. 27, 2005, at A01.

[62] Rumsfeld v. Padilla, 542 U.S. 426 (2004) (Stevens, J., dissenting).

justified to prevent persons from launching or becoming missiles of destruction. It may not, however, be justified by the naked interest in using unlawful procedures to extract information. Incommunicado detention for months on end is such a procedure. Whether the information so procured is more or less reliable than that acquired by more extreme forms of torture is of no consequence. For if this Nation is to remain true to the ideals symbolized by its flag, it must not wield the tools of tyrants even to resist an assault by the forces of tyranny.[63]

As the preceding discussion illustrates, there are no clear definitions regarding the detainees. The most effective way to respond is not to eloquently form some phrase aimed at encompassing the entirety of the modern situation, rather, categorization can be accomplished by determining the rights, privileges, and obligations owed them. Discussion of these three issues leads to additional significant questions, such as appropriate judicial process, the limits of interrogation,[64] the limits of detention,[65] and standard of review.[66]

The Current Combatant Paradigm

What then is the status of the detainees? The standards originally articulated by the Bush administration serve as one extreme. This extreme suggests that an enemy combatant, as defined by the Bush administration, is any individual who has been in contact, passively or actively, with a terrorist organization. This definition denies the detainee basic constitutional rights.[67] At the other extreme would be a system aimed to afford the detainee the full panoply of possible rights, either under the criminal law paradigm or the prisoner of war paradigm. Neither extreme is practicable or appropriate. As the discussion below indicates, the hybrid paradigm lies between these extremes.

---

[63] *Id.*

[64] *See* Amos N. Guiora & Erin M. Page, *The Unholy Trinity: Intelligence, Interrogation and Torture*, 37 Case W. Res. J. Int'l L. 427 (2006) in addition, I am addressing this issue in a work in progress tentatively entitled, *Hamdan as Heir to the Bram-Brown Progeny*.

[65] Hamdi v. Rumsfeld, 124 S. Ct. 2633 (2004).

[66] *See* Amos N. Guiora & Erin M. Page, *Going Toe to Toe: President Barak's and Chief Justice Rehnquist's Theories of Judicial Activism*, 29 Hastings Int'l & Comp. L. Rev. 51 (2005).

[67] This assumes that they are entitled to constitutional rights.

Hamdan v. Rumsfeld

The continued definitional uncertainty is evidenced by the U.S. Supreme Court's decision in *Hamdan v. Rumsfeld*,[68] which represents the Court's most recent foray into the question of detainee status and rights. The *Hamdan* ruling signaled that the Bush administration could not, under the guise of executive wartime powers, create its own definitions to apply to newly established military commissions for terror detainees.[69] Although the full impact of this decision has yet to become evident, the decision is highly relevant for the hybrid paradigm.[70]

The Military Commissions Act of 2006

In response to *Hamdan*, the United States Congress passed the Military Commissions Act of 2006.[71] Although this legislation takes a step in the direction of addressing the Court's concerns in *Hamdan*, it is ultimately insufficient in formulating proper interrogation standards. Rather than specifically articulating permissible interrogation methods, the Military Commissions Act grants the executive branch of the government the authority to interpret the scope and application of Common Article III of the Geneva Convention. The evasiveness of the Military Commissions Act potentially leads to abuses on the battlefield.

Possible Solutions

Six years after 9/11, the issue of detainee status and rights remains unclear and open to interpretation. From *Milligan* to *Quirin* to the Executive

---

[68] 126 S. Ct. 2749 (2006).
[69] The Court signaled the Bush administration that the rules currently governing the Guantanamo Bay military commissions were illegal and in need of revamping. The Court held this by indicating that the Authorization for the Use of Military Force was not a blank check for the administration to set up these commissions but rather was more like the lowest ebb of power, similar to *Youngstown Steel*, requiring further Congressional approval for such commissions.
[70] *See* Amos N. Guiora, *Where Are Terrorists to Be Tried: A Comparative Analysis of Rights Granted to Suspected Terrorists*, 56 CATH. U. L. REV. 805 (2007) and Amos N. Guiora, *Interrogation of Detainees: Extending a Hand or a Boot?*, 41 U. MICH. J.L. REFORM (forthcoming 2008).
[71] 120 Stat. 2600 (Oct. 17, 2006).

Order and the subsequent Supreme Court decisions, the question of how to define the detainees is far from resolved. Furthermore, the failure to sufficiently define or determine the detainee's status significantly inhibits the ability to articulate the rights granted to the detainee. This double failure ultimately affects the development of clearly defined limits of interrogation.

Rather than rely on the variety of terms adopted by the Supreme Court in various decisions or the unarticulated, vague, and problematic terms that the Bush administration has applied (resulting in violations of international and domestic law alike), the hybrid paradigm regime proposes an approach that clearly and concisely addresses and resolves these issues. The hybrid paradigm, in conjunction with the proposed historical analogy offers a viable solution for lawful coercive interrogation.

CHAPTER 3

Application of the Hybrid Paradigm

Although there are a number of critical, fundamental assumptions this book makes—including the *leap of faith* regarding relevance of the historical analogy—one clear assertion is that the present system of interrogations and detainee status requires our collective and immediate attention. To that end, the hybrid paradigm was created. Although not a perfect solution to a complicated problem, the hybrid paradigm proposes an alternative that addresses the dilemma of how to balance legitimate civil and political rights of the individual with the equally legitimate national security rights of the state. Accordingly, the detainee held by the United States in Guantanamo Bay and similar facilities will be granted certain constitutional rights, in particular those based on the Fifth, Eighth, and Fourteenth Amendments.

The operative words in this chapter are granting *certain rights* to non-Americans held by the United States *outside the United States*. The inherent internal contradiction of only certain granting rights and privileges on a limited basis is admittedly problematic. The discussion of how much to curtail is critical to the development and ultimate implementation of the paradigm. Such an analysis facilitates an examination of whether the proposal sufficiently protects the rights of those it presumes are a constitutionally *protected class*.

The hybrid paradigm, however, begs an important question: Are the detainees to be granted any rights, and if yes, why? The answer is that the detainees are a protected class, but not a *fully* protected class. That is to say, as individuals they are entitled to some protections, but not full constitutional protections. It is both legally and morally wrong to assign the detainees to a black hole, both literally and figuratively. To do so, stains the United States. The hybrid paradigm seeks to protect those who would otherwise be subject to the whims and fancies of their captors with no recourse or protection. It establishes a practical, alternative structure predicated on standards and criteria regarding interrogation guidelines specifically articulated for the scenario at hand.

Status and rights cannot be determined if we cannot agree on a definition by which to refer to a class of individuals subjected to our interrogations. However, prior to addressing interrogations it is necessary to finish developing and articulating the hybrid paradigm.

Given the dissatisfaction with the present legal regime, and subscribing to the legitimacy of comparative global constitutionalism, examining and perhaps borrowing from other civil, democratic states in an effort to resolve this dilemma is a worthwhile endeavor. To that end, the Israeli legal regime serves as a potential model for the post-9/11 American legal paradigm, albeit subject to limitations inherent to comparative legal analysis.

Israel applies a two-track approach to Palestinians suspected of having committed acts of terrorism.[72] Following the June 1967, Six Day War, the Israel Defense Force (IDF) established Military Courts in the West Bank and the Gaza Strip[73] for the purpose of trying Palestinians residing in either area[74] suspected of having committed acts of terrorism.

---

[72] The focus of this section will be Palestinian residents of the West Bank and the Gaza Strip with two caveats: (1) there are a number of outstanding legal questions concerning the status of residents of the Gaza Strip post-disengagement, and (2) Israeli citizens suspected of having committed acts of terrorism are brought before civil courts only and, for policy reasons, are not subject to the jurisdiction of the military courts. However, they may be placed in administrative detention (similar to residents of the West Bank and the Gaza Strip) although the procedure is different than that in place for Palestinians. Jewish and Arab citizens of Israel alike have been placed in administrative detention over the years. For purposes of clarity, Palestinians residing in the West Bank and the Gaza Strip will be referred to as Palestinians.

[73] As these lines are written, the courts' name has not been changed following disengagement.

[74] According to the Geneva Convention Relative to the Protection of Civilian Persons in Time of War, articles 64–71, the occupying power may establish courts to try residents of the occupied area for offences committed against the public good/security; courts

Military judges were appointed by military commanders who had command responsibility over the West Bank and the Gaza Strip; military prosecutors were similarly appointed.[75] Palestinians are represented before the courts by civilian defense attorneys, Palestinians and Israelis alike.

Palestinians brought before the court are interrogated initially by the General Security Service (GSS) (in Hebrew: *SHABAK*)[76] and afterwards by the Israel police.[77] The charge sheet, based either on the individual's confession or on the testimony of others, is submitted to the court by the military prosecutor. The case is heard by a panel consisting either of one or three judges.[78] The trial is conducted according to Rules of Criminal Procedure and Evidence akin to those in Israeli civilian courts and would be very familiar to American trial lawyers. If convicted, the defendant can appeal to the Military Court of Appeals; the prosecution can appeal if the court has acquitted the defendant. During the course of the interrogation, Israel can deny the suspect the right to see an attorney for up to thirty-one days.[79]

---

with jurisdiction over civil matters that were in existence prior to the occupation must be allowed to continue. 75 U.N.T.S. 287.

[75] As Israel has never annexed the West Bank and the Gaza Strip, the Commander of the IDF Forces in the West Bank is in essence the head of the Military Government in the West Bank, and until disengagement, his counterpart in the Gaza Strip was the Officer in Command of the Gaza Strip. This author's appointment as Prosecutor in the West Bank Military Court was signed by then Major General (later, Lt. General, ret.) Ehud Barak (OC—Central Command); an appointment to serve as a military judge in the Gaza Strip Military Court was signed by Major General (ret.) Matan Vilnay (OC-Southern Command).

[76] A number of High Court of Justice opinions have been written regarding various interrogation measures. The seminal opinion is H.C. 5100/94, Public Comm. Against Torture in Israel v. State of Israel & General Sec. Serv.

[77] The Israel police commander in the West Bank while serving under the Director General of the Israel police, is under the command of the IDF area commander, with the exception of internal disciplinary affairs.

[78] The size of the panel will be determined by the severity of the charge sheet. Regarding the composition of the panels, until recently the presiding judge was a lawyer serving in the IDF Judge Advocate General's (JAG) Corps and in those cases where the panel was composed of three judges the two additional judges were reserve officers who were not lawyers. Recently two significant changes have been made: (1) the judges (unlike the prosecutors) no longer serve in the JAG; rather they serve in the IDF Military Court Unit, and (2) lawyers serving in the reserves have replaced nonlawyers as the two additional judges. The IDF School of Military Law (when this author was its commander) instituted a training program for newly appointed judges.

[79] U.S. Department of State Country Report on Human Rights Practices 2004—Israel and the occupied territories—Feb. 2005, Sect. 1(d), *available at* http://www.unhcr.org/cgi-bin/texis/vtx/rsd/rsddocview.html?tbl=RSDCOI&id=4226d98a9.

The second track that has been implemented by Israel over the course of the past forty years is administrative detention. Administrative detentions, unlike the criminal process, are not punitive; rather, an individual is detained if available intelligence information indicates the individual is involved in the preparation of a future attack.[80] In such instances, a senior IDF commander[81] will sign an administrative detention order on receipt of a recommendation from the GSS and a legal opinion from an IDF legal advisor. The legal opinion will analyze the intelligence information and attempt to gauge whether the High Court of Justice will deny a petition should the detainee file one. Administrative detentions are codified in article 85 of the Defense Emergency Regulations Act (1945).[82] The maximum detention is for renewable six-month periods subject to judicial review,[83] and there is no statutorily determined time period limiting the number of detentions.

Administrative detention has been heavily criticized[84] for a number of reasons. Primarily, the criticism has concentrated on two critical issues: the detainee's inherent inability to confront his or her accuser and the resultant fishing expedition his or her lawyer is required to conduct. However, unlike the Military Commission mechanism established by President Bush's Executive Order,[85] the military commander's decision regarding the administrative detention of an individual is subject to independent judicial review by the High Court of Justice.[86]

---

[80] Administrative sanctions are deterrent-driven rather than punitive determinant.

[81] Generally, the commander who signs the orders is the commander of the IDF in the West Bank (a brigadier general); in extreme cases, the commander of the IDF for the Central Command (a two-star general) will sign, during a large scale military operation, a regional commander (full colonel) will sign.

[82] When the IDF occupied the West Bank, these regulations were in place as they had been introduced by the British in the Mandate period (1917–1948). As international law does not allow the occupying power to erase existing laws, the IDF inherited the regulations from the Jordanians who ruled the West Bank from 1948–1967.

[83] The process repeats itself in its entirety.

[84] See, e.g., Orna Ben-Naftali & Sean S. Gleichgevitch, *Missing in Legal Action: Lebanese Hostages in Israel*, 41 HARV. INT'L L.J. 185 (2000); Eitan Barak, *With the Cover of Darkness: Ten Years of Games with Human Beings as "Bargaining Chips" and the Supreme Court*, 8 PLILIM 77, 81 (1999) (Heb.)

[85] See Detention, Treatment, and Trial of Certain Non-Citizens in the War Against Terrorism, Military Order of Nov. 13, 2001, 66 Fed. Reg. 222 § 4 (Nov. 16, 2001).

[86] Salama v. IDF Commander in Judea and Samaria, HCJ 5784/03, Marab v. IDF Commander in the West Bank, HCJ 3239/02.

Trials of Detainees

The trials can take place in either of two different venues: civilian courts or IDF military courts. The IDF military courts, convened for the purpose of trying detainees, are distinguished from courts martial, before which soldiers stand for trial.

An overwhelming majority of Palestinians accused of terrorism acts are tried in the Military Court, even if the act was committed in Israel proper (the pre-1967 borders). The primary reason for this is substantive: if the act was planned in the West Bank, the participants reside in the West Bank, and the cells' activities primarily occur in the West Bank, the Military Courts are deemed to have proper jurisdiction over the matter.

The trial process is similar to the American criminal system. The defendant is innocent until proven guilty, the state submits a charge sheet, and the defendant can admit guilt. Similar to large American cities, approximately 90% of defendants plead out. The most notable difference is the lack of a jury trial in the Israeli system.

Similar to the constitutionally guaranteed right to confront the accuser, secret intelligence information cannot be submitted to the court for purpose of conviction. However, it can be the basis both for a suspect's initial detention and the extension of remand. In Israel, a suspect who has been arrested must be brought before a judge within twenty-four hours. In the West Bank, as amended in 1997, a Palestinian can be held for up to eight days without seeing a judge.[87]

Administrative Hearings for Detainees

Administrative sanctions include deportations, assigned residence, and administrative detention. The administrative detention process is initiated when the GSS receives intelligence information from one or more

---

[87] Military Order 378. In Israel, according to section 9.3.3 of the Penal Code, a detainee must be brought before a judge within twenty-four hours. http://64.233.167.104/search?q=cache:HUTfhlzLL7sJ:www.heuni.fi/uploads/j6hs303ru64zn5.pdf+detention+in+israel+according+to+the+penal+code&hl=en. The West Bank and the Gaza Strip have never been annexed to the State of Israel, which is why the government is a military government; in addition, the laws of the state do not apply to the two areas. The legislation of the areas is drafted by the officers of the Judge Advocate General Corps and signed into being by the commander of the Central Command or by the commander of the Southern Command (both are major generals; the equivalent to two-star generals).

informants regarding a particular individual. If the GSS determines that the information cannot be submitted to an open court of law then a recommendation will be made to the IDF commander that the individual be administratively detained.[88]

Should the military commander sign the detention order, the individual will be brought before a military judge. This is not a trial—neither the detainee nor his attorney has the right to examine the information on which the detention is based. During the course of the hearing, the judge fulfills a double role—that of judge and defense attorney. The detention order, if approved by the judge, is then reviewed by a higher ranking judge. Petitions can then be filed against these decisions to the High Court of Justice.[89]

The detention for six months is indefinitely renewable; however, an extension order is subject to mandatory review by an independent judiciary. That is, the detention can be unlimited (the longest one was for a number of years), but each time the process is renewed in full. Renewability, however, requires a showing that the detainee continues to present a viable security threat. In the overwhelming majority of cases, the basis for extension of the initial detention order is the *same* intelligence information that had served as the basis for the military commander's initial decision.

In implementing the additional track—as problematic as it is—Israel recognizes that terrorists, although they possess certain rights, cannot be granted full criminal law rights in every instance. Granting all terrorists full criminal rights would foreclose the state's right to detain individuals when only classified information is available. The state's requirement to protect itself requires the development of mechanisms whereby the state grants terrorists rights, although not the full panoply of criminal rights.

---

[88] Article 85 of the Defence Emergency Regulation of 1945 as described in David A. Kirshbaum, *Israeli Emergency Regulations & The Defense (Emergency) Regulations of 1945*, http://www.geocities.com/savepalestinenow/emergencyregs/essays/emergencyreg sessay.htm.

[89] I have sat in on these hearings, and decisions of mine have been appealed to the High Court of Justice.

Application

On April 14, 2002, the IDF arrested Marwan Barghouti in Ramallah.[90] Barghouti, who was the head of the Tanzim,[91] challenged the jurisdiction

---

[90] http://www.mfa.gov.il/MFA/MFAArchive/2000_2009/2002/4/Information%200n%20 Marwan%20and%20Ahmed%20Barghouti%20-%2015-Apr, The Tel Aviv District Court described Barghouti as follows:

The Defendant, who is a resident of Ramallah, is the head of the Terrorist Organizations in the Judea and Samaria area. He is their leader and was a central partner in their decision making.

The Defendant was subordinate to Yasser Arafat, who is head of the Terrorist Organizations.

During the Relevant Period for the Indictment, the Terrorist Organizations engaged in intensive Acts of Terror against Israeli targets, in accordance with the policy established by the leadership of the organizations.

The Defendant led, managed and operated Acts of Terror against Israeli targets by conspiring with senior field operatives, who were responsible for the actual implementation of the Acts of Terror, according to the aforesaid established policy, which the Defendant was engaged in implementing.

Senior and key terror activists with whom the Defendant conspired to commit the Acts of Terror under his leadership were, among others: Nasser Aweis, Ahmed Barghouti, Nasser Abu Hamid, Ra'ad Karmi, Muhaned Diria (Abu Halawa), Muhammad Musalah (Abu Satha), Mansour Shrim and Mahmoud Titi (hereinafter: "the Field Commanders"). Ahmed Barghouti (hereinafter: Ahmed) also served as the Defendant's right hand man and his liaison in contacts with the other Field Commanders.

The field commanders committed the Acts of Terror by conspiring with the field activists who were subordinated to them, were under their command and operated according to their orders (hereinafter: "Terror Activists").

Each time a decision was made by the leadership of the Terrorist Organizations to halt the Acts of Terror due to various constraints, political and otherwise, the Defendant instructed the Field Commanders and their subordinated activists to halt the Acts of Terror.

The end result of this pattern of activity was that during the Relevant Period for the Indictment, since no explicit order was given by the Defendant to halt the Acts of Terror, the Commanders and their subordinate Terror Activists continued to carry out Acts of Terror in accordance with the policy of the leadership of the Terrorist Organizations throughout that entire period, as detailed above.

Within the conspiracy to commit Acts of Terror and with the intention of promoting this conspiracy, the Defendant and his subordinates carried out a series of actions that caused, promoted and enabled the implementation of the Acts of Terror. http://www. israel.org/MFA/MFAArchive/2000_2009/2002/12/State%200f%20Israel%20vs%20Mar wan%20Barghouti-%20Ruling%20by%20Jud

[91] The "Tanzim"—an organizational framework through which the activity of the Fatah members was implemented in the Judea and Samaria region and in Gaza. In the Relevant Period for the Indictment, the organization has waged a violent and armed struggle while committing acts of terror against Israel, its civilians and its soldiers. The Tanzim is a terrorist organization as defined in the Prevention of Terrorism Ordinance (quoted from the Gurfinkel decision). http://www.israel.org/MFA/MFAArchive/2000_2009/ 2002/12/State%200f%20Israel%20vs%20Marwan%20Barghouti-%20Ruling% 20by%20Jud.

of the Tel Aviv District Court to try his case arguing five fundamental points:

1. The authority of the State of Israel to try Palestinians who attack Israelis was negated upon the signing of the Oslo Accords.
2. The rules of international law reject Israel's right to try the Defendant, since he is a freedom fighter opposing occupation. All forms of opposition have been defined as legitimate, including the use of violent force. If such a fighter is apprehended, he is to be defined as a prisoner of war and not as a criminal.
3. The Defendant was kidnapped from Ramallah by IDF soldiers contrary to the Oslo Accords and international law.
4. The Defendant holds immunity negating the right of the State of Israel to put him on trial.
5. The indictment is political and constitutes an indictment against the entire Palestinian people.[92]

Although Barghouti was a resident of the West Bank, a politically based decision was made to bring him to trial in an Israeli civilian court rather than before the West Bank Military Court.[93] In the context of the two-track approach implemented by Israel, Barghouti was to be tried before a court of law rather than subjected to the administrative detention process. In determining which track to apply, the criminal law process is preferable both legally and policy-wise as the defendant's basic rights are guaranteed. However, operational and intelligence considerations *may* conceivably outweigh legal considerations. In addressing

---

[92] State of Israel v. Marwan Barghouti, Ruling by Judge Zvi Gurfinkel, Dec. 12, 2002, *available at* http://www.israel.org/MFA/MFAArchive/2000_2009/2002/12/State%200f%20Israel%20vs%20Marwan%20Barghouti-%20Ruling%20by%20Jud (last visited Oct. 18, 2006).

[93] The overwhelming majority of Palestinians who commit acts of terrorism are brought to trial in the Military Courts even if they committed or were responsible for others having acts of terror in Israel. The decision regarding Barghouti was based on political considerations—it was assumed that there would be overwhelming media interest in the trial given his preeminent position, his relationship with Arafat, and that he counted among his friends members of the Israeli left. In light of this expected media interest it was felt that the civilian court system would be a more appropriate venue. According both to various media reports and information to which this writer is privy, there was opposition to this decision within the security apparatus. It was felt that military judges who had been sitting in terrorist cases for years would be more competent in handling the issues Barghouti was expected to raise and that the process would be both more efficient and more effective were the case not brought before the civilian court.

Barghouti's status, the Tel Aviv District Court (Judge Zvi Gurfinkel) examined the international law issue:

> The Defendant claims that he is to be considered a prisoner of war, and, accordingly, the Occupying Power is forbidden to prosecute him under criminal law.
>
> The Defendant is not to be considered a prisoner of war.
>
> Terrorists who attack a civilian population do not fall within the framework of "lawful combatants" entitled to the status of "prisoners of war," since they do not meet the conditions, in accordance with international law, that a lawful combatant is required to meet. The heads of the Palestinian terror organizations, of whom the Defendant is one, systematically violate the rules of war.
>
> International law distinguishes between two groups of combatants who undertake hostile actions against the State of Israel.
>
> The first group of elements that undertake hostile actions against the State comprises persons who are part of regular armies that engage in combative actions against the State of Israel in accordance with the rules of war.
>
> Combatants who act within the framework of this group and are apprehended receive the status of prisoners of war. Prisoners of war are not prosecuted in accordance with criminal law for their participation in combative actions, provided that they acted in accordance with the rules of war. If, however, they acted contrary to the rules of war, they may be prosecuted on account of war crimes.[94]

The two-track Israeli model enables the state to determine which judicial regime to apply to a particular defendant depending on the nature of the information available. If the information is evidence based, enabling cross-examination in open court of witnesses, then the defendant will be charged in a criminal trial. However, if the case is predicated on intelligence information, the individual will be administratively detained.

---

[94] State of Israel v. Marwan Barghouti, ruling by Judge Zvi Gurfinkel, Dec. 12, 2002, *available at* http://www.israel.org/MFA/MFAArchive/2000_2009/2002/12/State%200f%20Isr ael%20vs%20Marwan%20Barghouti-%20Ruling%20by%20Jud (last visited Oct. 18, 2006).

Although administrative detentions deny the individual the right to confront his or her accuser, independent judicial review guarantees both procedural and substantive oversight. In direct contrast to the Executive Order establishing the military commissions or the recently enacted Military Commissions Act, independent judicial review is institutionalized in Israel. The two-tier process described above is predicated on a clear definition of terrorism, and the status and rights of terrorists.

The Hybrid Paradigm Applied Specifically to Interrogations

In discussing interrogation, the relevant questions are who can be interrogated subject to what rules, regulations, and criteria. In other words, what contribution does the hybrid paradigm make to the interrogation of a detainee suspected of involvement in terrorist activity? As an example: Will individuals detained in Guantanamo Bay be granted Miranda rights prior to their interrogations? In the context of seeking to articulate the limits of interrogation, the question is posed seriously and analyzed accordingly.

Whether Miranda rights are to be granted is highly relevant to the hybrid paradigm discussion for it highlights the complexity of the debate. Under traditional criminal law, detainees would be entitled to Miranda rights. In contrast, under the POW paradigm, detainees would not be entitled to Miranda rights. This is the paradox that the hybrid paradigm—in the interrogation context—seeks to resolve.

The litany of Supreme Court cases decided in the aftermath of 9/11 insufficiently articulate the regime relevant to the detainees. In *Padilla, Rasul, Hamdi, In re Guantanamo Bay Detainees*, and *Hamdan*, the Court failed to articulate or create a clear set of rules regarding rights to be granted detainees undergoing interrogations. Although the limits of interrogation were not necessarily the primary focus of these cases, the Supreme Court's primary concern should have been to clearly and unequivocally articulate a rights-based regime to facilitate the limits of interrogation.

Where does all this leave us? As we examine the historical paradigm on which the foundation of this book rests, it is important to remember that while significant basic differences exist between the African American detainee of the 1930s and an individual suspected of involvement in terrorism in 2007, significant similarities persist. In the present context, the failure of all three branches of the U.S. government to adequately address—much less resolve—the issue of the status and rights of the detainees has left a gaping hole. That uncertainty and ambiguity, accentuated by a failure to define terms, ultimately manifests itself in the inability to adequately and concretely determine the limits of interrogation.

These limits will be explored in the next chapter by examining the African American experience in the Deep South of the 1930s and 1940s.

CHAPTER 4

Interrogations in the History of American Criminal Law:

Adding Historical Perspective from an Examination of

African American Interrogations in the Deep South

Exploring the Deep South: *Bram, Brown,* and Their Progeny

B ased on similarities between the current treatment of detainees and African Americans in the Deep South, the constitutional standards established by the Supreme Court[95] are applicable and germane to the discussion regarding the current *armed conflict short of war*. The starting point for examining domestic jurisprudence of interrogation methods is what I term the "*Bram-Brown* progeny."[96] This progeny examines the Supreme Court's extension of constitutional protections in response to interrogations of African American suspects imprisoned in the Deep South.

In the Deep South,[97] those detained by law enforcement officials were predominantly poor, illiterate African Americans subjected to threats, cumulative mistreatment, and additional interrogation methods that violated Constitutional safeguards. The Deep South interrogation methods in many instances were even reminiscent of the Star Chamber;[98]

---

[95] See discussion below of *Bram, Brown, White, Ward, White,* and *Ashcraft*.
[96] The word is used here to refer to the line of cases, beginning with *Bram v. United States*, which have formed the domestic jurisprudence regarding interrogation standards.
[97] As referenced earlier to consist of the early to mid-1900s.
[98] The *Star Chamber* is a term used to describe the room in Westminster Palace where the King of England's council met, because of the star painted on the ceiling of that room.

such treatment continued until the Supreme Court eventually mandated the extension of Fifth and Fourteenth Amendment protections to this previously unprotected class. Similarly, the detainees in Guantanamo Bay are typically poor, do not speak the language of their surroundings, have little or no access to attorneys, and are subject to threats and abuses from detaining authorities.

As will be shown, in spite of the differences between the African Americans who were historically considered to be three-fifths of a citizen,[99] and the detainees who are not U.S. citizens, the similarities between these two unprotected classes are ultimately more germane than the differences. Specifically, the African American experience in the interrogation cells, in the woods, and in the back seats of the local sheriff's car, have an eerie resemblance to the experience of the detainee captured in the aftermath of 9/11 and held in Guantanamo Bay, Abu Ghraib, Bagram, and "black sites."[100]

Before moving forward, however, I wish to acknowledge other differences in my historical comparison. First, the detainees are subjected to coercive interrogation not simply because of who they are, as was the case for African Americans in the Deep South, but also in the pursuit of information. Secondly, the torturing of African Americans in the Deep South was caused solely by racism, whereas the current detainees are subjected to abuses as the *enemy* in the context of armed conflict. However, the similarities in treatment and the lessons learned far outweigh differences. Specifically, just as allegations of rights violated in the early to mid 1900s led to the establishment of the Wickersham Commission,[101] the post-9/11 experience of interrogating detainees has yielded numerous allegations

---

The court of equity had jurisdiction over criminal matters, and as it was intended to be a streamlined alternative to common-law courts, it became a byword for unfair judicial proceedings. *See* the *Columbia Encyclopedia* 2704 (6th ed., Paul Lagasse ed., 2000).

[99] See U.S. Const. art. I, § 2, cl. 3, amended by U.S. Const. Amend. XIV, § 2.

[100] That expression has been used to describe detainees held in so-called "black sites" as exposed by Dana Priest, *CIA Holds Terror Suspects in Secret Prisons*, WASH. POST, Nov. 2, 2005 at A1.

[101] President Hoover established the commission in response to the American public's increasing worries about crime, and a concern about publicity emerging from gang wars in Chicago.

of violations of human and civil rights,[102] ranging from minor[103] to major,[104] mandating the development of new and clear standards. The practical recommendations this book proposes, founded on the hybrid paradigm, a historical analogy, and the need to balance powerful competing interests, would facilitate both more effective interrogations in the future while also addressing many of the failures of the past six years. Although not akin to a Wickersham Commission, adoption of the recommendations premised on the guidelines suggested would reflect an effort to learn from the past and to effectively move forward.

With those differences admitted and addressed, it is time to set the stage regarding the conditions and circumstances of African Americans in American history. Only by first engaging in this examination will the later correlation be possible, thereby contributing to practical policy recommendations based on a reading of history and an analysis of the law.

During the late 1800s and 1900s,[105] African Americans were constant victims of lynchings, merciless whippings (with and without the complicity of local law enforcement officials), and other mistreatments in the local jails.[106] In this timeframe, African Americans were often "rounded-up"[107]

---

[102] See generally U.S. Soldiers Tell of Detainee Abuse in Iraq, HUM. RTS. WATCH (July 23, 2006); "No Blood, No Foul": Soldiers' Account of Detainee Abuse in Iraq, 18 No. 3(G) HUM. RTS. WATCH (July 2006); More Than 600 Implicated in Detainee Abuse, HUM. RTS. WATCH (Apr. 26, 2006); Michelle Voeller-Gleason, Soldier Pleads Guilty to Detainee Abuse, Others Face Charges, ARMY NEWS SERVICE, May 25, 2004; and Steven C. Welsh, Detainee Abuse: Abu Ghraib Court Martial: Staff Sgt. Ivan Frederick, INT'L SEC. LAW PROJ. (Oct. 26, 2004), http://www.cdi.org/news/law/abu-ghraib-courts-martial-frederick.cfm (last viewed July 25, 2006).

[103] Including photographs and stress positions.

[104] Including beatings and personal degradation.

[105] Bram was decided in 1897 and although the defendant was not an African American, it represents the first time the Supreme Court addressed the issue of the limits of interrogation. The cases subsequently discussed in the book were decided between 1920 and 1940.

[106] For example, there were 3,385 documented mob lynchings of African Americans in the United States between 1882 and 1935. MARK CURRIDEN & LEROY PHILLIPS, JR., CONTEMPT OF COURT, THE TURN OF THE CENTURY LYNCHING THAT LAUNCHED 100 YEARS OF FEDERALISM 354–355 (Anchor Books 2001). Further, historian W. Fitzhugh Brundage's study of lynchings in Georgia found that 441 of 460 victims of lynchings between 1880 and 1930 were African Americans. See W. FITZHUGH BRUNDAGE, LYNCHING IN THE NEW SOUTH: GEORGIA AND VIRGINIA, 1880–1930, at 262 (Urbana: Univ. of Illinois Press 1993).

[107] Although the phrase, "round up the usual suspects" was popularized by the movie Casablanca, it is highly relevant both to the African American experience as discussed in this book, and as evidenced by the number of detainees released from Guantanamo it would seem to be equally relevant to those detained in Afghanistan. For instance, of the 760 detainees brought to Guantanamo Bay in 2002, the military has released 180

without evidentiary justification.[108] The accusation by a white woman that an African American male had sexually assaulted her sealed his fate regardless of proof. An accusation that he was merely "looking" may well have doomed him to "mob rule."[109]

In the same vein, many of the detainees in the ill-defined "War on Terrorism"[110] have been detained on the shaky ground of rounding up the

---

without ever charging any of them. A report authored by Seton Hall Law Professor Joshua Denbeaux found that: (1) 55% of the detainees are not charged with having committed any hostile acts against the United States. (2) Only 8% of the detainees were characterized as Al Qaeda fighters, and of the remaining detainees, 40% have no definite connection with Al Qaeda at all, and 18% have no definitive ties with either Al Qaeda or the Taliban. (3) The government has detained numerous individuals based merely on affiliations with large groups that are not on the Department of Homeland Security watch list, as only 8 % are detained because they were deemed to be "fighters." (4) Only 5% of the detainees were even captured by U.S. forces. "The government has detained these individuals for more than four years, without a trial or judicial hearing, and has had unfettered access to each detainee for that time," said the report, written by lawyers who represent two of the detainees. The lawyers—Mark Denbeaux, a law professor at Seton Hall University in New Jersey, and Joshua Denbeaux—were assisted by Seton Hall law students." See http://law.shu.edu/ for full report (last viewed Aug. 9, 2006).

[108] This is illuminated in countless stories from the early and mid-1800s. For example, the 1831 case of Nat Turner (see HERBERT APTHEKER, A DOCUMENTARY HISTORY OF THE NEGRO PEOPLE IN THE UNITED STATES 119 (New York: Citadel Press, 1951)), involved thousands of slaves acting in rebellion. In this case there was a uprising in which 60 white men lost their lives, as did 100 black men. The white response, indicative of the time, was not to search out the guilty parties for trial in the courts, but rather to hang all black men who either participated, or were thought to have participated. Further, night riders were organized with police authority to put down any groupings they determined to be secret meetings. John A. Davis, *Black, Crime, and American Culture*, 423 ANNALS AM. ACAD. POL. & SOC. SCI., CRIME AND JUSTICE IN AMERICA: 1776–1976, at 89–98 (Jan. 1976).

[109] The Scottsboro Case, which has become the paradigm for "black on white" rapes, is a case where the accuser's "whiteness" overrode any consideration of her gender or sexual history. In 1931, two white women were hitchhiking on a train across the state border to find work. When two police officers entered the car, the women, out of fear of being arrested for violating the law prohibiting transporting women across state lines for illicit purposes, immediately told the police officers that they had been raped by nine black men, who were all sitting in the same train car. These accusations lead to the quick formation of a mob that was only restrained by the promise of a speedy trial. This ensuing trial ended with quick death sentences, despite the lack of evidence regarding any rape. Even as the case went through appeal, and the women recanted their stories, the local population did not believe in the innocence of the nine men. Further, despite evidence of the women's involvement in prostitution and adultery, one spectator told a reporter that the "victim might be a fallen woman, but by God she is a white woman." See LISA LINDQUIST DORR, WHITE WOMEN, RAPE, AND THE POWER OF RACE IN VIRGINIA 1900–1960, (University of North Carolina Press, 2004).

[110] President Bush's use of the term "war" reaped unintended consequences. Although it was no doubt aimed at galvanizing the nation, the fact that in international law war can only be between states, he inadvertently promoted Al Qaeda to the level of a state.

usual suspects. Unfortunately, many of the means used in current detainee interrogations are all too familiar to the African American experience in the Deep South.[111]

In 1931, the Wickersham Commission Report on Lawlessness in Law Enforcement[112] was established by President Herbert Hoover for the specific purpose of examining the veracity of numerous reports regarding the conduct of police departments in interrogations throughout the United States. In the end, the Commission's members concluded that suspects had been regularly subjected to "the third degree."[113] Specifically, the Commission determined that willful infliction of pain onto criminal suspects was both widespread and pervasive. The Commission further determined that the abusers included not just interrogators, but the entire system: police officers, judges, magistrates, and other officials. The commission found such violations by examining illegal arrests, bribery, coercion of witnesses, fabrication of evidence, and the aforementioned "third degree."

The history of African Americans in southern jails has been well documented and the subject of much commentary.[114] Furthermore, the

---

[111]   The techniques authorized by U.S. Secretary of Defense Rumsfeld include: the use of stress positions, isolation, hoods over head, removal of comfort items, forced grooming, removal of clothing, and using detainees' phobias to induce stress. See *Impunity for the Architects of Illegal Policy*, HUM. RTS. WATCH, Apr. 2005. http://www.hrw.org/reports/ 2005/us0405/6.htm (last viewed Aug. 2, 2006). Further, on Dec. 25, 2002, the *Washington Post* reported that persons held at Bagram were kept kneeling for hours in black hoods as well as being deprived of sleep with 24-hour bombardments of lights. Further, this article quoted one official as saying that "we don't kick the [expletive] out of them, we send them to other countries so they can kick the [expletive] out of them."

[112]   The *Report on Lawlessness in Law Enforcement* was one of fourteen reports published by the National Commission on Law Observance and Enforcement (the Wickersham Commission). For a discussion of the Commission's report, *see* http://www.lexisnexis. com/academic/guides/jurisprudence/wickersham.asp (last accessed July 25, 2006). President Hoover established the commission in response to American public's increasing worries about crime, and a concern about publicity coming from gang wars in Chicago.

[113]   The Wickersham Commission defines this term as "the use of physical brutality, or other forms of cruelty, to obtain involuntary confessions or admissions." NATIONAL COMMISSION ON LAW OBSERVANCES AND ENFORCEMENT, REPORT ON LAWLESSNESS IN LAW ENFORCEMENT 4 (Washington, D.C.: Government Printing Office, 1931).

[114]   John C. Knechtle, *When to Regulate Hate Speech*, 110 PENN. ST. L. REV. 539 (2006); Mitchell P. Schwartz, *Compensating Victims of Police-Fabricated Confessions*, 70 U. CHI. L. REV. 1119, Summer 2003; Peter B. Rutledge, *The Standard of Review for the Voluntariness of a Confession on Direct Appeal in Federal Court*, 63 U. CHI. L. REV. 1311, Summer 1996; and Seth F. Kreimer, *"Torture Lite," "Full Bodied" Torture, and the Insulation of Legal Conscience*, 1 J. NAT'L SECURITY L. & POL'Y 187, 2005.

"conspiracy of silence"[115] among the relevant communities contributed to abuses, if not death. Even more troubling, many lynchings were conducted with either the active or passive participation of local law enforcement.[116]

Beyond the similarities in the interrogation methods used against the African Americans in the Deep South and the current detainees, there is a further poignancy to this comparison. Specifically, just as African Americans in the Deep South often died as a result of the physical mistreatment, such tragedies occur in current detainee interrogations as well. According to charges filed by the U.S. military against Chief Warrant Officer Lewis Welshofer Jr., Major General Abed Hamed Mowhoush of the Iraqi army was killed by Welshofer during the course of an interrogation.[117]

Additionally, a Department of Defense report documents further instances of abuses inflicted by U.S. personnel beyond Abu Ghraib.[118] Major General Antonio Taguba's investigation identified the following violations of detainee human rights:

> Punching, slapping, and kicking detainees; jumping on their naked feet; Videotaping and photographing naked male and female

---

[115] Amos N. Guiora & Erin M. Page, *Going Toe to Toe: President Barak's and Chief Justice Rehnquist's Theories of Judicial Activism*, 29 HASTINGS INT'L & COMP. L. REV. 51 (2005).

[116] *See* W. FITZHUGH BRUNDAGE, LYNCHING IN THE NEW SOUTH: GEORGIA AND VIRGINIA, 1909–1950, at 18; Sherrilyn A. Ifill, *Creating a Truth and Reconciliation Commission for Lynching*, 21 LAW & INEQ. J. 263, 281 (2003); and Muneer I. Ahmad, *A Rage Shared by Law: Post-September 11 Racial Violence as Crimes of Passion*, 91 CAL. L. REV. 1259 (2004).

[117] Chief Warrant Officer Welshofer was ultimately reprimanded in court but not given jail time for this charge. See *No Prison Time for Soldier Held in Iraqi's Death*, N.Y. TIMES, Jan. 24, 2006, § A. Also, for instances of more detainee deaths, see Tim Golden, *In U.S. Report, Brutal Details of 2 Afghan Inmates' Deaths*, N.Y. TIMES, May 20, 2005, at A1 (detailing the deaths of two Afghan detainees tortured by their Army captors); Tim Golden, *Army Faltered in Investigating Detainee Abuse*, N.Y. TIMES, May 22, 2005, at A1.

[118] For discussion of the events of Abu Ghraib and elsewhere, *see generally* Frank Rich, *Supporting Our Troops Over a Cliff*, N.Y. TIMES, Jun. 4, 2006; Carlotta Gall & David Rhode, *The Reach of War: The Prisons; Afghan Abuse Charges Raise Questions on Authority*, N.Y. TIMES, Sept. 17, 2004; Eric Schmitt, *The Conflict in Iraq: Abuse*, Sept. 9, 2004; Eric Schmitt, *The Reach of War: Capitol Hill*, N.Y. TIMES, July 16, 2004; Josh White, *Memo Shows Officer's Shift on Use of Dogs*, WASH. POST, Apr. 14, 2006; James W. Smith III, *A Few Good Scapegoats: The Abu Ghraib Courts-Martial and the Failure of the Military Justice System*, 27 WHITTIER L. REV. 671 (2006); John T. Parry, *Just for Fun: Understanding Torture and Understanding Abu Gharaib*, 1 J. NAT'L. SECURITY L. & POL'Y 253 (2005). For a discussion of the historical use of lynchings, *see generally* Robert Peltz, *Contempt of Court, The Turn-of-the-Century Lynching That Launched 100 Years of Federalism*, 57 U. MIAMI L. REV. 221 (2002); William S. McFeely, *A Legacy of Slavery and Lynching: The Death Penalty as a Tool of Social Control*, 21-NOV CHAMPION 30 (1997); and Anne S. Emmanuel, *Lynching and the Law in Georgia Circa 1930: A Chapter in the Legal Career of Judge Elbert Tuttle*, 5 WM. & MARY BILL RTS. J. 215 (1996).

detainees; Forcibly arranging detainees in various sexually explicit positions for photographing; Forcing detainees to remove their clothing and keeping them naked for several days at a time; Forcing naked male detainees to wear women's underwear; Forcing groups of male detainees to masturbate themselves while being photographed and videotaped; Arranging naked male detainees in a pile and then jumping on them; Positioning a naked detainee on a MRE Box, with a sandbag on his head, and attaching wires to his fingers, toes, and penis to simulate electric torture; Writing 'I am a Rapest' (sic) on the leg of a detainee alleged to have forcibly raped a 15-year old fellow detainee, and then photographing him naked; Placing a dog chain or strap around a naked detainee's neck and having a female Soldier pose for a picture; A male MP guard having sex with a female detainee; Using military working dogs (without muzzles) to intimidate and frighten detainees, and in at least one case biting and severely injuring a detainee.[119]

With respect to the ill-treatment in the Deep South, the Supreme Court finally entered the mix. In a series of monumental decisions predicated on the Fifth and Fourteenth Amendments, the Court held that the "Star Chamber" was a clear violation of the Constitutional rights of African Americans. The Court, in clear language, held that the government must immediately extend constitutional protections and due process to the interrogations of African Americans.[120]

Just as the Court in the *Bram-Brown* progeny demanded the extension of procedural protections to African American interrogations, the Court in *Hamdan* has now similarly articulated to the government that the regime established in the aftermath of 9/11 must be changed. Specifically, the Court in *Hamdan*, held that the detainees are entitled to Geneva Convention, Article III protections, stating that:

Even if al Qaeda was not signatory of Geneva Conventions, aliens captured in connection with United States' war with al Qaeda [are] entitled to protection of article of Geneva Conventions prohibiting "the passing of sentences and the carrying out of executions

---

[119] *See* "An open letter to President George W. Bush on the question of torture and cruel, inhuman or degrading treatment," Amnesty International, May 7, 2004. http://web. amnesty.org/library/Index/ENGAMR510782004 (last viewed Aug. 30, 2006).

[120] *See* discussion *infra* of "*Bram-Brown* Progeny."

without previous judgment pronounced by a regularly constituted court affording all the judicial guarantees which are recognized as indispensable by civilized peoples"; conflict with al Qaeda was a "conflict not of an international character" within meaning of article, which afforded some minimal protection to individuals associated with neither a signatory nor even a nonsignatory "Power" who were involved in a conflict "in the territory of" a signatory.[121]

To comply with *Hamdan*'s requirement that adequate procedures be established, the government would benefit by looking at the extension of the Fifth and Fourteenth Amendments to African Americans in the Deep South as expressed in the *Bram-Brown* progeny.

Case Law of the *Bram-Brown* Progeny

In *Bram v. United States*,[122] the Supreme Court made its initial foray into the interrogation setting. Although the case did not involve an African American, the Court's bright-line rule is particularly relevant to subsequent race-based cases. Bram was accused of committing murder on board an American vessel, the *Herbert Fuller*, sailing from Boston to South America.[123] The ship's crew overpowered Bram, the ship's first officer, and put him in irons until the vessel reached Halifax.[124] On reaching Halifax, Bram was brought to jail and interrogated by a detective from the Halifax Police Department.[125]

Bram's subsequent confession led to his conviction for the murder aboard the ship.[126] Bram appealed the conviction, claiming that the confession was coerced.[127] In the ensuing appeal, the interrogator testified that Bram had confessed fully to the murder without undue influence or coercion.[128] Bram's counsel, however, objected, arguing that Bram had

---

[121]   *Hamdan*, at 2794.
[122]   Bram v. United States, 168 U.S. 532.
[123]   *Id*. at 534.
[124]   *Id*. at 536.
[125]   *Id*. at 537. Although Bram was brought first to Hallifax, and, at the request of the American consul, interrogated by the Hallifax authorities, the American consul eventually requested that Bram be brought to Boston. It was in the United States, then, that Bram was formally charged with murder.
[126]   *Id*. at 534.
[127]   *Id*. at 539.
[128]   *Id*. at 538–539.

been brought to the detective's private office where he was stripped and interrogated. Because of these circumstances, according to the defendant's counsel, "no statement made by the defendant while so held in custody and his rights interfered with to the extent described was a free and voluntary statement, and no statement as made by him bearing upon this issue was competent."[129]

Although the case does not illustrate an egregious threat, the Court's decision to reverse Bram's conviction established a bright-line test with respect to threats made during interrogation:

> A confession can never be received in evidence where the prisoner has been influenced by any threat or promise; for the law cannot measure the force of the influence used, or decide upon its effect upon the mind of the prisoner, and therefore excludes the declaration if any degree of influence has been exerted.[130]

As the progeny is further developed below, it is important to note that the strict *Bram* test has not been overturned,[131] but rather has been reiterated through its adaptation into a broader test. The "totality of the circumstances"[132]

---

[129] *Id.* at 539.

[130] *Bram*, at 543.

[131] See Alan Hirsch, *Threats, Promises, and False Confessions: Lessons of Slavery*, 49 HOW. L.J. 31 (2005); Marvin Zalman, *The Coming Paradigm Shift on Miranda: The Impact of Chavez v. Martinez*, 39 No. 3 CRIM. LAW BULLETIN 4 (2003); and Mark A. Goodsey, *The New Frontier of Constitutional Confession Law—The International Arena: Exploring the Admissibility of Confessions Taken by U.S. Investigators From Non-Americans Abroad*, 91 GEO. L.J. 851 (2003).

[132] *See generally* United States v. Etchison (not reported in F. Supp., 2005 WL 3088343) (Police interrogation of a suspect in custody threatens the Fifth Amendment where officers compel confessions through coercive interrogation or exposure to "inherently coercive" environments created by custodial interrogation.); State v. Swanigan (279 Kan. 18 (Supreme Court of Kansas 2005)) (Police officers' threats during interrogation to tell county attorney of defendant's lack of cooperation was inconsistent with defendant's Fifth Amendment right against self-incrimination but did not render his confession involuntary per se.); *Riley* (while a pretrial detainee was painfully tightly handcuffed, an officer inserted a pen into a pretrial detainee's nose and threatened to rip it open. The officer also slapped the detainee, causing his head to snap to one side and raising welts on his face. The detainee subsequently suffered depression and nightmares. The court found these injuries to be no more than *de minimus*, necessitating judicial action); *Taylor* (while attempting to remove a driver's license from a pretrial detainee's mouth, an officer "placed his knee in the lower part of [plaintiff's] back and at the same time grabbed [plaintiff] by the head and started pulling his head backwards until his back popped." The detainee also claimed that the officer "shoved a small wooden object into [the detainee's] nose with such force that it caused his nose to hemorrhage and then shoved it into [the detainee's] mouth." The court found the injuries to be *de minimus* at most. The Court held that there are only two exceptions to the rule that plaintiff's

test articulated by the Court in *Ashcraft*,[133] which then morphed into the "shocks the conscience" test[134] for determining whether an interrogation violated a suspect's Fifth and Fourteenth Amendments rights builds on *Bram*.[135]

---

injuries must be more than *de minimus* to sustain a claim of excessive force. The first is under extraordinary circumstances where the officer's conduct is "repugnant to the conscience of mankind. The second exception from the rule requiring more than *de minimus* injury is under a claim of excessive force employed during interrogation); *Gray v. Spillman* (the pretrial detainee was tightly handcuffed, which caused swelling and injury to his right hand; kicked in the foot, which caused severe pain and swelling; and shoved up against a wall, which injured his lip and loosened three of his front teeth. *Id.* at 91. The court held that even if these injuries were *de minimus*, in the context of interrogation, a plaintiff has only to prove the use of *any* physical force to coerce an incriminating statement.); Bartram v. Wolfe (152 F. Supp. 2d 898 (U.S. Dist. Ct., S.D. West Virginia 2001)) (Beating and threatening a person in the course of custodial interrogation violates the Fifth and Fourteenth Amendments of the Constitution.)

[133] Ashcraft v. State of Tennessee, 322 U.S. 143 (1944); Later, in *Arizona v. Fulminante*, (Arizona v. Fulminante, 499 U.S. 279 (where the Court held a jailhouse confession to have been coerced because defendant confessed to a government, agent who was posing as a fellow prisoner, who offered to protect defendant from jailhouse violence in exchange for the truth)) for instance, the Court wrote:

> We deal first with the State's contention that the court below erred in holding Fulminante's confession to have been coerced. The State argues [under *Schneckloth*] that it is the totality of the circumstances that determines whether Fulminante's confession was coerced, but contends that rather than apply this standard, the Arizona court applied a "but for" test, under which the court found that but for the promise given by Sarivola, Fulminante would not have confessed. In support of this argument, the State points to the Arizona court's reference to *Bram v. United States.* Although the Court noted in Bram that a confession cannot be obtained by "any direct or implied promises, however slight, nor by the exertion of any improper influence," it is clear that this passage from Bram, which under current precedent does not state the standard for determining the voluntariness of a confession, was not relied on by the Arizona court in reaching its conclusion.

[134] Edward L. Fiandach, *Miranda Revisited*, 22 CHAMPION (Nov. 2005) ("With Brown establishing the outer parameter of what would commonly be known as the Due Process voluntariness test, the next two decades would see the Court move closer to the rationale of Bram. In so doing, the Court's focus would inexorably shift from an examination of the statement's truthfulness to the motivation to make the statement and whether the decision to testify against one's self was "free and voluntary."); David Aram Kaiser, United States v. Coon: *The Detrimental Reliance for Plea Agreements?*, 52 HASTINGS L.J. 579 (2001) ("While Bram was decided before Brown and its progeny, for the middle third of the 20th century [the Court] based the rule against admitting coerced confessions primarily, if not exclusively, on notions of due process. [The Court] applied the due process voluntariness test in some 30 different cases decided during the era that intervened between *Brown and Escobedo v. Illinois*."); and MaryAnn Fenicato, *Miranda Upheld by U.S. Supreme Court*, 2 No. 19 LAWYERS J. 2 (2000) ("Although Bram preceded Brown, the latter prevailed because the Fifth Amendment was not considered incorporated by the Fourteenth Amendment and applicable to the states until 1964. Thus, the due process test was utilized in approximately thirty different cases thereafter, and continually refined into an inquiry examining whether a defendant's will was overborne by 'weighing the circumstances of pressure against the power of resistance of the person confessing.'")

[135] In applying the Fourteenth Amendment to the criminal law interrogation setting, the Supreme Court has addressed the core issues of voluntary confessions and the totality

The Court's bright-line rule in *Bram* specifically acknowledged not only the applicability of the Fifth Amendment, but also that "there can be no doubt that long prior to our independence the doctrine that one accused of crime could not be compelled to testify against himself had reached its full development in the common law ... as resting on the law of nature, and was imbedded in that system as one of its great and distinguishing attributes."[136] This rule was then adapted and applied to cases involving police departments in the Deep South.

The following cases represent the core of the Supreme Court's intervention in the interrogations of African American suspects requiring application of the Fifth and Fourteenth Amendments.[137] After the enunciation of the rule in *Bram*, the Supreme Court's initial Deep South interrogation case was *Brown v. Mississippi*.[138] *Brown* presented the question of whether convictions based solely on confessions that are shown to have been extorted by state officers through brutality and violence are consistent with the Fourteenth Amendment's due process requirement.[139] The due process doctrine for police interrogations was developed by the Court's dramatic creation of a Fourteenth Amendment exclusionary rule in *Brown*.[140]

In *Brown*, upon discovery of the dead body of a white planter named Raymond Stewart, the local sheriffs went to the home of an African American tenant farmer, Ed Brown. The sheriff asked Brown to accompany him to the house of the deceased where, unbeknown to Brown, a mob of white men had gathered to accuse him of the crime. On Brown's

---

of the circumstances. What the Court referred to in Rochin v. California, 342 U.S. 165 (1952), as "shocks the conscience" is the test for determining whether an interrogation violated the Fifth and Fourteenth Amendments. This test stands for the proposition that the police cannot procure evidence from for a criminal prosecution in a particularly offensive manner (in *Rochin*, the methods objected to included a forced stomach pump looking for drugs in the defendant's stomach).

[136]   *Bram*, at 545.

[137]   Whether the Court could have intervened earlier is for scholars to debate; that being said, I have argued elsewhere (*See* Amos N. Guiora & Erin M. Page, *Going Toe to Toe: President Barak's and Chief Justice Rehnquist's Theories of Judicial Activism*, 29 HASTINGS INT'L & COMP. L. REV. 51 (2005)) that judicial review in armed conflict must be active and immediate. The judicial review philosophy advocated in the article is based on the Israeli model as espoused by the former President of the Israeli Supreme Court, Aharon Barak (see Aharon Barak, *A Judge on Judging: The Role of a Supreme Court in a Democracy*, 116 HARV. L. REV. 16 (2002)).

[138]   Brown v. Mississippi, 297 U.S. 278 (1936).

[139]   *Id*. at 279.

[140]   Catherine Hancock, *Due Process Before Miranda*, 70 TUL. L. REV. 2195 (1996).

denial, the mob seized him, with the sheriff's assistance, and hung him by a rope. The mob let the petitioner down before hanging him a second time.

This process continued while Brown repeatedly protested his innocence. The mob then tied Brown to a tree, whipping him as he consistently denied the accusations. At this point, the mob finally released Brown, and, despite the severe abuse he had just endured, managed to stagger home.[141] Other suspects were then brought to the jailhouse where they were made to strip and lay over chairs while their backs were cut to pieces with a leather strap containing buckles. It was made clear to the victims that the whippings would continue unless and until they confessed.[142]

After a few days, the sheriff returned to Brown's home and arrested him again. In the process of taking Brown to jail in the adjoining county, the sheriff stopped and severely whipped him, threatening that he would continue the whipping until Brown confessed. At this point, Brown finally acceded to the demands, and confessed.[143] Nevertheless, the whippings continued until the confession's specific language was in accordance with that desired by the officers. Ultimately, the petitioners were arrested, indicted, tried, convicted, and sentenced to death within exactly one week.[144]

The Supreme Court in *Brown* held that the trial court should have excluded the confessions because of the brutality used to procure them. Specifically, the Court used the "totality of the circumstances" approach:

> There was thus enough before the court when these confessions were first offered to make known to the court that they were not, beyond all reasonable doubt, free and voluntary; and the failure of the court then to exclude the confessions is sufficient to reverse the judgment, under every rule of procedure that has heretofore been prescribed, and hence it was not necessary subsequently to renew the objections by motion or otherwise.[145]

The extension of constitutional protections was achieved through the use of two constitutional principles: the Fifth Amendment right

---

141   *Brown*, at 282.
142   *Id.*
143   *Id.* 280–282.
144   *Id.* at 279.
145   *Brown*, at 463.

against self-incrimination articulated in *Bram*, and the Fourteenth Amendment's due process clause articulated in *Brown*.[146]

The following cases enable us to draw conclusions pertinent to detainee interrogation. These cases, were not only chosen for their show-ing of the progressive application of the Fifth and Fourteenth Amendments to African Americans, but also for the similarities to current detainee treatment.

White v. Texas

In *White v. Texas*,[147] the defendant, a black farmhand working on a plan-tation outside of Livingston, Texas, was convicted of rape and subse-quently sentenced to death.[148] The defendant was called in from the field while picking cotton to go to the brother of the prosecutrix "where fifteen or sixteen Negroes of the vicinity were at the time in custody without warrants or the filing of charges."[149] White was then taken to a local jail where each night armed officers took him into the woods, asked him to confess, whipped him, and warned him not to tell anyone what transpired.[150]

The defendant, who was illiterate, eventually signed a written confes-sion. Although the officer who was identified by petitioner as the indi-vidual who whipped him nightly in the woods denied doing so, he did not specifically deny taking the petitioner into the woods to be interro-gated.[151] In reversing the defendant's conviction, the Supreme Court held that "due process of law, preserved for all by our Constitution, commands that no such practice as that disclosed by this record shall send any accused to his death."[152]

---

[146] MaryAnn Fenicato, *Miranda Upheld by U.S. Supreme Court*, Law. J., Sept. 2000, at 2, *available at* Westlaw 2 No. 19 Lawyersj 2. Referring to *Brown*, Laura Magid, com-mented that "[i]n 1936...with *Brown v. Mississippi*, the Court turned to the Due Process Clause of the Fourteenth Amendment as the basis for examining the voluntariness of confessions in dozens of state cases. The Court held that police use of violence was 'revolting to the sense of justice,' stating that '[t]he rack and torture chamber may not be substituted for the witness stand." Laura Magid, *Deceptive Interrogation Practices: How Far is Too Far?*, 99 Mich. L. Rev. 1168, 1172 (2001).

[147] White v. Texas, 310 U.S. 530 (1940).

[148] *Id.* at 530.

[149] *Id.* at 532

[150] *Id.*

[151] *Id.* at 533.

[152] *Id.*, citing Chambers v. Florida, 309 U.S. 227 (1940).

Ward v. Texas

In another example of coercive interrogation in the Deep South, the defendant in *Ward v. Texas*,[153] a black man accused of killing a white man, appealed his murder conviction, arguing that it was based on a coerced confession. On arrest, the police told the defendant that mobs of white men were waiting for him in various towns. Based on the supposed presence of these mobs, the police took the defendant from town to town under the cover of night, not allowing him to sleep.[154] Further, the defendant contended that he only offered a confession after "he had been arrested without a warrant, taken from his home town, driven for three days from county to county, placed in a jail more than 100 miles from his home, questioned continuously, and beaten, whipped and burned by the officer to whom the confession was finally made."[155]

The *Ward* Court held that accepting the defendant's confession into evidence was a denial of his due process rights because of the cumulative mistreatment to which he was subjected. Specifically, the Court spoke of "cumulative mistreatment"[156] when it indicated that:

> The effect of moving an ignorant negro by night and day to strange towns, telling him of threats of mob violence, and questioning him continuously is evident from petitioner's statement to County Attorney Rolston that he would be glad to make any statement that Rolston desired. Disregarding petitioner's claims that he was whipped and burned, we must conclude that this confession was not free and voluntary but was the product of coercion and duress, that petitioner was no longer able freely to admit or to deny or to refuse to answer, and that he was willing to make any statement that the officers wanted him to make.
>
> This Court has set aside convictions based upon confessions extorted from ignorant persons who have been subjected to persistent and protracted questioning, or who have been threatened with

---

[153] Ward v. Texas, 316 U.S. 547 (1942).
[154] *Id.* at 549.
[155] *Id.*
[156] Finding cumulative mistreatment requires a case by case analysis where the court must focus on particular circumstances (amount of movement, specific length of time, number of people, gender, etc.) to make a determination of when the "continuousness" breaks the individual's will.

mob violence, or who have been unlawfully held incommunicado without advice of friends or counsel, or who have been taken at night to lonely and isolated places for questioning. Any one of these grounds would be sufficient cause for reversal. All of them are to be found in this case.[157]

Ashcraft v. Tennessee

In 1944, the petitioners in *Ashcraft v. Tennessee*[158] claimed that their convictions had been improperly extorted by law enforcement officials. The defendants were questioned continuously for more than thirty-six hours by a relay of police officers. In reversing the convictions, the Ashcraft Court held that, under the totality of the circumstances test, the confessions were compelled through cumulative mistreatment. As previously indicated, the question in *Bram* was whether the defendant had been compelled, or coerced, to make a self-incriminatory statement, contrary to the Fifth Amendment. The question in *Ashcraft*, furthering *Brown*, was whether the defendant's Fourteenth Amendment privileges were violated when he was coerced to confess.

The particular importance of *Ashcraft* is its factual distinction from the previous cases. The conviction was overturned not because of physical abuse, but rather, because of cumulative mistreatment, as "it appears that Ashcraft from Saturday evening at seven o'clock until Monday morning at approximately nine-thirty never left this homicide room of the fifth floor."[159]

The *Ashcraft* dissent, however, raises concerns that the majority's position may be construed to mean that *any* lengthy interrogation is inherently coercive. The dissent argued that although confessions resulting from a lengthy interrogation should be held as *prima facie* involuntary, a court must still focus on the actual coerciveness of the interrogation. More specifically, the question is what interrogation methods can be used on the detainee to facilitate the receipt of actionable intelligence without violating the individual's rights. Accordingly, it is critical to examine specific interrogation methods. The specific measures are the

---

[157] *Ward*, at 555.
[158] Ashcraft v. Tennessee, 322 U.S. 143 (1944).
[159] *Id*. at 149.

most accurate measure of the actual coerciveness to which the detainees are subjected.

The *Bram-Brown* Progeny and the Hybrid Paradigm

The detainees currently held by the United States, similar to the African Americans, have, in many instances, been rounded up and detained based on vague and unarticulated suspicion of guilt. They have been subjected to violent and degrading interrogations, held until their will is broken, often times leading to untrustworthy confessions and intelligence. With the above facts and discussion in hand, we turn to the Constitutional discussion regarding extending Constitutional protections to noncitizens.

In addition to this discussion of *whether* and *how* to extend such protections, the preceding question of *why* must always be kept in mind. A regime of protection needs to be extended because of the abuses, most notably in Abu Ghraib and Guantanamo Bay. However, protecting human rights is mandatory, regardless of whether abuses have occurred to date or not. Even if the past six years had been abuse free, the newness of the situation combined with the national trauma in the aftermath of 9/11 requires the executive branch and legislature to articulate the limits of interrogation. The abuses during the past six years are direct results of a system hesitant to use meaningful guidelines, favoring illusive and undefined standards.

Bram, Brown, Ashcraft, White, and *Ward* addressed a recurring theme: the mistreatment of African Americans in the Deep South by local law enforcement officials, either directly or indirectly (turning a *blind eye*). The methods used—beatings, whippings, lynchings—were predicated on coercion, cumulative mistreatment, threats, and cruelty. Whether the interrogation was information-based or racism-based, the means used violated the detainee's basic constitutional rights. The mistreatment was pervasive, institutionalized, and normative from a societal perspective. A retrospective analysis of the times suggests that mistreatment of African Americans was socially acceptable and legitimized by the political and judicial establishments. Wherever he was whipped, the African American had literally no recourse to the courts, the media, or the conscience of the largely acquiescing majority. Whether the acquiescence was based on racism or predicated on ignorance (some would argue the two are inherently related), the result is that the interrogations of the African American detainee violated legal and moral norms alike.

Although the Supreme Court held that the interrogation in *Brown* violated Brown's constitutional rights, the Court's reticent approach is similar to that advocated by late Chief Justice Rehnquist with respect to judicial review during armed conflict. The Supreme Court of the 1920s and 1930s was hesitant to interfere in *normative behavior* that consistently violated the civil rights of American citizens. In seeking to define the limits of interrogation, the threats, cumulative mistreatment, coercion, and cruelty were largely, and tragically, unchecked by the Supreme Court. This damning indictment holds true for the Congress and executive branch alike.

However, as it was the Supreme Court that *finally* sought to protect the African American detainee, the relevant question in our discourse is how does the *Bram-Brown* progeny impact the Guantanamo Bay detainee? Given, in large part, the deafening silence of the Congress, the executive, media, and public, the Court is our guiding light in seeking to articulate the limits of interrogation. The question before us is what relevance does 1930s and 1940s case law pertaining to African Americans have for the detainee of today in the interrogation setting?

What Does the *Bram-Brown* Progeny Mean for Detainees?

Interrogations are paradoxical in that they are simultaneously matters of great complexity and simplicity. There is universality to the interrogation setting that encompasses Montgomery, Alabama and Abu Ghraib, Iraq alike. An absence of clearly articulated limits is what characterized interrogations of the Deep South of the 1930s and 1940s and detainee abuses that directly resulted from the Bybee memos.

Over the years, the Supreme Court has applied a series of tests for the limits of interrogation designed to determine the voluntariness of the confession. The interrogation setting is inherently unfair because the interrogator is in complete control. The interrogatee cannot leave when they desire, they may not excuse themselves to the bathroom, they cannot tell the interrogator that they do not feel like talking and cannot tell their families they will be home shortly. In addition to the basic denials of freedom, the interrogated have been stripped of individuality; they wear the same clothes as other interrogatees, their hair may have been closely cut, and they may well have a number on the chest of their uniforms. At the end of the interrogation (a time to be determined solely by the interrogator without consulting the interrogatee), they will be returned to their cells where awaits them a cellmate whose purpose is to take full advantage of the interrogatee's basic need to talk after having been subjected to stressful conditions.

And who is this fellow cellmate? If the interrogation itself is not sufficiently stressful then the return to the cell is when the interrogatee needs to be truly on guard. His or her fellow cellmate may well be a mole specifically placed in the cell for the sole purpose of eliciting information from the tired, not fully on guard interrogatee. The cellmate, in this scenario a well-placed mole, is an integral part of the interrogation process. Therefore, in discussing the limits of interrogation and applying the tests discussed by the Supreme Court, the setting must be fully appreciated.

However, there is more than just the interrogator and the mole with whom the interrogatee must contend. The conduct of the guards also significantly affects the mood and behavior of the interrogatee. That is, in seeking to determine whether the *totality of the circumstances shocks the conscience*, or the *voluntariness* test applies, the analysis needs to go beyond the detainee's mere questioning. The context must be viewed in whole, rather than in part.

The African American in whichever context interrogated (back woods, back seat, jail) knew he would be subjected to methods that ranged from coercive interrogation to torture. The actors were all the officials who came in contact with individual. Confessions were rarely voluntary and would not be admissible by today's evidentiary and moral standards.

What causes the lack of institutional controls, whether deliberate or not, is unclear but also irrelevant. The lack of institutionalized oversight by choice or otherwise, the "banality of evil,"[160] was clearly true with respect to how African Americans were interrogated. They are clearly true with respect to how some detainees were interrogated post 9/11. Although the horrors visited on Brown, White, Ashcraft, and Ward were significantly different from the interrogations some detainees have been subjected to, the lessons history offers in the interrogation context are instructive.

---

[160]   Hannah Arendt's well known and oft-repeated phrase regarding the ease with which Nazi Germany executed the Holocaust.

Were all post-9/11 detainees tortured? No, but some clearly were, and most damning of all is that then Secretary of Defense Rumsfeld directly facilitated torture when he authorized a legal opinion stating that detainees could be subject to measures that include water-boarding. In that context, the written institutionalization of torture is profoundly disturbing for it suggests an administration openly disdainful of and in open violation of international law conventions.

The interrogations of the 1930s were more often than not carried out by largely uneducated individuals steeped in blind hatred of the black man. Premised on age-old stereotypes, the Deep South of that era represents the truly darkest days of American history. That hatred was based on ignorance, blind racism, and evil. That combination directly led to the interrogations and lynchings addressed in the cases discussed above.

The memos authorizing the means of interrogation were written by highly trained lawyers sitting in their offices and authorized by senior policy and decision makers, graduates of America's finest educational institutions. It is hard to know which is more troubling—the blind racism of the mob or the willful violations of the law by the educated. Without clearly articulated guidelines for interrogations, the *Brown* of yesterday will become the *Brown* of tomorrow.

CHAPTER 5

Interrogation Standards of the Fifth and Fourteenth Amendments Applied to Both Citizens and Noncitizens

Why should constitutional protections be extended to any noncitizen in the first place? Some argue that any alien (legal or illegal) residing in the United States is entitled to full constitutional guarantees and protections.[161] According to Professor David Cole:

> As politically tempting as the trade-off of immigrants' liberties for our security may appear, we should not make it. As a matter of principle, the rights that we have selectively denied to immigrants are not reserved for citizens. The rights of political freedom, due process, and equal protection belong to every person subject to United States legal obligations, irrespective of citizenship.[162]

The Supreme Court addressed this issue in the *Dred Scott* case, holding that the Fifth Amendment was not limited to the geographic boundaries of the states, but rather such protections were extended to all incorporated territories of the United States.[163] In the 150 years since *Dred Scott*, the Court has discussed two distinct lines of demarcation relevent for determining detainee rights. These two jurisprudential lines

---

[161] David Cole & James Dempsey, Immigrants' Rights and American Freedoms in the War on Terrorism (New Press 2003).

[162] David Cole, *Enemy Aliens*, 54 STANFORD LAW REVIEWS 953, 953 (2000)

[163] See Dred Scott v. Sandford, 60 U.S. 393 (1857).

are: distinguishing between individuals inside and outside of the United States and distinguishing between citizens and noncitizens.

For this first distinction, case law slowly extended Constitutional protections to include noncitizens, provided that cognizable ties to the United States could be demonstrated. The most commonly applied tie was physical location within the border of the United States.[164] If it is held that Guantanamo Bay is a territory of the United States, then this judicial precedent dictates that fundamental rights, such as the Fifth and Fourteenth Amendments, should apply. But, if not held to be a U.S. territory, then Constitutional protections would not be extended.[165]

For the second distinction, the Court looked to the applicability of Constitutional protections to citizens, no matter where they were physically located. Despite the traditional view that the Constitution has no reach beyond U.S. territory, the *Insular Cases* initiated expanding the reach. Specifically, the Insular Cases addressed four important points: (1) They offered explicit legal justification of American endeavors in Puerto Rico; (2) the cases created a system by which America, as a state, could exert power over a foreign entity; (3) they defined the *legitimate* framework for later political struggles relating to the issue of the political status of Puerto Rico and the granting of legal and political rights to Puerto Ricans; and (4) they created a framework that facilitated the establishment of practices which recognized, and validated, the colonial project in Puerto Rico.

As the Supreme Court further developed this second distinction, the question of citizenship, it increasingly held that citizens carry their constitutional rights outside of the territory of the United States. In 1990,

---

[164]   United States v. Tiede, 86 F.R.D. 227 (D. Berlin 1979).

[165]   The historical litany of this distinction began in 1891 with the case of *In re Ross* (140 U.S. 453 (1891)). In *Ross*, an American seaman was suspected of murder on an American ship in Japan. The defendant then was tried and convicted by a consular court in Japan, appealed based on a Fifth Amendment claim, and the Supreme Court denied the appeal because the trial took place outside of the United States, and thus the Fifth Amendment did not apply). In that case the Court acknowledged that it was a valid question to inquire whether the person asserting constitutional protection was inside or outside of the United States. This line of cases continued, then, with the Insular Cases running from 1901–1922. Specifically, cases considered to be within the progeny of the Insular Cases dealt with the land acquired by the United States during the Spanish-American War. This was, for the first time, where the Court noted that some constitutional rights could be extended out to U.S. territories, but only some rights would be here extended, as the territory was not fully incorporated. Downes v. Bidwell, 182 U.S. 244 (1901).

the Court held in *United States v. Verdugo-Urquidez*[166] that the Fifth Amendment, in particular, applied to any "person" or "accused" as opposed to the more restrictive Fourth Amendment protection of "the people."[167]

The *Eisentrager* Court[168] noted a slow and steady progression in the increase of rights to be granted to aliens. In noting this progressive trend, the *Eisentrager* Court held that physical presence *alone* in the country creates an implied guarantee of certain rights, which become even more extensive when an active statement of intent to become a citizen is made.[169] Specifically, the Court noted that "in extending constitutional protections beyond the citizenry, the Court has been at pains to point out that it was the alien's presence within its territorial jurisdiction that gave the Judiciary power to act."[170]

Applying these principles to the debate about Guantanamo detainees, the court in *Khalid v. Bush*[171] held that Guantanamo Bay detainees do not possess any cognizable rights because, the District Court noted, noncitizens detained by the United States beyond the domestic borders (as the court argued to be the case with Guantanamo Bay) cannot avail themselves of constitutional protections. However, *Rasul v. Bush*[172] offers a more appropriate modern frame of reference on the question of the interplay between the decisions of Guantanamo's territorial status and the proper extension of constitutional protections. *Rasul* stands for the proposition that the federal courts have jurisdiction to hear a detainee's habeas petition *whenever* they are held in a place where the "United States exercises complete jurisdiction and control."[173]

In further arguing for constitutional protections for detainees, the *In re Guantanamo Detainees*[174] court cited *Rasul* as recognizing the precedent from *Eisentrager* barring claims of an alien seeking to enforce the

---

[166] 494 U.S. 259, at 265–66.

[167] Moving forward momentarily, the current Congressional immigration debates enable further analysis. In the immigration context, illegal immigrants working in the United States are subjected to the aspects of the Constitution that benefit the government, such as taxation. Thus, the argument can be made that if the government is going to apply Constitutional guarantees when beneficial to its interests, then Constitutional protections, as discussed later in this book, must be extended.

[168] *Johnson v. Eisentrager,* 339 U.S. 763 (1950).

[169] *Eisentrager,* at 771.

[170] *Id.*

[171] *Khalid,* 355 F. Supp. 2d 311 (D.D.C. 2005) (foreign nationals captured on the battlefield and brought to Guantanamo Bay filed petitions for writ of habeas corpus).

[172] *Rasul* 542 U.S. 466, 467 (2004).

[173] *Id.*

[174] 355 F. Supp. 2d 443, 453–454 (D.D.C. 2005).

U.S. Constitution in a habeas corpus[175] proceeding outside of a sovereign territory of the United States.[176] However, the *In re Guantanamo Detainees* court held that the *Eisentrager* decision that denied German detainees constitutional rights was inapplicable to the Guantanamo detainees because the detainees, unlike the Germans, "have been imprisoned in territory over which the U.S. exercises exclusive jurisdiction and control."[177]

Thus for the question at hand, in light of the jurisprudence of the *Eisentrager* decision, the issue turns on the territorial status of Guantanamo Bay. Guantanamo detainees must be granted constitutional protections if Guantanamo Bay is accepted as a territory of the United States.

The discussion regarding the applicability of constitutional rights to the detainees must be grounded on the understanding that, although we are not talking about *legal aliens*, we are also not talking about *illegal aliens*, as the term is commonly understood.[178] Rather, we are talking about a third class of aliens: detainees. This class of individuals was brought within the jurisdiction of the United States, specifically to Guantanamo Bay, which is tantamount to U.S. soil, against their will by U.S. soldiers acting on the orders of their commander in chief.[179]

---

[175] A writ of habeas corpus is a judicial mandate to a prison official ordering that an inmate be brought to the court so it can be determined whether or not that person is imprisoned lawfully and whether or not he should be released from custody. In Brown v. Vasquez, 952 F.2d 1164, 1166 (9th Cir. 1991), cert. denied, 112 S. Ct. 1778 (1992), the court observed that the Supreme Court has "recognized the fact that'[t]he writ of habeas corpus is the fundamental instrument for safeguarding individual freedom against arbitrary and lawless state action." Harris v. Nelson, 394 U.S. 286, 290–91 (1969). "Therefore, the writ must be 'administered with the initiative and flexibility essential to insure that miscarriages of justice within its reach are surfaced and corrected.'" *Harris*, 394 U.S., at 291, http://www.lectlaw.com/def/h001.htm (last visited June 4, 2007).

[176] *In re Guantanamo Detainees*, at 449.

[177] *Id*. at 476. The German detainees were held and tried by the U.S. Army in the "China Theatre." However, on their convictions they were sent to Germany to serve their sentences. *Eisentrager*, at 766.

[178] This term usually refers to individuals who have illegally crossed the borders in an effort to get around the lengthy immigration process.

[179] *See generally* Juliet Stumpf, *Citizens of an Enemy Land: Enemy Combatants, Aliens and the Constitutional Rights of the Pseudo-Citizen*, 38 U.C. Davis L. Rev. 79 (2004); Valerie L. Barth, *Anti-Immigrant Backlash and the Role of the Judiciary: A Proposal for Heightened Review of Federal Laws Affecting Immigrants*, 29 St. Mary's L.J. 105 (1997); and Wendy R. St. Charles, *Recognizing Constitutional Rights of Excludable Aliens: The Ninth Circuit Goes Out on a Limb to Free the "Flying Dutchman,"* 4 J. Transnat'l L. & Pol'y 145 (1005).

The Fifth Amendment Right Against Self-Incrimination

The protections of the Fifth and Fourteenth Amendment are inextricably tied to the interrogation setting within the domestic criminal law paradigm. The Fifth Amendment of the U.S. Constitution specifically protects an individual from being forced to incriminate himself.[180] For this discussion, the ultimate question regarding the Fifth Amendment is whether the right against self incrimination should be extended to post 9/11 detainees. Although the suggestion that an individual arrested in the zone of combat[181] should be read the traditional Miranda rights is unreasonable given its impracticability, it remains to be examined whether such rights and protections should be granted to the detainee once he is in the interrogation setting.[182]

In analyzing the *Bram-Brown* progeny, it is clear that the Supreme Court extended the Fifth Amendment to the indigent, illiterate African American in the jailhouse of the Deep South. In the aftermath of *Hamdan*, the right against self incrimination needs to, at least partially, be extended

---

[180] Specifically, "nor shall be compelled in any criminal case to be a witness against himself." U.S. Const. amend. V. Scholars and Supreme Court cases alike have analyzed the significance of this right in various contexts: For scholarship discussing the Fifth Amendment in relation to police interrogation methods, *see generally* Alexander J. Wilson, *Defining Interrogation Under the Confrontation Clause After* Crawford v. Washington, 39 Colum. J.L. & Soc. Probs. 257 (2005); Paul G. Alvarez, *Taking Back Miranda: How Seibert and Patane Can Keep "Question-First" and "Outside Miranda" Interrogation Methods in Check*, 54 Cath. U. L. Rev. 1195 (2005); Russell D. Covey, *Interrogation Warrants*, 26 Cardozo L. Rev. 1867 (2005). For scholarship discussing the Fifth Amendment in relation to court testimony, *see generally* H. Mitchell Caldwell & Carlo Spiga, *Crippling the Defense of an Accused: The Constitutionality of the Criminal Defendant's Right to Testify*, 6 Wyo. L. Rev. 87 (2006). For scholarship discussing the Fifth Amendment in relation to confessions, *see generally* Eric English, *You Have the Right to Remain Silent, Now Please Repeat Your Confession:* Missouri v. Seibert *and the Court's Attempt to Put and End to the Question-First Technique*, 33 Pepp. L. Rev. 423 (2006); and Ronald J. Allen, *Miranda's Hollow Core*, 100 Nw. U. L. Rev. 71 (2006).

[181] This is a much used, perhaps misused and misunderstood, term of art. In traditional warfare, the zone of combat was where armies faced each other: infantry and armored corps units on the battleground; air forces in the air and navies on the high sea. In "armed conflict short of war," the zone of combat has been significantly expanded to include the civilian population and urban residential areas. The training of the soldier for the zone of combat is significantly different than for traditional warfare.

[182] *See* Rinat Kitai, *A Custodial Suspect's Right to the Assistance of Counsel: The Ambivalence of the Israeli Law Against the Backdrop of American Law*, 19 BYU J. Pub. L. 205 (2004); *Executive Branch Memoranda on Status and Permissible Treatment of Detainees*, 98 Am. J. Int'l L. 820 (2004); and Jonathan F. Lenzner, *From a Pakistani Stationhouse to the Federal Courthouse: A Confession's Uncertain Journey in the U.S.-Led War on Terror*, 12 Cardozo J. Int'l & Comp. L. 297 (2004).

to the detainees as well.[183] Although never directly addressing the detainees' rights regarding self-incrimination, the *Hamdan* Court's opinion is a scathing criticism of the military commissions as a whole, incorporating the complete lack of Fifth Amendment protections into its criticism. The Bush administration would clearly disagree with such a proposition. It had previously indicated that "it is not practicable to apply in military commissions under this order the principles of law and the rules of evidence generally recognized in the trial of criminal cases in the United States district courts."[184]

Although it can be argued that a detainee *may* possess intelligence information of operational importance, the Supreme Court has clearly linked the Fifth Amendment's protections against self-incrimination to a limitation of acceptable interrogation methods. Despite the Bush administration's "new day of executive detentions,"[185] the dismissal regarding the possibility of extending Fifth Amendment protections to the detainees may be easier said than done. Granting this right to noncitizens is an issue with which the Court and scholars will continue to wrestle.

---

[183] *See* Bob Herbert, *The Definition of Tyranny*, N.Y. Times, July 17, 2006; Adam Liptak, *Scholars Agree That Congress Could Reject Commissions, but Not That It Should*, N.Y. Times, July 15, 2006; Kate Zernike & Sheryl Gay Stolberg, *Detainee Rights Create a Divide on Capitol Hill*, N.Y. Times, July 10, 2006; Rosa Brooks, *Orwell Has Nothing on This White House*," LA Times, July 14, 2006, *Enemy Combatants at Guantanamo Bay*, LA Times, July 2, 2006.

[184] Detention, Treatment, and Trial of Certain Non-Citizens in the War Against Terrorism, Military Order of Nov. 13, 2001, 66 Fed. Reg. 222 § 1(f) (Nov. 16, 2001).

[185] Timothy Lynch, *Power and Liberty in Wartime*, 2004 Cato Sup. Ct. Rev. 23 2004:

President Bush shocked the American legal community by asserting what was essentially a "new day of executive detentions." But absent an invasion or rebellion on American soil, it is farfetched to suggest that any person in America can be imprisoned on the mere say-so of the president.

However, it is not unreasonable or implausible to suggest that wartime circumstances can mean a change in the rules, methods, and procedures by which the government can deal with the problem of illegal aliens. American law generally denies the benefit of a transaction to one who procures the transaction with fraud. Thus, why should an individual who has entered the United States surreptitiously or through false pretenses benefit from that wrong by acquiring the full panoply of constitutional rights that are accorded to citizens and long-term permanent residents?

Before a nonresident alien can acquire standing to assert constitutional protections against detention and imprisonment, the first order of business ought to be an examination of the prisoner's immigration status. "If that status was obtained by fraud, misrepresentation or other unlawful means, then it should be deemed void ab initio. Such an alien should be treated under the law as if he never was lawfully admitted to the United States—because in a very real sense he was not."

For instance, in *Zadvydas v. Davis*[186] the Supreme Court reaffirmed the tradition of applying due process to aliens present within the United States, regardless of their legal status.[187] Specifically, the Court held the Fifth Amendment is incongruent with a law permitting the indefinite detention of a noncitizen on domestic soil. Thus, "once present in the country, aliens can claim due process protections."[188]

In an additional immigration case law, the Court in *Verdugo-Urquidez*,[189] denied a motion to suppress evidence seized by agents of the Drug Enforcement Agency while searching the home of a Mexican citizen without a warrant.[190] Although the Court held that Fourth Amendment rights are not to be extended to noncitizens,[191] Justice Kennedy's concurrence stated the defendant would be entitled to Due Process Clause protection under the Fifth Amendment when his case finally went to trial.[192]

Specifically, the Court ruled that Fourth Amendment protections did not extend to the home of a Mexican citizen in Mexico. The Court, however, made a point to distinguish its holding from one which would have occurred had the appeal been regarding the Fifth Amendment. In looking at the language of the Fourth Amendment, the Court noted that the Amendment's application was only to "the people," as discussed therein. The Fifth and Sixth Amendments, however, apply to "persons" or "the accused," respectively.[193] The Court, although not explicitly extending Fifth Amendment protections to noncitizens, used dicta to indicate that such a holding is not beyond the pale.[194] Although Professor Cole convincingly argues that legal and illegal aliens should be entitled to the same rights and protections, it is important to note that his position is not uniformly accepted. Those opposed to Professor Cole argue that the extension of Constitutional protections to noncitizens is only permissible when such an individual has "some substantial connection to the

---

[186] 533 U.S. 678 (2001).
[187] Shirin Sinnar, *Patriotic or Unconstitutional: The Mandatory Detention of Aliens Under the USA Patriot Act*, 55 Stan. L. Rev. 1419 (2003).
[188] *Id.*
[189] 494 U.S. 25.
[190] *Verdugo-Urquidez*, at 274–275.
[191] *Id.* at 265.
[192] Brenner A. Allen, *A Cause of Action Against Private Contractors and the U.S. Government for Freedom of Speech Violations in Iraq*, North Carolina Journal of International Law and Commercial Regulation, 31 N.C. J. Int'l L & Com. Reg. 535 (2005).
[193] *Id.* at 265–66.
[194] United States v. Verdugo-Urquidez, 494 U.S. 259 (1990).

United States."[195] Those who subscribe to this view argue that the law of the United States holds that only aliens within the U.S. territory are "persons" and that such status is wholly unavailable to any alien outside of the American border.[196]

In examining the extension of Fifth Amendment rights and protections to detainees in the interrogation setting, the question relevant for our purpose is whether the application of rights granted to African Americans in the Deep South is applicable to the hybrid paradigm. Specifically, we must determine whether a detainee subject to coercion is entitled to Fifth Amendment privileges regarding self-incrimination. In the wake of the *Bram-Brown* progeny holdings, which granted this right to African Americans, I submit that extending the right to detainees is both constitutionally appropriate and necessary. Although the detainees are not American citizens, their interrogation takes place in American custody, on soil that is as American as possible without actually being within the American borders.

As the preceding discussion illuminates, consensus regarding extending constitutional protections to noncitizens has not yet been reached. However, it appears clear that the Supreme Court is inclined to extend Fifth Amendment safeguards to all persons subject to control of the United States government. This argument is strengthened when discussing detainees who, unlike immigrants, did not willingly come to be under U.S. control.

It is arguable that by taking up arms against the United States, the detainees were combatants who placed themselves in this situation and therefore not entitled to constitutional protections. However, as the detainees are innocent until proven guilty, they are solely defined as *suspects* at the interrogation stage. Suspects, regardless of what crime they may *potentially* be found guilty of, are entitled to the Fifth Amendment right against self-incrimination. This principle holds true for African Americans in the Deep South, for all noncitizens living in the United States, and for detainees held by the United States.

---

[195] Austen L. Parrish, *Sovereignty, Not Due Process: Personal Jurisdiction Over Nonresident Alien Defendants*, 41 WAKE FOREST L. REV. 1 (2006).

[196] *Id.*

The Fourteenth Amendment Right to Due Process

In addition to extending Fifth Amendment protections to African Americans, the *Bram-Brown* progeny also stands for the proposition that the African Americans of the Deep South were to be extended the Fourteenth Amendment guarantee of due process.[197] As noted earlier, the discussion of extending constitutional protections to noncitizens has involved the Fourteenth Amendment at almost every turn.[198] Those

---

[197] Specifically, "nor shall any State deprive any person of life, liberty, or property, without due process of law." U.S. Const. amend. XIV. For discussion on the applicability of the Fourteenth Amendment Due Process rights to detainees, *see* Tamara Huckert, *The Undetermined Fate of Guantanamo Bay Detainees' Habeas Corpus Petitions*, 9 Gonz. J. Int'l L. 236 (2005–2006); Michael I. Greenberger, *Three Strikes and Your Outside the Constitution: Will the Guantanamo Bay Alien Detainees be Granted Fundamental Due Process?*, 37 APR Md. B.J. 14 (2004); Jeffery F. Addicott, *Into the Star Chamber: Does the United States Engage in the Use of Torture or Similar Illegal Practices in the War on Terror?*, 92 Ky. L. J. 849 (2003).

[198] In Kwon v. Colding, 344 U.S. 590 (1953) and Jean v. Nelson, 472 U.S. 846 (1985) the court noted that "As a general rule, aliens who are physically present in the United States are accorded the full panoply of traditional due process rights, while aliens merely seeking to enter the country do not enjoy such protection and find much less process due an adjudication of their right to admission."

In Medina v. O'Neill, 838 F.2d 800 (5th Cir. 1988), Lynch v. Cannatella, 810 F.2d 1363 (5th Cir. 1987) the court held that even though inadmissible aliens cannot challenge admission decisions, and the like, "they are entitled under the Due Process Clauses of the Fifth and Fourteenth Amendments to be free of gross physical abuse at the hands of state or federal officials."

In Johnson v. Eisentrager, 339 U.S. 763 (1950), the Court, in discussing the constitutional rights of aliens, has stated in domestic matters that "[m]ere lawful presence in the country creates an implied assurance of safe conduct." The Supreme Court ultimately held that the petitioners in *Eisentrager* had no standing to file a claim for habeas relief in a United States court. In *In re Guantanamo Detainees Cases* 355 F. Supp. 2d 443 (D.D.C. 2005) the Court upheld a decision that was based on an interpretation that *Eisentrager* barred claims of any alien seeking to enforce the United States Constitution in a habeas proceeding unless the alien is in custody in sovereign United States territory. Recognizing that Guantanamo Bay is not part of the sovereign territory of the United States, the District Court dismissed the cases for lack of "jurisdiction to consider the constitutional claims that are presented to the Court for resolution." After issuing a show cause order as to why an additional pending habeas case filed by a Guantanamo detainee, Habib v. Bush, 02-CV-1130 (CKK), should not be dismissed in light of the decision in *Rasul* and *Al Odah*, the District Court also dismissed that case, and all three cases were appealed to the United States Court of Appeals for the District of Columbia Circuit. The Supreme Court reversed the D.C. Circuit's decision (which had upheld the District Court) and held that the District Court did have jurisdiction to hear the detainees' habeas claims. The majority noted several facts that distinguished the Guantanamo detainees from the petitioners in *Eisentrager* more than fifty years earlier: "[The Guantanamo petitioners] are not nationals of countries at war with the United States, and they deny that they have engaged in or plotted acts of aggression against the United States; they have never

discussions illuminate the fact that the drafters of the Constitution actually intended the Fourteenth Amendment to apply to noncitizens as opposed to the unclear history of the Fifth Amendment. Specifically, the Congressional debates surrounding the adoption of the Fourteenth Amendment show that the drafters had a close familiarity with the provisions of the Articles of Confederation, a document that noted a strict line of demarcation between *citizens* and *persons*. The framers of the Fourteenth Amendment, then, did not use the term *citizens*, but rather made frequent reference to *persons*, which can be interpreted to include noncitizens.[199] This is highly relevant to analyzing whether the Supreme Court's holdings regarding due process can be applied to the category of persons the hybrid paradigm seeks to protect: detainees.

---

been afforded access to any tribunal, much less charged with and convicted of wrongdoing; and for more than two years they have been imprisoned in territory over which the United States exercises exclusive jurisdiction and control." Emphasizing that "[b]y the express terms of its agreements with Cuba, the United States exercises 'complete jurisdiction and control' over the Guantanamo Bay Naval Base," and highlighting that the government conceded at oral argument that "the habeas statute would create federal-court jurisdiction over the claims of an American citizen held at the base," the Court concluded, "Aliens held at the base, no less than American citizens, are entitled to invoke the federal courts' authority under [the habeas statute]." The Supreme Court expressly acknowledged that the allegations contained in the petitions for writs of habeas corpus "unquestionably describe 'custody in violation of the Constitution or laws or treaties of the United States'" as required by the habeas statute, and concluded by instructing: Whether and what further proceedings may become necessary after respondents make their response to the merits of petitioners' claims are matters that we need not address now. What is presently at stake is only whether the federal courts have jurisdiction to determine the legality of the Executive's potentially indefinite detention of individuals who claim to be wholly innocent of wrongdoing. Answering that question in the affirmative, we reverse the judgment of the Court of Appeals and remand for the District Court to consider in the first instance the merits of petitioners' claims.

The court in Hamdi v. Rumsfeld, 316 F.3d 450 (4th Cir. 2003) held that the President constitutionally detained the petitioner, a United States citizen, as an enemy combatant pursuant to the war powers entrusted to him by the United States Constitution, the court noting that one who takes up arms against the United States in a foreign theater of war, regardless of his citizenship, may properly be designated an enemy combatant and treated as such. This annotation collects and discusses the cases that have considered the executive branch's designation of a person as an unlawful or enemy combatant.

Also, see David Cole and James Dempsey, Immigrants' Rights and American Freedoms in the War on Terrorism (New Press 2003).

199   Cong. Globe, 37th Cong., 2nd Sess. 1638 (1862).

Constitutional Rights and Due Process in the Hybrid Paradigm

In discussing the application of the Fifth and Fourteenth Amendments in the context of the hybrid paradigm, case law suggests the application of both the *totality of the circumstances* and *voluntariness* tests. In the totality of the circumstances test, the Court examines all of the factors surrounding a confession to independently determine its validity. The voluntariness test specifically examines whether the defendant independently chose to confess.

The voluntariness test, finds its roots in English common law and early American jurisprudence.[200] Evolving from early tests, American courts began to recognize two constitutional bases for the requirement that a confession be voluntary: the Fifth Amendment right against self-incrimination and the Fourteenth Amendment Due Process Clause.[201] The important question regarding the voluntariness test is how deferential[202] a test adopted for detainees interrogated in the context of "armed conflict short of war"[203] should be.

As an example: should interrogators be allowed to apply physical force to get the detainee to talk? Do the Constitution and case law enable interrogators to threaten the detainee in the name of national security so that all sense of balance between the rights of the state and the equally

---

[200] *See* King v. Rudd, 168 Eng. Rep. 160, 161 (1783) (stating that the English courts excluded confessions obtained by threats and promises); King v. Warickshall, 168 Eng. Rep. 234 (1783) ("A free and voluntary confession is deserving of the highest credit, because it is presumed to flow from the strongest sense of guilt...but a confession forced from the mind by the flattery of hope, or by the torture of fear, comes in so questionable a shape...that no credit ought to be given to it; and therefore it is rejected.")

[201] *See Bram* (stating that the test "is controlled by that portion of the Fifth Amendment... commanding that no person shall be compelled in any criminal case to be a witness against himself) and *Brown* (reversing a conviction under the Due Process Clause because it was based on coerced confession.)

[202] Deferential as understood to provide the interrogators great latitude in their efforts to seek a confession from the suspect and consequently understood to be a minimizing of his Fifth Amendment right not to self-incriminate. For instance, see Justice O'Connor's words in *Hamdi*: "the Constitution would not be offended by a presumption in favor of the Government's evidence, so long as that presumption remained a rebuttable one and fair opportunity for rebuttal were provided."

[203] The Israeli government created this term to address the nebulous type of conflict that is not quite war and not quite a police action. *See* First Statement of the Government of Israel, Sharm El-Sheikh Fact-Finding Committee (Dec. 28, 2000), *available at* http:// www.mfa.gov.il/NR/exeres/FCFDA57E-15AB-4F50-AFBD-BDCE6A289FA8.htm (last visited July 11, 2006). I will be using it in this book to refer to the post-9/11 conflict.

legitimate rights of the individual is skewed?[204] Is cumulative mistreatment to be applied until the detainee breaks down and *spills the beans*—regardless of the truth of the information?

Under common law, there were originally no constraints on permissible methods for gaining a confession. However, the Supreme Court grew concerned regarding the reliability of these confessions when physical abuse had been involved. Thus, in *Brown*, the Court found that the interrogation methods led to a false confession. Nevertheless, despite the growing concerns over such practices, law enforcement continued to employ the third degree.[205] In the detainee context, it is clear that a modern-day version of the third degree is at play in Guantanamo, Abu Ghraib, and Bagram.

In discussing the dilemma faced by courts examining a confession, Prosecutor and Professor Laurie Magid suggests the use of the totality of the circumstances:

> The totality of the circumstances test required courts to consider: the conduct and actions of the officers; the physical surroundings of the interrogation; and the characteristics and status of the defendant, including both physical and mental condition. Some types of police conduct were deemed so coercive that no examination of the particular susceptibilities of the suspect was even necessary. Most notably, physical violence and threats, whether implicit or explicit, could not be directed against any suspect. Physical mistreatment, such as extended periods of interrogation without intervals for sleep, also provided grounds for finding involuntariness.[206]

In the alternative, Magid discusses a third test, the "shocks the conscience" test:

> The Court has suggested that a "shock the conscience" standard may be useful for determining when police deception during interrogation

---

[204] For a discussion regarding balancing in counterterrorism, *see* Amos N. Guiora *Transnational Comparative Analysis of Balancing Competing Interests in Counterterrorism*, 20 TEMP. INT'L & COMP. L.J. 363 (2006).

[205] See Laurie Magid, *Deceptive Interrogation Practices: How Far is too Far?*, 99 Mich L. Rev, 1168 (2001). "Due process required interrogation procedures that would yield voluntary, and therefore reliable, statements. Courts used a 'totality of the circumstances' analysis to determine whether 'the interrogation was...unreasonable or shocking, or if the accused clearly did not have an opportunity to make a rational or intelligent choice.'"

[206] *Id.*

goes too far. The Court applied the shock the conscience standard when it considered police deception not towards a suspect, but towards the attorney for the suspect who was interrogated. In 1986, in *Moran v. Burbine*,[207] the Court heard a claim that the police violated due process: (1) by failing to inform the defendant that an attorney, retained by his sister, was trying to contact him; and, (2) by falsely telling the attorney that the suspect would not be questioned that day. The Court rejected the claim, finding that "egregious ... police deception might rise to a level of a due process violation," but that the conduct in Moran "falls short of the kind of misbehavior that so shocks sensibilities of civilized society as to" violate due process.

Under a shock the conscience standard, techniques cannot be considered shocking simply because they are successful in convincing suspects to give truthful confessions. The shock the conscience standard bars only those few techniques that, even though they do not involve physical coercion clearly forbidden under the voluntariness test, and even though they do not implicate the concerns of the reliability rationale, nevertheless violate "canons fundamental to the traditions and conscience of our people." Although the hypothetical involving the imposter chaplain is not the only technique that shocks the conscience by violating a fundamental value, it is one of only a small group.[208]

I propose that, in applying aspects of the criminal law paradigm to the hybrid paradigm, the voluntariness test and totality of the circumstances tests are the most appropriate. They are the most articulate tests for determining whether the specific interrogation tactics used broke the detainees' will in a manner that violated constitutional rights and protections.

Applying These Tests

In light of southern sheriffs and deputies interrogating African Americans while exposing them to the brutality of mob rule, the Supreme Court

---

[207]   475 U.S. 412 (1986).
[208]   *Id.*

held that such actions violated both the Fifth and Fourteenth Amendments. The most important aspect of this is that the violations of the constitutional rights of African Americans were addressed through a progressive and active implementation of the Fifth and Fourteenth Amendments.[209] This transformative moment in American constitutional law, initiated by the Supreme Court, led to a fundamental restructuring of basic rights. This is evidenced by the fact that, rather than allow officials to continue the mistreatment, the beatings, whippings, degradations, and humiliations, the Supreme Court mandated the extension of the Fifth and Fourteenth Amendments.[210] Ultimately, the criminal law paradigm was held to be applicable not only to whites, but also to the *not fully citizen* blacks.

We find ourselves today at yet another transformative moment in American society, which must lead to a restructuring of basic constitutional guarantees. Again, it is important to acknowledge possible criticism of the proposition that constitutional protections are to be extended to the detainees although they are not citizens.[211] When the Court indicated that the continued abuse of African Americans was impermissible, the remedy was the extension of the Fifth and Fourteenth Amendments. Thus, if the Fifth and Fourteenth Amendments were deemed to be tools to protect the rights of a discriminated and oppressed group, then the same jurisprudential standard should be extrapolated for detainees. It follows that although detainees are suspected of having committed serious crimes, the operative word is *suspected*. Although it would be inappropriate to suggest that the full panoply of criminal law and procedure

---

[209] *See* Laura Magid, *Deceptive Interrogation Practices: How Far is Too Far?*, 99 Mich. L. Rev. 1168, 1172 (2001); David E. Berstein, *Fifty Years After* Bolling v. Sharpe: *Bolling, Equal Protection, Due Process, and Lochnerphobia*, 93 Geo. L.J. 1253 (2005); Jacobus Tenbroek, Equal Under the Law, (Collier Books, 1965); Akil Reed Amar, *Forward: The Document and the Doctrine*, 114 Harv. L. Rev. 26 (2000); Richard A. Primus, *The Riddle of Hiram Revel's*, 119 Harv. L. Rev. 1680 (2006); Richard L. Aynes, *Unintended Consequences of the Fourteenth Amendment and What They Tell Us About Its Interpretation*, 39 Akron L. Rev. 289 (2006); and Jack M. Balkin, *Wrong the Day It Was Decided: Lochner and Constitutional Historicism*, 85 B.U. L. Rev. 677 (2005).

[210] *Id.*

[211] I have discussed the limits of those constitutional rights in *Quirin to Hamdan: Creating a Hybrid Paradigm for the Detention of Terrorists*, 19 FLA. J. INT'L L. 2 (forthcoming 2008). The discussion of the *limits* of those rights has been made inevitable by the Supreme Court's decision in *Hamdan;* rather than the Bush administration's initial theory of granting minimal rights to the detainees, the Court has forced the White House and Congress alike to engage in active debate regarding what rights must be granted the detainees. Although this book does not address the limits of all rights to be granted, it does seek to delineate detainee rights in the interrogation setting.

guarantees granted to American citizens are appropriate for battlefield detentions,[212] at least minimum and basic guarantees should be extended to the interrogation of suspects.

The Fourteenth Amendment Right to Due Process

Speaking more concretely, what does due process mean in the context of a detainee interrogated in Guantanamo Bay? The detainee subject to interrogation by American personnel in Guantanamo Bay is to be granted due process rights *as if* he were an American citizen interrogated by the local police department. The granting of due process, however, needs to extend beyond the interrogation setting to the entire detention process. In other words, the general application of the Fourteenth Amendment to a detainee in Guantanamo Bay would address many of the Supreme Court's criticisms in *Hamdan* regarding President Bush's Executive Order and the subsequently issued instructions published by the Department of Defense (DoD).

Before specifically addressing the interrogation of detainees, it is important to understand the context in which they are being held and tried, as interrogation is only one part of the detainees' experience. Otherwise, a discussion regarding the limits of interrogation is a nonstarter.

In establishing the military commissions, President Bush intended to remove from the battlefield, or zone of combat, all individuals involved in terrorism. To that end, Guantanamo Bay military commissions were established. The initial DOD instructions, in concert with the Bybee and Yoo memos, stripped the detainees of any due process. It was as if the Fourteenth Amendment was tossed out the window for detainees. Individuals were subjected to a judicial regime that included indefinite detention with the possibility of indictment for crimes and sentences specified neither in the Executive Order nor the DOD instructions.

Given the inherent violations of rights endemic to this newly established judicial regime, how could their interrogations be anything but problematic? A paradigm premised on limiting the rights of a detainee is most dangerous specifically in the interrogation setting. It is there, away from the spotlight of the judiciary, media, and attorneys that the individual is most susceptible to the power of the state.

---

[212] *Miranda* is a notable exception.

Interrogation, as I articulate it, is not restricted to the questioning of the individual. Rather, the nonquestioning phase of the interrogation must be considered an essential aspect of a prisoner's interrogation. To that end, insufficiently trained guards will—as seen in Abu Ghraib—humiliate the detainees, resulting in violations of the 1984 Convention Against Torture.

Throughout this entire chapter and possibly the book, a reader might object with the fundamental premise that detainees are entitled to rights. Perhaps this adds a moralist spin to our discussions. To that end, the discussion turns not only on the legal aspects of interrogations and the legal rights of the detainee but also on the moral, ethical requirements of the state with respect to operational counterterrorism.

Establishing a judicial regime that explicitly denies detainees basic due process rights and guarantees for interrogation, as illustrated by incidents in Abu Ghraib and Guantanamo Bay, is replete with both significant human rights and moral violations. Addressing moral violations in an armed conflict short of war is difficult, but crucial to establishing limits. The effort is all the more critical in the interrogation setting. For it is there that a completely vulnerable individual comes in contact with the full power of the state. In many lectures to soldiers and officers alike—in Israel and the United States—the issue of morality in armed conflict has increasingly received attention. An article in the *Washington Post* entitled "Troops at Odds with Ethics Standards"[213] addressed a Pentagon report issued May 4, 2007, regarding ethics and the U.S. military.[214]

In this continuing discussion of proper methods to be used for interrogations, I suggest that morality is another tool in the commander's toolbox. It is no less significant than traditional operational capability as confirmed by the Pentagon report.

Teaching morality and ethics during armed conflict to combat units, however, presents unique challenges to military educators and commanders alike. It must be understood that the ultimate responsibility of

---

[213] Thomas E. Ricks & Ann Scott Tyson, *Troops at Odds With Ethics Standards*, Wash. Post, at A01, May 5, 2007, http://www.washingtonpost.com/wp-dyn/content/article/2007/05/04/AR2007050402151.html?hpid=topnews.

[214] The report addresses issues I have discussed in two articles, with Professor Martha Minow, *National Objectives in the Hands of Junior Leaders: IDF Experiences in Combating Terror, in Countering Terrorism in the 21st Century*, (James J. F. Forest ed., Praeger Security International 2007); and Amos N. Guiora, *Teaching Morality in Armed Conflict—The Israel Defence Forces Model*. Case Legal Studies Research Paper (No. 05–24, Aug. 2005) *available at* www.ssrn.com.

morality and ethics is the commander's. If the commander is unwilling to go beyond *talking the talk*, or if his actions contradict what he has instructed his forces regarding issues of morality, the potential for violations is great.

In the context of armed conflict short of war, operational considerations have expanded to include subject areas not traditionally associated with military operations and training. However, the reality of modern combat is that states will rarely be engaged in warfare with other states. Rather, states will be engaged in combat with nonstate entities, comprised of individuals dressed like innocent civilians.

Accordingly, the tool box of the contemporary junior commander must include skills not critical to the operational success of his predecessor forty years ago. These skills must include an understanding of cultural mores of the local peoples, an ability to communicate on a basic level with the local population, an understanding of morality in armed conflict and international law, and an appreciation for the power of the media. Furthermore, the junior commander is required to integrate these skills in stressful conditions in a foreign land while facing a hostile, local population.

The interrogation setting, for the reasons articulated throughout this book, is more complicated than the specific point of engagement between a soldier and an individual suspected of terrorism. That individual *may* possess a weapon whereas the interrogatee absolutely does not. Conversely, the interrogatee who the interrogator knows very little about *may* possess information the interrogator and his superiors believe critical to saving lives. The dilemma regarding the limits of interrogation potentially contributes to moral violations. These violations have significant tactical and strategic considerations alike.

CHAPTER 6

Coercive Interrogation, Threats, and Cumulative Mistreatment

I n the previous chapters we discussed the interrogation setting with respect to the Deep South and, by analogy, to the post-9/11 world. In this chapter, the discussion turns to specific interrogation methods facilitating analysis of the limits of interrogation. This discussion focuses on differentiating between various categories of interrogation, which will provide the framework for the proposed recommendations. This analysis requires distinguishing between interrogation, coercive interrogation, and torture.

Torture is illegal, immoral, and does not lead to actionable intelligence. However, it is important to encourage the detainee to provide information that will either prevent future acts of terrorism or contribute to the conviction of those responsible for acts committed. To that end, it is vital to create a lawful interrogation regime that enables balancing legitimate civil and political rights of the individual with the equally legitimate national security considerations of the state. Ultimately, the information received in accordance with that balancing requirement is the most accurate and reliable.

It is important to articulate that differences, subtle yet significant, exist between interrogation and coercive interrogation. Just as importantly, differences exist between coercive interrogation and torture. In the conceptualization this book proposes, coercive interrogation is not "torture lite." Rather, it is lawful interrogation that includes—when

justified and conducted in accordance with the safeguards proposed—
measures more stressful than interrogation as presently understood in
the criminal law paradigm. However, those measures are not illegal.

Articulating the differences requires sensitivity, for coercive interrogation involves the imposition of discomfort on another human being.
However, such tactics *may* be required in the state's legitimate effort to
protect its citizens. Accordingly, we are obligated to candidly and frankly
engage in debate regarding this issue, regardless of how uncomfortable it
might make us. The critical caveat is that a discussion addressing interrogation limits must be devoid of spin and politicization. Otherwise, we
will not be providing interrogators tools predicated on the rule of law
and a moral compass.

In seeking to articulate the limits of interrogation, there are a number
of critical assumptions that must be made and explained. Although some
of these assumptions have been previously discussed, it is important to
revisit them in the context of this chapter. The following assumptions are
not intended as a checklist, rather, they are recommended *guides* for the
broader discussion of threats and cumulative mistreatment in coercive
interrogation:

1. Who is the interrogatee and how much background information
   does the interrogator possess about the individual (personal
   status, job, family, medical history)? Has the individual been
   subjected to interrogation(s) in the past and, if yes, what means
   and methods were used and to what effect?
2. What information is he or she believed to possess?
3. How timely is the information he or she is believed to possess, and
   does it relate to an imminent threat?
4. Are other individuals going to be questioned regarding the same
   attack and/or planned attack, and are there other methods of
   obtaining this information?
5. What interrogation methods have proved successful with respect
   to the interrogatees' cell (if he or she belongs to one), other family
   members (if they have been detained)?
6. Have previous interrogation means used been challenged by the
   public, media, or courts?
7. How has the intelligence service director defined effectiveness and
   reasonable expectations?

8. How does the respective intelligence service define *threat* and *cumulative mistreatment?*
9. Has torture been explicitly banned or has interpretation premised on a "wink and a nod" been implicitly authorized?

Coercive Interrogation

Clear and concise definitions are of paramount importance when the state decides to limit the freedoms of an individual (citizen and noncitizen alike) and subject him to an interrogation process that is inherently unpleasant. Interrogation is the questioning of an individual by authorized state representatives for the purpose of obtaining information relevant to a previous act of terrorism or future act. It is predicated on the belief that the individual is in possession of information with respect to either alternative.

To that end, the interrogator may, but is not obligated to, impose measures that cause the interrogatee discomfort for a limited period of time. That is the essence of coercive interrogation. The means used and the length of time the measures are imposed is within the purview and discretion of the director of the national intelligence services. However, the director must be subject to legislative oversight, active judicial review, and strict scrutiny by authorized members of the executive branch. All instructions given by the Director regarding implementation of coercive interrogation must be in writing. In addition, the detainee's medical and psychological condition is subject to constant monitoring by an on-site licensed physician who bears criminal liability and responsibility if harm befalls the interrogatee. Furthermore, the physician is not within the intelligence community's chain of command. The coercive interrogation methods I suggest as lawful are:

1. Sleep deprivation
2. Modulation of room temperature
3. Stress position
4. Placing a sack over the head
5. Playing loud, cacophonous music

The above measures, while admittedly controversial (both in sum and in part) are *distinguishable* from torture (as defined in the 1984 Convention Against Torture). Similarly, they are distinct from the interrogation paradigm as portrayed on television in *Law and Order*. In the traditional criminal law paradigm, the suspect is granted full constitutional law privileges and protections. The proposed hybrid paradigm advocates the adoption of coercive interrogation *while* granting the suspect certain constitutional protections and privileges. Specifically, coercive interrogation is the imposition of moderate methods—in a highly controlled environment—intended to enable the interrogator to receive information using means that although potentially causing detainees discomfort, does not cause them severe mental and physical pain. The distinction between coercive interrogation and torture is not semantic. It is substantive and should not be subjected to political spin.

Torture is intended to cause severe pain either for purposes of sadism or information gathering. Although coercive interrogation is also intended to gather information, similarities to torture end there.

To that end, the five permissible coercive interrogation measures can be applied in conjunction with the hybrid paradigm. Although distinct from the traditional criminal law paradigm, the hybrid paradigm does not, under any circumstances, endorse a torture-predicated interrogation regime. However, it does recommend an interrogation paradigm that allows lawful, carefully monitored implementation of interrogation methods more severe than the traditional criminal law paradigm. The implementation of additional methods is a direct reflection of the reality of the post-9/11 world. However, torture must not be allowed to enter the interrogation setting *under any circumstance*.

An additional safeguard is the incorporation of Miranda protections, regardless of where the interrogation physically takes place. That is, should the individual wish to exercise his right to remain silent as guaranteed by the Supreme Court, then the interrogator is prohibited from interrogating until and unless the detainee voluntarily waives his or her right.

The Fifth Amendment right against self-incrimination is incorporated into the hybrid paradigm. Otherwise, the interrogatee would be subject both to coercive interrogation (distinct from the criminal law paradigm) and denied the self-incrimination privilege (distinct from the criminal law paradigm).

In determining which criminal law paradigm interrogations standards are applicable to hybrid paradigm interrogations, threats and cumulative mistreatment serve as our roadmap. Although other aspects of traditional interrogation are equally applicable, threats and cumulative mistreatment best enable an analysis of the proposed hybrid model. Both have long been a mainstay of criminal law interrogations and have been subject to critique and analysis for many years.

In determining permissible or impermissible threats in interrogation, the Rehnquist Court provided some guidance. As Professor Welsh White wrote:

> Indeed, the limitations of the pre-Miranda voluntariness test prompted the Court to seek "some automatic device by which the potential evils of incommunicado interrogation [could] be controlled." Simultaneously, those concerned with restraining pernicious interrogation practices sought a constitutional rule that would impose effective, general restraints on the police. Miranda represented the solution to these problems. To the extent that the Court intended Miranda to replace the due process voluntariness test, however, the *Miranda* Court did not contemplate the important role that the due process voluntariness test would continue to play in regulating post-waiver interrogation practices.[215]

What is a Threat?

Threats can take many forms: threatening to harm detainees' relatives, threatening to move them from jurisdiction to jurisdiction,[216] turning the suspect over to an angry mob (particularly when the African American suspect is accused of having killed or desired to kill a white person),[217] or threatening suspects with physical harm unless they confess.[218] The determination of whether specific language amounts to a threat will depend on the circumstances of its use. In making this determination, a court would employ a totality of circumstances test including whether the accused's will was overborne at the time he or she confessed.[219] If it is determined that an interrogator did in fact threaten the individual, it is of

---

[215] Welsh S. White, *Miranda After Dickerson: The Future Concession of Law*, 99 MICH. L. REV. 1211 (2001).

[216] *See infra* for a discussion of *Brown.*

[217] *See infra* for a discussion of *Ward.*

[218] *See infra* for a discussion of *White.*

[219] *Threats in Interrogation; Voluntariness of Confessions*, CORPUS JURIS SECUNDUM— CRIMINAL LAW, § 908.

no consequence whether that threat specifically produced fear in the interrogated individual. Any threat that yields apprehension of harm will suffice for the invalidation of the confession. More specifically, if the threat is of a violent nature, there is no need to measure the specific impact on the will of the victim, as a violent threat is per se improper.[220]

However, an examination of relevant threat jurisprudence[221] leads to the conclusion that *threats* are neither definitively nor consistently defined. Whether the test is akin to Justice Stewart's definition or pornography[222] is perhaps an open question. In the context of the hybrid paradigm, threats are defined as "interrogation methods inducing a suspect to provide his interrogator(s) with information when under the impression that to do otherwise will result in penalty either to himself or to others."[223]

Professor Ronald Allen, a leading expert on evidence and procedure[224] offers a middle ground approach with respect to interrogations and threats. Allen suggests that "an interrogation was proper that was not obtained through physical violence or its threat, and did not overbear the will of the suspect; 'overbearing the will' in turn was best defined by tactics that might lead an innocent person to confess."[225] In proposing his own definition, Allen emphasizes the *will* of the suspect and whether threats used in the interrogation setting overcame that will.

Testing the Impact of a Threat on a Confession—The Voluntariness Test

As noted earlier, the interrogation room represents complete inequality as the state assumes the inherently threatening position. As such, the battle cannot be a fair fight. The question in analyzing threats is whether

---

[220] *Id.*

[221] *See* Frazier v. State, 107 S0.2d 16 (1958); State v. Bernard, 106 So. 656 (1925); Schneckloth v. Bustamonte, 93 S. Ct. 2041 (1973); United States v. Robinson, 698 F.2d 448 (1983); Stephen v. State, 11 Ga. 225 (1852); and Stein v. People of State of New York, 73 S. Ct. 1077 (1953).

[222] Justice Stewart in Jacobellis v. State of Ohio, 378 U.S. 184, 197 (1964), in which the majority commented regarding pornography that "I know it when I see it."

[223] In proposing this definition, I seek to balance between legitimate and lawful interrogation methods and unlawful measures which violate the detainee's constitutional rights. Furthermore, the definition intends to articulate clear criteria and parameters of the *limits of the permissible*. The definition both draws on the enormous contributions of others and on my own professional interrogation experiences.

[224] Ronald Allen, *In Praise of Yale Kasmir*, 2 OHIO ST. J. CRIM. L. 9 (Fall, 2004).

[225] *Id.* at 17.

an interrogator's actions increased this inherently threatening situation by imposing undue force on the individual's will to confess to a crime he may not have committed.

Fred Inbau and John Reid—two of the nation's leading experts on confessions and interrogations—make clear that the distinctions between permissible and impermissible interrogation methods are a matter of degree. "Under any test of confession admissibility ... a confession was legally invalid if it had been obtained after a suspect had been led to believe that *unless* he confessed he was in danger of loss of life or bodily harm."[226] A particularly manipulative example of a threat that would nullify a confession is telling a suspect that unless he confesses the police will apprehend and accuse his wife, mother, or some other person close to him.[227]

Application Regarding Threats

In applying criminal law principles to the hybrid paradigm, the focus returns to the voluntariness test. In the absence of clear use of force or threat of force, the test seeks to determine whether the confession was voluntary. In making this determination, a court must assess both the interrogators' actions during the interrogation and the suspect's individual characteristics. This is critical in seeking to determine whether the suspect's will was overcome.[228]

If the confession is determined to be involuntary, then the court must rule the statement inadmissible. Thus, the proper remedy would be similar to, if not analogous to, the exclusionary rule. Conversely, if legitimate threats led to the confession, then the statement may be useable. According to criminal law jurisprudence, voluntariness is the critical variable in determining admissibility.

In determining whether, after a threat has been made, the confession was voluntary, I suggest the following spectrum: At one end are implied or direct threats to family members[229] which, if leading to a confession,

---

[226] Fred E. Inbau & John E. Reid, Criminal Interrogation and Confessions 187 (The Williams and Wilkins Company 1967) (emphasis added).

[227] *Id.* at 188.

[228] Welsh S. White, *Miranda After Dickerson: The Future Concession of Law*, 99 Mich. L. Rev. 1211 (2001).

[229] In 1988, when serving as a prosecutor in the West Bank Military Court, I received the following phone call on a Friday night from an attorney representing a Palestinian

would be ruled impermissible. At the other extreme are legitimate threats, such as the mentioning of possible prison sentence for obstructing justice.

Inbau and Reid offer the following insight on delineating lawful threats:

> Advising or imploring a subject to tell the truth is never considered objectionable. Some difficulty arises when the interrogator uses such language as "It would be better for you to confess;" "You had better confess;" "It would be better for you to tell the truth;" or "You had better tell the truth." A number of courts have held that such statements as "You had better confess" or "It would be better for you to confess," constitute threats or promises which will nullify a confession. Some courts have gone so far as to hold that the same rejection rule applies even when the suspect is merely told "it would be better to tell the truth."[230]

Concern that adoption of these restrictive criminal law principles to detainee interrogations will handicap the interrogator in his effort to protect national security is legitimate. However, this would be no truer than for the police detective. Society has determined that police can effectively investigate murders and rapes under a set of standards that do not allow for harsh interrogation methods. Detainee interrogators should be able to similarly interrogate with the caveat that the five coercive interrogations methods can be implemented, if necessary.

As Professor Seth Kreimer, a leading Constitutional Law scholar, has recently argued:

> In reconciling order and liberty, American traditions have denounced the use of torture and its cognates not because such measures are irrational, but because they corrode the core of our

---

suspected of having committing an act of terrorism: "Have you guys (the reference was to the IDF/General Security Services) gone crazy…my client tells me you threatened to arrest his sister and mother with the implied threat that their modesty will be violated." I promised to intervene in the matter, spoke with relevant security officials, was assured no such threat had been made and accordingly updated the attorney who seemed reassured by my response. As I heard nor received any additional complaint regarding the matter, I viewed the matter as closed. I bring this to the reader's attention to highlight the extraordinary sensitivity in Islam to such threats, the requirement to assure that interrogators do not "cross the line" and the need to establish clear guidelines.

[230]   *See* Inbau and Reid, at 190.

liberty and of our national identity. Even the Bush administration is unwilling to claim publicly that "cruel, inhuman or degrading treatment" is consistent with American values. It maintains that its policy is to treat prisoners "humanely," while, with the fine hypocrisy that marks the homage of vice to virtue, it defines "torture lite" as humane.[231]

Although Kreimer's comments address torture, they are applicable to the model this book proposes. In short, no theories that allow for *wiggle room* should be accepted. The acceptance of such a model, which includes *torture lite*, creates a system permitting government to abuse a detainee.

The limits of interrogation, however defined and in whatever paradigm, are the core issue in any discussion addressing the question of how to obtain necessary information. The Supreme Court's articulation of the limits of interrogation was critical in the context of the abuses suffered by African Americans in harsh, cruel, and violent settings. Those same principles are also relevant to the interrogation setting of armed conflicts: today and tomorrow. The threats interrogators have made to detainees since 9/11 are disturbingly similar in nature to those made seventy years ago in a different context.[232] The fear, disconnect, and vulnerability felt by suspects in the Deep South is existentially and psychologically similar to that felt by the detainees.[233]

---

[231]   *See* Kreimer.
[232]   *See* Table of Interrogation Techniques Recommended/Approved by U.S. Officials, Human Rights Watch, for a discussion of specific threatening actions permitted in the interrogation of detainees, *available at* http://hrw.org/backgrounder/usa/ 0819interrogation.htm (last accessed Feb. 5, 2007).
[233]   I have, over the course of my nineteen-year career, met with Palestinian detainees in various stages of the process: from those just arrested, to remand hearings that I conducted, to trials that I both appeared in as a prosecutor to those I conducted as a judge. In addition, I have met with detainees in the context of visits conducted by various human rights organizations to prisons. I feel qualified to state the following: The system, which is ultimately comprised of individuals serving in a wide range of security related positions, attempts to balance the legitimate needs of the detainees with pressing, sometimes urgent matters of state security. Most of the detainees understand the "rules of the game" and are well aware of the process, particularly those who have been arrested, if not tried, in the past. Nevertheless, a certain percentage of the detainees are clearly under pressure and in stress mode. When threatened, they are more susceptible to providing sometimes critically needed information to their interrogators. Are the interrogations conducted in such as a way as to accommodate the prisoner's comfort zone? The answer is obviously no. That being said, I am of the belief that most of the individuals involved in the process understand what I refer to as "the limits of the interrogation" and are conscious of the illegality of unlawful threats. It should be added that

The application of criminal law principles regarding threats to the hybrid paradigm leads to an explicit rejection of the views espoused in the Bybee memos. This rejection is the essence of the theory proposed here. Mild threats, such as those implicit in any interrogation setting (informing the defendant of the possible consequences awaiting him), are constitutionally permissible aspects of the criminal law paradigm. But, that only satisfies stage one of the threat analysis. After determining that a threat was on its face permissible, the next test is whether the resulting confession was voluntary. If held to be involuntary in response to a threat, then the confession is inadmissible. Supreme Court precedent has unequivocally instructed law enforcement officials regarding the limits of power with respect to threats. In extrapolating from the criminal law paradigm, I suggest that the same test applies to the hybrid paradigm.

Cumulative Mistreatment

Although courts and scholars have discussed and defined *threats* in the context of the interrogation setting, the same cannot be said for *cumulative mistreatment*. Cumulative mistreatment occurs when law enforcement officials either hold a detainee for an extended period of time, subject him to seemingly endless interrogations, or deprive the detainee of basic needs for a significant period of time.[234] In short, cumulative mistreatment is any *prolonged interrogation incorporating illegal methods*

---

during my IDF service I was involved in the training of various units involved in the process. There was a clear understanding that limits had to be taught and retaught. Nevertheless, there is no doubt that excess occurred and continues to occur. That is perhaps a tragic inevitably of the conflict. The theory espoused in this monograph is that ultimately our sense of morality must be the true guide in assisting us determine the limits of power and unlawful threats are just that, unlawful.

[234] One pointed example of cumulative mistreatment, solitary confinement, raises issues of the Eighth Amendment. How, then, do these standards apply to the discussion of the Eighth Amendment's prohibition of cruel and inhuman punishment? Although such discussion is typically confined to postconviction, a setting basically inapplicable to this book's discussion of interrogation, acts/punishments *prior* to conviction raise the Eighth Amendment are relevant.

The primary example of the application of the Eighth Amendment to the pre-conviction setting is solitary confinement. The typical focus on such analysis is the psychological effect solitary confinement has on the detainee. It can be used, just as cumulative mistreatment, as a way to break a detainee's will, leading to a confession that is coerced and false. The Court in *In re Medley*, 134 U.S. 161 (1890), through dicta, discussed the particularly horrific conditions historically attributed to solitary confinement:

resulting in an involuntary confession. Cumulative mistreatment can be identified by asking whether the continuousness and cumulativeness of the interrogation was the specific factor that broke down a detainee's will.

Voluntariness Is Again the Standard

An example that illustrates the above definition is *McNabb v. United States.*[235] In *McNabb,* the defendants were questioned while in custody prior to appearing in front of a magistrate. This was in violation of existing law, which required the arresting officers to bring the individuals before the nearest judicial officer for an initial hearing. The officers, however,

---

The peculiarities of this system were the complete isolation of the prisoner from all human society, and his confinement in a cell of considerable size, so arranged that he had no direct intercourse with or sight of any human being, and no employment or instruction....But experience demonstrated that there were serious objections to it. A considerable number of the prisoners fell, after even a short confinement, into a semifatuous condition, from which it was next to impossible to arouse them, and others became violently insane; others still, committed suicide; while those who stood the ordeal better were not generally reformed, and in most cases did not recover sufficient mental activity to be of any subsequent service to the community. It became evident some changes must be made in the system.

The Court's decision, then, in Estelle v. Gamble, 429 U.S. 97 (1976), was the first Supreme Court case to apply the Eighth Amendment cruel and unusual punishment clause to deprivations not specifically part of a prisoner's sentence. In Estelle, the plaintiff claimed that he received inadequate medical treatment from prison personnel after sustaining an injury. "Failure to do so may actually produce physical 'torture or a lingering death,' which the Eighth Amendment originally prohibited." The Court stated that "[t]he infliction of such unnecessary suffering is inconsistent with contemporary standards of decency as manifested in modern legislation."

Lastly, in Rhodes v. Chapman, 452 U.S. 337 (1981), the Court added a totality of the circumstances test regarding conditions in solitary confinement. The Court announced that "[c]onditions...alone or in combination, may deprive inmates of the minimal civilized measure of life's necessities." The Rhodes Court, however, noted that the Constitution does not mandate comfortable prisons, and therefore, provided great deference to the legislature and prison officials in allowing them to determine and implement effective measures of prison reform."

Although many discussion of solitary confinement and the Eighth Amendment center on a postconviction analysis, the standards there set are directly applicable to the discussion of this article. If solitary confinement is held to be psychologically damaging to the inmate, then it can be extrapolated that an interrogator who moves a detainee into solitary confinement is inflicting the same psychological impact on the *preconviction* individual.

[235] McNabb v. United States, 318 U.S. 332 (1943).

subjected the defendants to pressure in violation of the law for an extended period of time.

Throughout the questioning, most of which was done by Taylor, at least six officers were present. At no time during its course was a lawyer or any relative or friend of the defendants present. Taylor began by telling each of them before they were questioned that we were Government officers, what we were investigating, and advised them that they did not have to make a statement, that they need not fear force, and that any statement made by them would be used against them, and that they need not answer any questions asked unless they desired to do so.[236]

McNabb as Applied to Detainees

Much like the Court finding the treatment of the defendants in *McNabb* unconstitutional, similar treatment in the detainee interrogation context is unconstitutional. The voluntariness test, as articulated by the Court[237] and commented on by scholars,[238] is appropriate to the hybrid paradigm in the cumulative mistreatment context. The Supreme Court's ruling in *McNabb* is on-point for the detainees, standing as an example of what to do with tainted evidence:

> Quite apart from the Constitution, therefore, we are constrained to hold that the evidence elicited from the petitioners in the circumstances disclosed here must be excluded. For in their treatment of the petitioners the arresting officers assumed functions which Congress has explicitly denied them. They subjected the accused to the pressures of a procedure which is wholly incompatible with the vital but very restricted duties of the investigating and arresting officers of the Government and which tends to undermine the integrity of the criminal proceeding. Congress has explicitly commanded

---

[236] *Id*. at 336.

[237] "While the connotation of voluntary is indefinite, it affords an understandable label under which can be readily classified the various acts of terrorism, promises, trickery and threats which have led this and other courts to refuse admission as evidence to confessions." *Id*. at 348.

[238] *See* Paul Marcus, *It's Not Just About Miranda: Determining the Voluntariness of Confessions in Criminal Prosecutions*, 40 Val. U. L. Rev. 601 (2006); Kimberly Burke, *Circumstances of a Voluntary Confession*, 25 J. Juv. L. 84 (2005); and Rutledge.

that "It shall be the duty of the marshal, his deputy, or other officer, who may arrest a person charged with any crime or offense, to take the defendant before the nearest United States commissioner or the nearest judicial officer having jurisdiction under existing laws for a hearing, commitment, or taking bail for trial."[239]

A discussion concerning *McNabb* is incomplete without addressing Justice Reed's dissent. Although Reed's argument is problematic from the interrogation perspective, it is not insignificant. Precisely because Justice Reed's dissent reflects what many believe the interrogation standards should be, it is relevant to this discussion:

> I find myself unable to agree with the opinion of the Court in this case. An officer of the United States was killed while in the performance of his duties. From the circumstances detailed in the Court's opinion, there was obvious reason to suspect that the petitioners here were implicated in firing the fatal shot from the dark. The arrests followed. As the guilty parties were known only to the McNabbs who took part in the assault at the burying ground, it was natural and proper that the officers would question them as to their actions.[240]

The adoption of Justice Reed's dissent would allow for *exceptions, special circumstances,* and *exigency.* As made clear by both the Court in *Hamdan* and the administration's subsequent decision holding that the detainees are entitled to Geneva Convention protections,[241] exceptions developed in the immediate aftermath of an event are ultimately nullified. Justice Reed's dissent would have facilitated law enforcement allowing itself judicially sanctioned excess *in response* to a particular event. Clearly delineated rules would allow no opportunity for such excess, whether in the criminal law paradigm or the hybrid paradigm.

An additional case similar to *McNabb* is *Upshaw v. United States.*[242] In *Upshaw,* the Court ruled a suspect's confession inadmissible after law

---

[239] *McNabb,* at 342.

[240] *Id.* at 347.

[241] As noted in the recent memorandum written to Department of Defense officials by Deputy Secretary of Defense England: "you will ensure that all DoD personnel adhere to these standards. In this regard, I request that you promptly review all relevant directives, regulations, policies, practices, and procedures under your purview to ensure that they comply with the standards of Common Article 3."

[242] Upshaw v. United States, 335 U.S. 410 (1948).

enforcement officials failed to comply with criminal procedure rules. In *Upshaw*, the officers did not bring the suspect before a magistrate within the requisite time:

> Where confessions were made during a thirty hour period while accused was held a prisoner after police had arrested him on suspicion and without a warrant and the delay was for the purpose of furnishing an opportunity for further interrogation, the confessions were inadmissible.[243]

The petitioner in *Upshaw* was convicted of larceny based on a confession, which he argued was coerced.[244] His confession was made at the end of a thirty-hour period during which he had been held in prison, without any charges filed or warrant requested.[245]

The Court further addressed the issue of cumulative mistreatment in *Anderson v. United States:*[246]

> While the petitioners, with at least thirteen others, were thus held in custody at the Y.M.C.A. by the state officers, they were questioned by the federal agents intermittently over a period of six days during which they saw neither friends, relatives, nor counsel. Incriminating statements from six of the petitioners were the fruit of this interrogation.
>
> The question for decision is whether these confessions—repudiated when those who made them took the witness stand at the trial—were properly admitted in evidence against all the petitioners, including Anderson and Ellis who did not confess. In the McNabb case we have held, that incriminating statements obtained under the circumstances set forth in that opinion cannot be made the basis of convictions in the federal courts. The considerations which led to that decision also govern this case. The detention of the petitioners by state officers was, as the Government concedes, in violation of the Tennessee statute which provides that "No person can be committed to prison for any criminal matter, until examination thereof be first had before some magistrate."[247]

---

[243] *Id.* at 411.
[244] *Id.* at 410.
[245] *Id.*
[246] Anderson v. United States, 318 U.S. 350 (1943).
[247] *Id.* at 355.

As both *Upshaw* and *McNabb* illustrate, examining whether a detainee's interrogation is tantamount to cumulative mistreatment must be viewed under a broad totality standard. This analysis enables the court to accurately determine whether such treatment broke the suspect's will, leading to an involuntary confession.[248] The question to address is whether the actions inside post 9/11 interrogation rooms violate this standard.

There are many aspects of current detainee interrogation that violate established rules of both threats and cumulative mistreatment. Amnesty International has indicated, the "[t]he very conditions in which the detainees are held—harsh, isolating and indefinite—can in themselves amount to torture or cruel, inhuman or degrading treatment."[249] The report asserts that interrogation teams employ such tactics by having access to the medical files of the detainees, which provide sensitive information regarding physical and mental vulnerabilities of individual detainees. The interrogator's power is asserted through lengthy and cumulative use of sleep deprivation, stress positions, isolation, hooding, sensory deprivation, and the use of dogs to induce fear.[250] Although some of these measures are similar to the methods proposed in these chapters, there are critical differences: The use of dogs is a clear violation of international norms. Furthermore, institutionalized control and oversight is a key component of lawful coercive interrogation. To date, the interrogations in Abu Ghraib and Guantanamo have been devoid of both.

Cumulative Mistreatment: Just as Violative of Rights as Threats

Before moving forward in this discussion, it is worth noting that, on its surface, cumulative mistreatment might not come across as damaging as

---

[248] What is of interest in this section is the sum total of a particular interrogation; not only water-boarding specifically imposed on a detainee but whether that detainee's entire interrogation process (as compared to a single act) was reflective of coercive interrogation based on cumulative mistreatment resulting in an admissible confession. The analysis in this section, accordingly, is of the interrogation in the "overall" rather of a particular act during the course of an interrogation.

[249] *Guantanamo: An Icon of Lawlessness*, Amnesty International, Jan. 6, 2005, http://web.amnesty.org/library/Index/ENGAMR510022005 (last accessed Feb. 7, 2007).

[250] *Guantanamo: An Icon of Lawlessness*, Amnesty International, Jan. 6, 2005, http://web.amnesty.org/library/Index/ENGAMR510022005 (last accessed Feb. 7, 2007).

more easily defined and understood physical threats. The Supreme Court, although, explicitly held that cumulative mistreatment is as violative of a defendant's constitutional rights as are threats. The holding of a defendant for a number of days prior to bringing him or her before a judge,[251] the repeated transfer of an African American suspect from county to county without sleep,[252] the holding of a suspect in a hotel for a number of days for the purposes of intermittent interrogation,[253] the continued whipping of the African American suspect in the woods,[254] and the beatings imposed on a suspect over the course of a number of days[255] are all illustrative of cumulative mistreatment as defined in this book. These cases are the criminal law version of what Amnesty International and other human rights groups have argued is the reality of Guantanamo Bay, Abu Ghraib, and Bagram. The hybrid paradigm cannot tolerate cumulative mistreatment, just as it cannot tolerate unlawful threats.

The Fifth and Fourteenth Amendments, as analyzed by the Supreme Court in the series of cases examined earlier, speak loudly to what needs to be done. The right to not incriminate oneself and the right to due process in the criminal law paradigm have been affirmed and reaffirmed by the Supreme Court. Threats, as the Court has made clear, violate both of those amendments in the context of the interrogation room.

Defining Coercive Interrogation

One proposed definition of *coercive interrogation* was suggested by Professors Posner and Vermeule:

> (1) The application of force, physical or mental (2) in order to extract information (3) necessary to save others. Coercive interrogation can range from the mild to the severe. At some point of severity, coercive interrogation becomes a species of "torture," which is flatly prohibited by domestic and international law. Coercive interrogation and torture are thus partially overlapping concepts; neither is a proper subset of the other. Mild coercive interrogation does not amount to legal "torture," which requires that a threshold of severity be met.

---

[251] *McNabb*, at 334.
[252] *Ward*, at 548–549.
[253] Zing Sung Wan v. United States, 266 U.S. 1 (1924).
[254] *White*, at 532.
[255] *Brown*, at 280.

And there are forms of torture that are not coercive interrogation—for example, when torture is used as a means of political intimidation or oppression, indeed for any purpose other than extracting information necessary to save third-party lives.[256]

Given the documented instances in which those in the field have applied a liberal application test to regulations, rules, and guidelines, proposed definitions and standards must be neither circular nor overburdened with legalese and technicalities. Continuing to promulgate memos with vague standards serves only to create an environment whereby detainees may be subjected to treatment similar to that forever seared in the collective conscience of millions of Arabs. It is likely that Lyndi England, the Abu Ghraib guard photographed abusing detainees, did not read either Jay Bybee's or John Yoo's memos and in all probability, neither did her immediate commanders receive copies. Although Lyndi England did not make operational decisions based on the arguments contained in the memos, what Bybee and Yoo wrote clearly affected the environment in which interrogations were conducted.

It is irrelevant whether the soldiers posing with the Iraqis in Abu Ghraib ever met Mr. Bybee or read his memo. It is equally insignificant whether their superiors were acquainted with it. What is relevant is that someone's superior read it and understood its true meaning—that the American government endorses and therefore encourages torture. The attempt to distinguish between various degrees of pain that may be inflicted (mental or physical), although interesting from a theoretical and intellectual perspective, does a fundamental disservice to the only individuals who matter—those in the field, who are on the front lines of counterterrorism and the detainees.

Counterterrorism is not an abstract legal exercise; rather it involves real decisions made by people in the field. The greatest disservice that can be done to these individuals—generally young people, men and women alike—is to place them in a situation with unclear and murky instructions. In files obtained by the *New York Times*, there is a clear demonstration of the failure of the command structure to teach those in the field what actions are and are not permissible regarding detainees.[257]

---

[256] Eric A. Posner and Adrian Vermeule, *Should Coercive Interrogation Be Legal?*, 104 MICH. L. REV. 671, 672–673 (2006).

[257] Tim Golden, *Army Faltered in Investigating Detainee Abuse*, N.Y. TIMES, May 20, 2005, at A1.

The documents quote the individuals in charge of detention centers asking for clarification from the staff judge advocate regarding what interrogations techniques can properly be used; however, no training was ever offered.[258] The Bybee memo is in direct conflict with that very important command principle of the commander telling his troops what is and is not acceptable.

The difficulty of those on the ground is exacerbated not only when their training is minimal, but also when those who have sent them seek plausible deniability. The President's oft-repeated comment, that America is a nation of laws and those involved in Abu Ghraib are "bad apples," is disingenuous. The conduct of Private Charles Graner Jr., Private First Class Lyndi England, Specialist Sabrina Harman, among others is inexcusable, criminal, and sadistic. However, the environment that allowed for the horrific abuses at Abu Ghraib, Guantanamo Bay, and Bagram was created by the administration's own manipulation of the definition of torture.

The Bybee memorandum's overly legalistic, almost painful to read, hairsplitting arguments attempting to find a justification for the torture of detainees reflects the most inappropriate and ultimately damaging response to 9/11. I would suggest that the pictures that shocked the world and caused America such enormous damage in the Middle East were a result—it is insignificant whether direct or indirect—of that memo. Even when soldiers in the field acted impermissibly, their commanders and the leadership of the United States did very little, if anything, to intervene or to secure justice for the victims until their inaction was disclosed by the media.[259] Not only is that most disturbing, but also, in the context of this book, it raises important questions that must be addressed.

Although responsibility, discretion, and judgment are the essence of command, the fine-lined approach proposed above by Professors Posner and Vermeule is problematic from the perspective of interrogation room

---

[258] Tim Golden, *Army Faltered in Investigating Detainee Abuse*, N.Y. TIMES, May 20, 2005, at A1. Abuses at the Bagram Detention Center in Afghanistan were poorly investigated, which allowed the same military intelligence unit that lacked command in Afghanistan to be deployed to Abu Ghraib three months later without any indication that proper training or direction as to permissible actions were given before the deployment to Abu Ghraib.

[259] The investigation, although still open, was at a standstill until a March 4, 2003 article in the *New York Times* reported that at least one of the deaths of a detainee had been reported as a homicide. Carlotta Gall, *U.S. Military Investigating Death of Afghan in Custody*, N.Y. TIMES, Mar. 4, 2003, at A1.

realities. It can be satisfactory to create vague and evasive standards when writing from the protected vantage point of American academia, but what must be taken into account is the impact such proposals will have when put into action on the ground. The political fallout that resulted from the soldiers' abuse of vague standards highlights the danger of leaving interpretation and implementation to those on the front lines.

The potential for improper application of guidelines is particularly poignant when one considers that the abuses occurred in spite of standards clearly articulated by the U.S. Army. Army Regulation 190–8, paragraph 2–1(d), contains a reference to allowable procedures:

> Prisoners may be interrogated in the combat zone. The use of physical or mental torture or any coercion to compel prisoners to provide information is prohibited ....Prisoners may not be threatened, insulted, or exposed to unpleasant or disparate treatment of any kind because of their refusal to answer questions.

Finally, and most definitively, Army Field Manual 34–52, the controlling doctrine on this subject, states:

> U.S. policy expressly prohibit[s] acts of violence or intimidation, including physical or mental torture, threats, insults, or exposure to inhumane treatment as a means of or aid to interrogations. Such illegal acts are not authorized and will not be condoned by the US Army. Acts in violation of these prohibitions are criminal acts punishable under the [Uniform Code of Military Justice].[260]

Although these regulations are seemingly clear and concise, they suffered from slippery-slope interpretation by commanders and soldiers alike. In short, when drafting rules and procedures, not only *should* they be clear, they *must* be clear. If the standards adopted are not clear and precise, they are destined for abuse and adaptive interpretation. Similar to the "void for vagueness" doctrine,[261] a set of standards and procedures that are overly vague must be held void for their lack of specificity as vague rules lead to the slippery slope.

---

[260] Dep't of the Army, Field Manual 34–52: Intelligence Interrogation 1–8 (1992), *available at* http://www.fas.org/irp/doddir/army/fm34-52.pdf

[261] *See* Andrew E. Goldsmith, *The Void-for-Vagueness Doctrine in the Supreme Court, Revisited*, 30 Am. J. Crim. L. 279 (2003).

The Military Commissions Act of 2006[262] represents a step in the right direction regarding unlawful coercive interrogation. However, despite Congress' efforts to address the Court's concerns in *Hamdan*, it is wholly insufficient in remedying the lack of interrogation standards.[263] Interrogation standards must be clear and specific so that interrogators precisely know what is permissible, and what is not. Thus, the Military Commissions Act lack of absolute clarity all but guarantees continued abuses.

In creating these standards, there is a delicate balance between legitimate national security interests and the equally valid interests and rights of the individual. These two interests can be effectively balanced by a clear articulation of permissible interrogation standards that permit the proposed five interrogation methods. Those measures, however, must be subject to control and oversight. The combination of clearly articulated limits and strict scrutiny is critical to establishing an interrogation paradigm that meets this balancing requirement.

Reality of Modern Day Coercive Interrogation

Much like the members of the Wickersham Commission were shocked to discover the realities of the third degree, American policymakers were equally shocked by the reality of Abu Ghraib.[264] The practical reality is that in any setting, interrogation clearly pits the power of the state against the power of the individual. Both the Supreme Court and scholars alike have commented that the setting is a fundamental mismatch.[265] This mismatch was particularly acute in the context of the fundamental violations of constitutional rights in the Deep South.

It is for that reason that Professors Posner and Vermeule's attempt to find a *middle ground* (an area where limits are not delineated) must be rejected. The quote below, reflective of their jurisprudential approach,

---

[262] 120 Stat. 2600 (Oct. 17, 2006).

[263] The Military Commission Act allows for executive interpretation of coercive interrogation standards, rather than a clearly articulation of the standards up front in the legislation.

[264] Frank Rich, *Saving Private England*, N.Y. TIMES, May 16, 2004. at AR1

[265] *See* Laura Hoffman Roppe, *True Blue? Whether Police Should Be Allowed to Use Trickery and Deception to Extract Confessions*, 31 SAN DIEGO L. REV. 729, 758 (1994); and William T. Pizzi & Morris B. Hoffman, *Taking Miranda's Pulse*, 58 VAND. L. REV. 813, 819 (2005).

is problematic in the real world of both Montgomery, Alabama and Guantanamo:

> All we suggest is that law should treat coercive interrogation the way it treats other grave evils. Law has a typical or baseline regulatory strategy for coping with grave evils that sometimes produce greater goods. That strategy involves a complex regulatory regime of rules-with-exceptions, involving a prohibition on official infliction of serious harms, permission to inflict such harms in tightly cabined [sic] circumstances, an immunity regime that requires officials to follow the rules in good faith but protects them if they do so, and review procedures to reduce error and enhance transparency. In this baseline regime, the circumstances in which serious harms may be inflicted are specified ex ante, rather than being remitted solely to the discretionary mercy of juries, judges, and the executive after the fact. Contrary to the academic consensus, we see no plausible reason for treating coercive interrogation differently.[266]

Such a middle ground approach cannot persist as coercive interrogation must be treated differently, rather than in the same way as "other grave evils," as Posner and Vermeule prefer. In an environment of such inherent unfairness, fine-lining is inappropriate given the numerous abuses that have occurred to date in the "War on Terrorism."

Sufficiency of the Military Commissions Act

In response to *Hamdan*, the United States Congress passed the Military Commissions Act of 2006.[267] Although the Act represents an effort to address the Court's concerns, it is ultimately insufficient in formulating proper interrogation standards. Rather than specifically articulating permissible interrogation methods, the Military Commissions Act grants the Executive the authority to interpret the scope and application of Common Article III of the Geneva Convention. The evasiveness of the Military Commissions Act regarding the limits of coercive interrogation suggest an inevitability of future on-the-battlefield abuses.

---

[266] *See* Eric A. Posner and Adrian Vermeule, *Should Coercive interrogation Be Legal?*, 104 Mich. L. Rev. 671, 707 (2006).

[267] 120 Stat. 2600 (Oct. 17, 2006).

So where does this discussion lead? Why does this discussion matter? It matters because if we do not carefully define the limits of interrogation, the next Abu Ghraib is right around the corner. The least the public owes the men and women charged with interrogating terror suspects is that we *have their back*. In the context of this book, having their back requires articulating and enforcing the limits of interrogation.

The *Bram-Brown* progeny developed in this book seeks to argue that the tests developed by the Supreme Court with respect to Alabama are relevant to Guantanamo Bay. Allowing for the distinction between the traditional criminal law paradigm and the hybrid paradigm and granting the inherent dissimilarity between a suspected criminal and a suspected terrorism, the constitutional law principles at play are ultimately more similar than not. Based on the constitutional law issues discussed and the tests developed through the cases discussed, this book suggests that for interrogations to be lawful, they must be devoid of unlawful threats and cumulative mistreatment, and the suspect must be granted his Miranda rights.

To that extent, the *Bram-Brown* progeny is a most valuable guide. However, the post-9/11 world, it is suggested, requires an additional interrogation paradigm more appropriate to the threat posed to American national security. However, as there must be limits on what is, in essence, an exception to the constitutionally mandated criminal law interrogation, the *Bram-Brown* progeny is applicable. It is applicable because the limits on interrogation developed in response to the horrors of the Deep South are by analogy—for all the reasons articulated in this chapter—relevant to Guantanamo Bay.

Coercive interrogation regime is lawful, *provided* the safeguards articulated are implemented. In the next chapter we will explore torture—not as a straw man but to more fully distinguish between the lawful and the unlawful, the moral and the immoral.

CHAPTER 7

Torture

What Is Torture?

Defining limits of coercive interrogation is put to the test when an interrogator is sitting across from someone who is not cooperating and the interrogator *knows* is in possession of information purported to be urgent. It is exactly at that moment that the previously established lawful limits of interrogation must be implemented, no matter the circumstance. Otherwise, excess will be permitted, encouraged, and will inevitably will occur. In an effort to satisfy commanders and to prevent a terrorist attack, the interrogator may be inclined to cross the line.

An objective discussion regarding torture is, unfortunately, all but impossible. The subject conjures up horrible images of human beings subjected to intolerable pain and suffering. The idea of a helpless person tied to the rack has, for centuries, been front and center in the debate regarding the limits of state power.

Although it is not this book's intent to contribute to the torture debate, it is impossible to address coercive interrogation without discussing torture. My personal views regarding torture are consistent and unwavering. They are largely premised on my professional experience in the Israeli Defense Force; an interrogation gone awry involves serious violations of human rights. The interrogator's zeal and commitment to elicit information from the detainee is to be respected. However, there is no justification for accepting the need-to-torture argument.

As discussed earlier, in the immediate aftermath of 9/11 Jay Bybee and John Yoo justified torture of detainees as necessary to protect America and American interests. Their legal analysis can best be described as hair-splitting, their moral compass, at best, as skewed. Although 9/11 was a significant terrorist attack on the United States, the articulation of a legal regime justifying torture—and therefore violating U.S. and international law alike—was patently unwarranted.

The correct response should have been the much harder one, the more intellectually and morally demanding: seeking to determine limits. Admittedly, the public and political climate did not easily lend itself to moderation, perhaps just the opposite. However, it is exactly at such moments that political leaders are judged: Did they engage in excess or did they exercise restraint? The argument advocating coercive interrogation, rather than torture, is predicated on balancing complicated, competing interests.

According to the *Constitutional Center for Rights Report*,[268] Iraqi prisoners were told by their American interrogators, "You are in a place where there is no law—we are the law."[269] From a legal and moral perspective alike, that quote suggests lawlessness, immorality, and what Dana Priest of the *Washington Post* termed, "the black hole." The articulation of the limits of interrogation is, in many ways, directed toward the avoidance— *at all costs*—of the black hole from which there is no return. Akin to the slippery slope, the concept of the black hole implies detaining individuals in what can only be referred to as the dungeons of the world far from the courts, the public, and the media.

Thus far, this book has addressed the limits of interrogation. In this chapter, torture is examined—concisely and clearly. It is important to candidly discuss torture so that the reader will understand it in its most concrete form, rather than in the abstract.[270]

---

[268] http://www.ccr-ny.org/v2/reports/docs/Torture_Report_Final_version.pdf (last visited Apr. 30, 2007).

[269] http://www.ccr-ny.org/v2/reports/docs/Torture_Report_Final_version.pdf (last visited Apr. 30, 2007).

[270] Although I have chosen not to incorporate in the text statements or pictures depicting torture, it is important that readers examine this material, which is readily available online; *see* http://www.slate.com/features/whatistorture/taxonomy.html? http://www.slate.com/features/whatistorture/Isolation.htm; and Nigel S. Rodley, *The Definition(s) of Torture in International Law*, http://www.asil.org/is060630/Rodley_Def_Torture_paper_06_06_30.pdf; and Center for Constitutional Rights, *CCR Publishes First Report on Torture at GTMO with Declassified Primary Accounts from Current Detainees and*

This chapter is divided into three subsections: (1) definitions of torture; (2) an analysis of interrogation methods based on an Israeli High Court of Justice (HCJ) holding; *Ireland v. United Kingdom*; and a 1984 Israeli Commission of Inquiry; and (3) an analysis of functional torture and sadistic torture.

Again, I posit unequivocally that torture is illegal, immoral, and does not lead to actionable intelligence.[271] I propose that torture be divided into three categories: (1) interrogation based; (2) functional torture, whereby a ruler, leader, or government demonstrates that there is a "new sheriff in town;" and (3) evil and sadistic torture. Although the methods might bear some similarity, it is important to understand that these categories have fundamentally different purposes.

In the widely cited Cleveland Principles, torture was succinctly defined as "any cruel, inhuman, or degrading treatment."[272]

In defense of torture, consider the arguments of Professors Bagaric and Clarke who speculate that torture may be acceptable in certain conditions:

> The only situation where torture is justifiable is where it is used as an information gathering technique to avert a grave risk. In such circumstances, there are five variables relevant in determining whether torture is permissible and the degree of torture that is appropriate. The variables are (1) the number of lives at risk; (2) the immediacy of the harm; (3) the availability of other means to acquire the information; (4) the level of wrongdoing of the agent; and (5) the likelihood that the agent actually does possess the relevant information. Where (1), (2), (4) and (5) rate highly and (3) is low, all forms of harm may be inflicted on the agent—even if this results in death.[273]

Attorneys, http://www.ccr-ny.org/v2/reports/report.asp?ObjID=p3CXx0ajAy&Content=791); and Conor Foley, Combating Torture: A Manual for Judges and Prosecutors http://www.essex.ac.uk/combatingtorturehandbook/manual/app1_10.htm "When President Bush last week signed the bill outlawing the torture of detainees, he quietly reserved the right to bypass the law under his powers as commander in chief."

[271] *See* Guiora and Page, *supra.*

[272] The Cleveland Principles emanated from the Torture and the War on Terror conference held at Case Western School of Law in Cleveland, Ohio on Oct. 7, 2005. The text of the resolution can be found at: http://www.law.case.edu/centers/cox/content.asp?content_id=85 (last accessed July 26, 2006).

[273] Mirko Bagaric and Julie Clarke, *Not Enough Official Torture in the World? The Circumstances in Which Torture is Morally Justified,* 39 U.S.F.L. Rev. 611 (2005).

Writing in response to Bagaric and Clarke, Professor Rumney asserts that the fundamental problem is the "end product."[274] Whether it is termed "actionable intelligence,"[275] or "bad information and false confessions,"[276] the bottom line is the same: Experience has shown that information received from a tortured detainee is overwhelmingly inaccurate, unreliable, and of minimal value in preventing acts of terrorism.[277]

Moreover, torture must be avoided as the intelligence it yields damages the investigatory process itself. In Alberto Gonzales' confirmation hearing, Douglas A. Johnson, executive director of The Center for Victims of Torture, claimed that arguing for the necessity of torture rests on "unproven assumptions based on anecdotes from agencies with little transparency."[278] According to Johnson:

> Well trained interrogators, within the military, the FBI, and the police have testified that torture does not work, is unreliable and distracting from the hard work of interrogation. Nearly every client at the Center for Victims of Torture, when subjected to torture, confessed to a crime they did not commit, gave up extraneous information, or supplied names of innocent friends or colleagues to their torturers. It is a great source of shame for our clients, who tell us they would have said anything their tormentors wanted them to say in order to get the pain to stop. Such extraneous information distracts, rather than supports, valid investigations.[279]

Further, commenting on the coercive interrogation techniques authorized by the Bush administration, Professor David Gottlieb states

---

[274] Phillip N.S. Rumney, *Is Coercive Interrogation of Terrorist Suspects Effective? A Response to Bagaric and Clark*, 40 U.S.F.L. Rev. 479 (2006).

[275] Amos N. Guiora and Erin M. Page, *The Unholy Trinity: Intelligence, Interrogation, and Torture*, 37 Case W. Res. J. Int'l L. Rev. 427, 428 (2006).

[276] Phillip N.S. Rumney, Is Coercive interrogation of Terrorist Suspects Effective? A Response to Bagaric and Clark, 40 U.S.F.L. Rev. 479 (2006).

[277] This assertion is predicated on my extensive professional experience as a prosecutor in the West Bank Military Court, judge in the Gaza Strip Military Court, legal advisor to the Gaza Strip, judge in Administrative Detention hearings and instructor in General Security Services courses. In addition, I have met with and spoken to numerous interrogators both in the United States and Israel regarding this issue; there is unanimity of opinion regarding this issue.

[278] Nomination of the Honorable Alberto R. Gonzales, Counsel to President George W. Bush, to be the Attorney General of the United States: Hearing Before the S. Comm. on the Judiciary, 109th Cong. 9–10 (2005) (testimony of Douglas A. Johnson).

[279] *Id.*

that: "[o]nce these powers were placed in the hands of poorly-trained reservists, they morphed into something more sinister."[280]

Lending credence to both Johnson and Gottlieb, the current allegations of improper treatment of detainees strongly suggests that allowing coercive techniques has led to even more serious abuses. This is supported by the testimony of a former military interrogator in Afghanistan, Chris Mackey. Mackey recounts how mental pressures imposed on detainees can further lead to the slippery slope:

> When we arrived in Afghanistan, I had an unshakable conviction that we should follow the rules to the letter: no physical touching, no stress positions, no "dagger on the table" threats, and no deprivation of sleep … but I knew that it was possible to make bad decisions in the heat of the moment, that it was easy for emotions to overwhelm good judgment. Following the rules to the letter was the safe route. Even entertaining the idea of doing otherwise was inviting "slippage."[281]

Mackey's words speak loudly of the inherent and implicit danger of the inevitable slippery slope. Even if moderate safeguards are instituted, as recommended by Professor Alan Dershowitz,[282] it is all but inevitable that an interrogator somewhere, sometime, will misunderstand or misinterpret his commander's instructions. Inevitably, he or she will be classified by an American President as a "bad apple who does not represent the American military."[283] In short, unclear or evasive guidelines lend themselves too easily to misinterpretation in the field. Clouding the interrogation debate—deliberately or not—ultimately leads to the pictures from Abu Ghraib. Scholarship, political spin, and media cautiousness—if not unwillingness—to directly address this issue does a disservice to interrogators and ultimately harms American interests and values.

This unfortunate reality is extenuated when noting that the Military Commissions Act[284] stops short of clearly and specifically delineating permissible and impermissible actions. Thus, the United States is still in great need of clear and concise standards.

---

[280] David J. Gottlieb, *How We Came to Torture*, 14 KAN. J.L. & PUB. POL'Y 449, 455 (2005).
[281] *See* Rumney, at 504–505.
[282] Tung Yin, *Ending the War on Terrorism One Terrorist at a Time: A Non-Criminal Detention Model for Holding and Releasing Guantanamo Bay Detainees*, 29 HARV. J. L. PUB. POL'Y 149, 157 (2005) (citing THE 9/11 COMMISSION REPORT 109 (2003); and Alan M. Dershowitz, *Why Terrorism Works* 138, 249 n.10 (2002)).
[283] *See Mr. Rumsfeld's Defense*, N.Y. TIMES, May 8, 2004.
[284] 120 Stat. 2600 (Oct. 17, 2006).

Interrogation-based torture is explainable both philosophically and practically. Harsh measures of interrogation, or what some would call torture, have been upheld by scholars and courts alike on the basis of legitimate self-defense in an effort to protect innocent lives. Furthermore, torture in certain interrogation settings is tempting. The frustration of sensing that the suspect is hiding something and not being able to coax the information can be overwhelming for an interrogator, particularly one under enormous pressure to provide his superiors with timely, relevant intelligence information that may well prevent the loss of innocent life.

Although that pressure may well be used to justify the imposition of illegal interrogation methods, the temptation must be resisted. It must be resisted regardless of how senior the official suggesting that a by-all-means-necessary approach is justified in light of the threat posed by the interrogatee.

Definitions of Torture

Webster's Dictionary defines torture as "the infliction of intense pain (as from burning, crushing, or wounding) to punish, coerce, or afford sadistic pleasure."[285] The U.S. Code makes it a criminal offense for any person outside the United States to commit or attempt to commit torture.[286] Torture is defined in the Code as "an act committed by a person acting under the color of law specifically intended to inflict severe physical or mental pain or suffering (other than pain or suffering incident to lawful sanctions) on another person within his custody or physical control."[287]

---

[285] MERRIAM-WEBSTER ONLINE DICTIONARY, www.m-w.com.

[286] 18 U.S.C. § 2340A (1994).

[287] 18 U.S.C. § 2340 (1994). *See id.* (defining "severe mental pain or suffering" as the "prolonged mental harm caused by or resulting from (A) the intentional infliction or threatened infliction of severe physical pain or suffering; (B) the administration or application, or threatened administration or application, of mind-altering substances or other procedures calculated to disrupt profoundly the senses or the personality; (C) the threat of imminent death; or (D) the threat that another person will imminently be subjected to death, severe physical pain or suffering, or the administration or application of mind-altering substances or other procedures calculated to disrupt profoundly the senses or personality."). *See also* Letter from John C. Yoo, Deputy Assistant Attorney Gen., Office of Legal Counsel, U.S. Dep't of Justice to Alberto Gonzales, Counsel to the President (Aug. 1, 2002), *reprinted in* MARK DANNER, TORTURE AND TRUTH 109 (New York Review of Books 2004) (To convict a person of torture, "the prosecution must

Common Article 3 of the Geneva Conventions prohibits the use of torture in any circumstance without actually defining what constitutes torture.[288] All four Geneva Conventions also dictate that the use of torture is a grave breach.[289] The 1984 Convention Against Torture and Other Cruel, Inhuman or Degrading Treatment, or Punishment (1984 Convention Against Torture, CAT) defines torture as:

> [A]ny act which by severe pain or suffering, whether physical or mental, is intentionally inflicted on a person for such purposes as obtaining from him or a third person information or a confession … or intimidating or coercing … when such pain or suffering is inflicted … with the consent or acquiescence of a public official …[i]t does not include pain or suffering arising only from, inherent in or incidental to lawful sanctions.[290]

CAT states that there are no exceptional circumstances that can be invoked as justifications of torture.[291]

The European Commission of Human Rights has stated that:

> (T)he notion of inhuman treatment covers at least such treatment as deliberately causes severe suffering, mental or physical. Further, treatment of an individual may be said to be degrading if it grossly humiliates him before others or drives him to act against his own will or conscience.[292]

---

establish that: (1) the torture occurred outside the United States; (2) the defendant acted under the color of law; (3) the victim was within the defendant's custody or physical control; (4) the defendant specifically intended to cause severe physical or mental pain or suffering; and (5) that the act inflicted severe physical or mental pain or suffering.").

[288] Geneva Convention for the Amelioration of the Condition of the Wounded and Sick in Armed Forces in the Field art. 3, Aug. 12, 1949, 6 U.S.T. 3114, 75 U.N.T.S. 31 [hereinafter Geneva I]; Geneva Convention for the Amelioration of the Condition of Wounded, Sick and Shipwrecked Members of Armed Forces, at Sea art. 3, Aug. 12, 1949, 6 U.S.T. 3217, 75 U.N.T.S. 85 [hereinafter Geneva II]; Geneva Convention Relative to the Treatment of Prisoners of War art. 3, Aug. 12, 1949, 6 U.S.T. 3316, 75 U.N.T.S. 135 [hereinafter Geneva III]; Geneva Convention Relative to the Protection of Civilian Persons in Time of War art. 3, Aug. 12, 1949, 6 U.S.T. 3516, 75 U.N.T.S. 287 [hereinafter Geneva IV].

[289] Geneva I, art. 50; Geneva II, art.. 51; Geneva III, art. 130; and Geneva IV.

[290] Convention Against Torture and Other Cruel, Inhuman or Degrading Treatment or Punishment art. 1, Dec. 10, 1984, 1465 U.N.T.S. 85 [hereinafter Torture Convention].

[291] Id. art. 2.

[292] See Nan Miller, International Protections of the Rights of Prisoners: Is Solitary Confinement in the U.S. a Violation of International Standards?, 26 CAL. W. INT'L L.J. 139 (1995).

The International Criminal Court's definition of torture is very similar to both the U.S. Code definition and CAT. It defines torture as "the intentional infliction of severe pain or suffering, whether physical or mental, on a person in the custody or under the control of the accused;"[293] It is important to note that although many international conventions prohibit the use of torture, very few actually define it.[294]

The U.S. Senate, when ratifying the CAT, gave consent to the Convention subject to its own definition of torture:

[I]n order to constitute torture, an act must be specifically intended to inflict severe physical or mental pain or suffering and that mental pain or suffering refers to prolonged mental harm caused by or resulting from: the intentional infliction or threatened infliction of severe physical pain or suffering; the administration or application, or threatened administration or application, of mind-altering substances or other procedures calculated to disrupt profoundly the senses or the personality; the threat of imminent death; or the threat that another person will imminently be subjected to death, severe physical pain or suffering, or the administration or application of mind-altering substances or other procedures calculated to disrupt profoundly the senses or personality.[295]

The United States became a party to CAT on November 20, 1994. Its ratification CAT made effective 18 U.S.C. §§ 2340, 2340A, and 2340B.[296] These provisions of the U.S. Code codified the U.S. obligation to prohibit and prevent torture as required by CAT.

---

[293] Rome Statute of the International Criminal Court art. 7(2)(e), July 17, 1998, 2187 U.N.T.S. 90.

[294] *See supra*, note 292. International Covenant on Civil and Political Rights, Dec. 16, 1966, 999 U.N.T.S. 171. U.N. Econ. & Soc. Council [ECOSOC], *Siracusa Principles on the Limitation and Derogation Provisions in the International Covenant on Civil and Political Rights*, Annex, U.N. Doc. E/CN.4/1985/4 (Sept. 28, 1984) [hereinafter *Siracusa Principles*].

[295] Sanford Levinson, *Brutal Logic*, VILLAGE VOICE, May 12, 2004, at 27 (quoting U.S. Reservations, Declarations, and Understandings to the Convention Against Torture and other Forms of Cruel, Inhuman or Degrading Treatment or Punishment, 136 Cong. Rec. 36 (1990)).

[296] Act of Apr. 30, 1994, Pub. L. No. 103–236, Title V, Part A, § 506(c), 108 Stat. 463 states that 18 U.S.C. § 2340 et seq. would become effective either on the later date between the date of enactment of the provision (Apr. 1994) or the date that the United States became a party to the 1984 Convention Against Torture (Nov. 20, 1994).

The Bybee memo was a "formal legal opinion of the Office of Legal Counsel," which interpreted CAT and the corresponding U.S. Code.[297] Prior to the Bybee memo, the U.S. military definition of torture was predicated on 18 U.S.C. § 2340A.[298] Based on the Bybee memo analysis, American armed forces narrowed the definition of "severe." It was re-defined as physical or mental pain that "must be of such a high level of intensity that the pain is difficult for the subject to endure."[299]

Unlike the codified U.S. definition of torture, the State of Israel's definition does not focus on the specific level of pain but rather defines torture as pressure that reaches the "level of physical torture or maltreatment of the suspect, or grievous harm to his honor, which deprives him of his human dignity."[300] Israel "has always maintained that the interrogation procedures used by the ...[GSS], to prevent acts of terrorism in Israel, do not constitute torture as defined by Article 1" of the 1984 Convention Against Torture.[301]

The British government defines torture as the intentional infliction of "severe pain or suffering on another at the instigation or with the consent or acquiescence—(i) of a public official; or (ii) of a person acting in an official capacity;" and the "official or other person is performing or purporting to perform his official duties when he instigates the commission of the offence or consents to or acquiesces in it."[302] According to

---

[297] John W. Dean, *The Torture Memo by Judge Jay S. Bybee that Haunted Alberto Gonzales's Confirmation Hearings*, FINDLAW, Jan. 14, 2005, http://writ.news.findlaw.com/dean/20050114.html.

[298] *Cf.* Human Rights First, *U.S. Law for Prosecuting Torture and Other Serious Abuses Committed by Civilians Abroad*, HUM. RTS. FRST., http://humanrightsfirst.org/us_law/detainees/us_torture_laws.htm (discussing military law and U.S. Code provisions that are applicable to members of the U.S. armed forces).

[299] Jess Bravin, *Pentagon Report Set Framework for Use of Torture: Security or Legal Factors Could Trump Restrictions, Memo to Rumsfeld Argued*, WALL ST. J., June 7, 2004, at A1.

[300] Alan Baker, Legal Adviser, Ministry of Foreign Affairs, Opening Statement to Second Periodic Report of Israel Concerning the Implementation of The Convention Against Torture (May 15, 1998), http://www.mfa.gov.il/MFA/MFAArchive/1990_1999/1998/5/Alan+Baker-+Opening+Statement+to+Second+Periodic+R.htm?DisplayMode=print.

[301] Yaakov Levy, Ambassador, Permanent Representative of Israel to the United Nations Office in Geneva, Opening Statement Consideration of Israel's Third Periodic Report to the Committee Against Torture (Nov. 20, 2001), http://www.mfa.gov.il/MFA/Foreign+Relations/Israel+and+the+UN/Speeches+-+statements/Opening+Statement+by+Ambassador+Yaakov+Levy-+Genev.htmhttp://www.mfa.gov.il/MFA/Foreign+Relations/Israel+and+the+UN/Speeches+-+statements/Opening+Statement+by+Ambassador+Yaakov+Levy-+Genev.htm

[302] Criminal Justice Act, 1988, c.33, § 134(a)(1)-(2), (b) (Eng.)

British law, "it is immaterial whether the pain or suffering is physical or mental and whether it is caused by an act or an omission."[303]

Interrogation-Based Torture

Although the emphasis in this book is coercive interrogation of detainees in the American context predicated on an analysis of the Constitution, it is instructive to engage—albeit briefly—in a comparative examination. Israel has been defined as the world's laboratory for the study of legal, policy, and operational aspects of counterterrorism. Engaging in a comparative analysis admittedly is not problem free as nations face dissimilar threats predicated on different paradigms and judicial and political regimes. Nevertheless, in explaining an issue of such importance as the limits of interrogation, an examination of a non-American experience is fruitful in the effort to develop a workable model. Such comparisons do not, naturally, lend themselves to a perfect one-to-one relationship. Nevertheless, in this case the similarities significantly outweigh the dissimilarities thereby justifying the comparison.

In the aftermath of the 1967 Six Day War and the subsequent establishment of the Israel Defense Force military government in the West Bank and Gaza Strip, the General Security Service (GSS) assumed responsibility for the interrogation of Palestinians suspected of terrorist activities. From 1967 to 1984, complaints regarding torture were regularly lodged, not only by Palestinians prisoners, but also by Palestinian and Israeli human rights groups. These complaints were largely dismissed as exaggerated.

In 1984, a National Committee of Inquiry[304] concluded that controlled, moderate physical duress could be allowed in "ticking bomb"

---

[303] *Id.* § 134(3).
[304] Known as the Landau Commission, named after Moshe Landau, a Supreme Court Justice, the Commission was established in the aftermath of the killing of a Palestinian terrorist by a senior member of the GSS. The terrorist was killed in the wake of an IDF rescue mission of a bus, which had been hijacked by Palestinian terrorists in Israel and then commandeered to the Gaza Strip. A newspaper photographer captured on film the GSS official and the terrorist leaving the bus. When the picture was published on the front cover of the newspaper, the media attempted to determine the identity and whereabouts of the detained terrorist. It was discovered that minutes after the picture was taken the Palestinian was brutally killed by the GSS official, who claimed that he was acting on the orders of the Head of the GSS. The Head in turn claimed that he was acting on orders he received directly from the Prime Minister, Yitzhak Shamir.

interrogations.[305] A "ticking bomb" interrogation occurs "when a bomb is known to have been placed in a public area and will undoubtedly explode causing immeasurable human tragedy if its location is not revealed at once."[306] Therefore, if the GSS strongly suspected that the detainee knew the location of the ticking bomb and the information in the detainee's possession could prevent that bomb from exploding, limited means of physical duress could be used. The report included a section available to the public as well as a confidential portion detailing permissible physical means.[307] According to various media reports, the Commission held that the following interrogation methods were legal: wall standing, the playing of loud music, sleep deprivation, physical discomfort through manipulation of room temperature, sitting in an uncomfortable position, and the wearing of a hood. Furthermore, and perhaps most importantly, in ticking bomb situations, the detainee could be violently shaken.[308]

Shaking Technique and the Ticking Bomb

Shaking has been defined by the HCJ as "the forceful shaking of the suspect's upper torso, back and forth, repeatedly, in a manner, which causes the neck and head to dangle and vacillate rapidly."[309] The consequences of shaking are disputed but can include serious brain damage and harm to the spinal cord, which can cause the suspect to "lose consciousness, vomit and urinate uncontrollably, and suffer serious headaches."[310]

During the course of its investigation, the Committee of Inquiry learned that GSS agents when called to testify in court concerning confessions made by suspected Palestinian terrorists systematically lied when asked whether suspects had confessed of their own free will and volition. Furthermore, the Commission discovered that one of its members, a senior GSS official, regularly updated the head of the GSS regarding the Commission's daily proceedings and prepared GSS agents prior to their testimony before the Commission. The Commission also discovered that the GSS had attempted to frame a Brigadier General for the murder of the terrorist.

[305] See HCJ 5100/94 Public Comm. Against Torture in Israel v. Israel, [1999] IsrSC 46(2), ¶ 16, *available at* http://www.derechos.org/human-rights/mena/doc/torture.html.
[306] *Id.* ¶ 14.
[307] B'Tselem, The Israeli Information Center for Human Rights in the Occupied Territories, Background on the High Court of Justice's Decision, B'Tselem, www.btselem.org/english/Torture/Background.asp [hereinafter Background on the High Court's Decision].
[308] See HCJ 5100/94 Public Comm. Against Torture in Israel v. Israel, [1999] IsrSC 46(2), ¶ 15, *available at* http://www.derechos.org/human-rights/mena/doc/torture.html.
[309] *Id.* at ¶ 9.
[310] *Id.*

In the aftermath of the Commission's report, the GSS implemented the shaking technique in ticking bomb cases. However, a series of petitions filed with the HCJ[311] argued that the ticking bomb case had been expanded to include virtually every Palestinian detainee instead of the imposition of duress being limited only to those cases where a ticking bomb truly existed. According to the petitions, torture became a "bureaucratic routine" for the GSS.[312] Nevertheless, the HCJ repeatedly denied the petitions[313] without addressing the legality of shaking.

Other countries also have allowed the use of torture or interrogation methods that harm the suspect, to stop a ticking bomb. Authorities in the Philippines received information that Ramzi Yousef, one of the masterminds of the 1993 World Trade Center bombing, planned to blow up a dozen jumbo jets over the Pacific Ocean.[314] The Philippine authorities were able to foil the plan after they tortured a suspected terrorist for sixty-seven days.[315]

Although this case has been heralded as an example of the effectiveness of implementing measures associated with the ticking time-bomb exception, it is not without controversy. It is arguable whether the interrogation—as compared to the actual detention—directly contributed to preventing the attack. According to counterterrorism experts, terrorist organizations modify, or even cancel, planned attacks if an individual with knowledge of the plans is detained. The reasons for this are clear—fear that in the course of interrogation the detainee will spill the beans. Therefore, the assertion that the ticking bomb exception successfully prevented the planned act *may* be correct, although to suggest it as *the* example justifying such measures may well be incorrect.

On at least one occasion in Israel, a detainee died during the course of his interrogation because of the shaking technique. The detainee's

---

[311] According to a 1968 legal opinion written by then Attorney General Meir Shamgar, Palestinians or those acting on their behalf, may seek redress against the executive in the HCJ regarding either actions taken or actions contemplated. Depending on the matter at issue, the Court may hear the petition immediately and issue a restraining order asking the executive to explain the considerations involved.

[312] Background on the High Court's Decision, *supra* note 23, www.btselem.org/english/Torture/Background.asp.

[313] *Id.*

[314] *See* Dershowitz, *supra.*

[315] *Id.* at 157–158 (citing Alan Dershowitz, *Why Terrorism Works* 137, 249 n.10 (2002)).

death led to discussions regarding both the legality and effectiveness of the shaking method.[316] Following his death, the HCJ explicitly ruled that "shaking is a prohibited investigation method" as it "harms the suspect's body ...[and] violates his dignity."[317] Thus, Israel no longer allows the shaking interrogation method.

High Court of Justice 5100/94

In *Public Committee Against Torture in Israel v. State of Israel and General Security Service*, the Israel Supreme Court sitting as the High Court of Justice ruled that although the GSS had the authority to conduct interrogations, their ability to employ certain methods would be restricted in the future.[318] As this book seeks to provide decision makers concrete recommendations, the importance of this case is that the Israel Supreme Court clearly articulated do's and don'ts in delineating the limits of interrogation. American policymakers are not—obviously—obligated to accept any of these guidelines. However, the importance of a Supreme Court articulating specific limits of interrogation cannot be minimized.

Seminal to our purposes, the Israel Supreme Court ruled that torture was illegal and mandated that under no circumstances can detainees be subjected to torture premised interrogation measures. If torture is illegal, then what? To that end, the court's decision is instructional and highly applicable to the very issue this book endeavors to address—the limits of interrogation.

The court limited the GSS interrogators to the same measures police officers can use, holding that neither "possess the authority to employ physical means which infringe on a suspect's liberty during the interrogation, unless these means are inherently accessory to the very essence of an interrogation and are both fair and reasonable."[319] The court specifically prohibited interrogators from forcing a suspect to crouch on the tips of

---

[316] *See* AMNESTY INT'L, COMBATING TORTURE: A MANUAL FOR ACTION (2002) (describing that Palestinian detainee Abd al-Samad Harizat was sent unconscious to the hospital twenty-four hours after his arrest by the GSS on April 22, 1995. He died three days later because of hemorrhaging within the skull overlying the brain, which results from sudden jarring movements of the head.).

[317] *See* HCJ 5100/94 Public Comm. Against Torture in Israel v. Israel, [1999] IsrSC 46(2), ¶ 24, *available at* http://www.derechos.org/human-rights/mena/doc/torture.html.

[318] *Id.* ¶ 38.

[319] *Id.*

his toes for five-minute intervals as "it does not serve any purpose inherent to an investigation."[320] With respect to placing a hood on the suspect's head, the court states that limiting the eye contact between suspects is a legitimate consideration, but having a hood that covers the entire head and causes the suspect to suffocate is forbidden. The court recommended that the GSS find a less harmful means to prevent eye contact and communication between detainees. According to the HJC, a ventilated sack allowing the suspect to breathe is insufficient.[321]

The HJC did not explicitly state that the use of loud music is always prohibited. Rather, the HJC held that in the circumstances of the current case, loud music when combined with an impermissible method is forbidden.[322] Furthermore, the HJC held sleep deprivation may be allowed as an "inevitable result of an interrogation, or one of its side effects."[323] However, the suspect cannot be "intentionally deprived of sleep for a prolonged period of time, for the purpose of tiring him out or 'breaking him.'"[324]

The court defined interrogation as "an exercise seeking to elicit truthful answers."[325] The court recognized that interrogations inherently infringe on a suspect's freedom even without the use of physical means. Although the court did not explicitly define torture, it held that the legality of interrogation techniques is "deduced from the propriety of ... purpose and from its methods."[326] Nevertheless, what is irrefutable is that the HCJ definitively held that physical duress cannot be implemented except in those very limited cases where the Head of the GSS personally authorizes such an exception. The test, according to the HJC, is whether a ticking bomb is genuinely suspected to exist. The HJC held that it is "prepared to assume that ... the 'necessity' defence is open to all, particularly an investigator, acting in an organizational capacity of the State in interrogations of that nature" and that "the 'necessity' exception is likely to arise in instances of 'ticking time bombs.'"[327]

---

[320] *Id.* ¶ 25.
[321] *Id.* ¶ 28.
[322] *Id.* ¶ 29.
[323] *Id.* ¶ 31.
[324] *Id.*
[325] *Id.* ¶ 18.
[326] *Id.* ¶ 23.
[327] *Id.* ¶ 34.

However, the Israel Supreme Court also stated that the physical means used must still be "inherently accessory to the very essence of an interrogation and ...[be] both fair and reasonable."[328] Therefore, the court held that although some instances of physical means are legitimate, their legality would be determined on a case-by-case basis. The important principle, according to the HJC, is that the necessity defense cannot inherently be used by interrogators justifying use of harsh measures.

The decision in HCJ 5100/94 has stood the test of time. Interrogators have commented that the ruling necessitated developing and honing advanced psychological interrogation methods in the place of more physical means.[329] Whether the ruling was popular among the intelligence community, who had to search for new lawful means of interrogation, is ultimately irrelevant. The critical point is that the Supreme Court articulated the limits of interrogation.

International Judicial Precedent

The Reagan administration relied on *Ireland v. United Kingdom* in arguing that the definition of torture is limited to "extreme, deliberate and unusually cruel practices."[330] In *Ireland*, the European Court of Human Rights analyzed methods of interrogation used by the United Kingdom when interrogating detainees suspected of terrorist activities in Northern Ireland.[331] The court held that although measures such as wall standing, hooding, subjection to noise, sleep deprivation, and deprivation of food and drink were inhuman and degrading, they did not amount to torture.[332] The court stated:

> Although the five techniques, as applied in combination, undoubtedly amounted to inhuman and degrading treatment, although their object was the extraction of confessions, the naming of others and/or information and although they were used systematically,

---

[328] *Id.* ¶ 38.

[329] Confidential conversations between author and senior GSS members.

[330] Memorandum from Jay S. Bybee, Assistant Attorney Gen., Office of Legal Counsel, U.S. Dep't of Justice to Alberto R. Gonzales, Counsel to the President, Standards of Conduct for Interrogation under 18 U.S.C. §§ 2340–2340A (Aug. 1, 2002), *reprinted in* DANNER, *supra* note 4, at 139 [hereinafter Bybee Memo] (quoting Ireland v. United Kingdom, 25 Eur. Ct. H.R. (ser. A) (1978)).

[331] *Id.*

[332] *Id.* ¶ 167. *See also* DANNER, at 139.

they did not occasion suffering of the particular *intensity* and *cruelty* implied by the word torture.[333]

U.S. Interrogation Methods

Section 2(c)(1) of a memo written by Lieutenant Colonel Jerald Pfifer on October 11, 2001, specified which Category III interrogation techniques[334] can be used against detainees held in Guantanamo. These include "the use of scenarios designed to convince the detainee that death or severely painful consequences are imminent for him and/or his family."[335] Also allowed, if approved "by the Commanding General with appropriate legal review and information to Commander," is the "use of a wet towel and dripping water to induce the misperception of suffocation."[336]

Water-boarding, a Category III technique, induces the detainee to believe that death is imminent. This technique requires that the detainee be strapped or held down to induce the sensation of drowning as either water is repeatedly poured down the individual's throat or his head is immersed in water. Detainees who have experienced water-boarding have universally expressed an overwhelming fear because the method prevents breathing. Furthermore, according to some reports, a number of individuals have died as a result of water-boarding.[337] There is little doubt that this technique is torture. Yet in a subsequent memo, Secretary of Defense Rumsfeld ordered water-boarding be used only in those cases he personally approved.[338]

---

[333] Ireland v. United Kingdom, 25 Eur. Ct. H.R. (ser. A) (1978) (emphasis added by DANNER, *supra* note 4, at 140).

[334] Category III techniques require special approval and are "required for a very small percentage of the most uncooperative detainees." They may be used in a carefully coordinated manner to help interrogate exceptionally resistant detainees. Memorandum from Jerald Phifer, Dir., J2 to Michael E. Dunlavey, Commander, Department of Defense Joint Task Force 170, Request for Approval of Counter-resistance Techniques (Oct. 11, 2002), *reprinted in* DANNER, at 168.

[335] *Id.*

[336] *Id.*

[337] Human Rights Watch, '*Stress and Duress*' *Techniques Used Worldwide*, June 1, 2004, http://hrw.org/english/docs/2004/06/01/usint8632_txt.htm. (In the submarine technique, the victim's head is covered with a cloth hood and intermittently forced into a vessel containing water; similar to water-boarding, it has been used by many countries, such as Argentina, Chile, Uruguay, Zimbabwe, and China. In several instances, for example in Zimbabwe and Uruguay, its use has lead to the death of the suspect.)

[338] Memorandum from Donald Rumsfeld, Sec'y of Def., U.S. Dep't of Def. to Commander, USSOUTHCOM, Counter-resistance Techniques (Jan. 15, 2003), *reprinted in* DANNER, at 183.

Controls on Interrogation Methods

Professor Alan Dershowitz advocates "controlling and limiting the use of torture by means of a warrant or some other mechanism of accountability."[339] The essence of this argument pertains to torture in the context of the ticking bomb theory. The argument, according to Dershowitz is philosophically and legally akin to self-defense. However, the distinction between torture and harsh interrogation methods referred to in *Ireland* and approved by the Israeli Commission of Inquiry is critical.

Were the ticking bomb argument is to be accepted as valid, which I advocate it should not be, its implementation should be limited to *only* those cases where a ticking time bomb actually exists, rather than as a catchall justification. However, implementation of the theory requires hands-on supervision and oversight by the head of the security services. Such matters cannot be left to the discretion of the individual interrogator, no matter how dedicated and skilled he or she might be.

The meeting place between the interrogator and the suspect, as described above, is fraught with tension. However, according to the Israel HJC, liberal democratic regimes must have self-imposed restraints. These restraints result in what former President of the Israeli Supreme Court, Aharon Barak has termed fighting terrorism with "one hand tied behind" the back.[340] Liberal democratic regimes must be vigilant at all times both with respect to the rule of law and moral and ethical considerations. These two principles were disregarded with respect to interrogations in Abu Ghraib, Guantanamo Bay, and Bagram.[341]

Functional Torture and Sadistic Torture

In the aftermath of 9/11, the Bush administration has been confronted with legal and moral dilemmas regarding the limits of counterterrorism. Did the United States, as a liberal democratic society, intend to fight with one hand behind its back, or would it fight with both hands and ignore

---

[339] ALAN DERSHOWITZ, *Tortured Reasoning, in* TORTURE: A COLLECTION 257 (Sanford Levinson ed., 2004). Professor Alan Dershowitz is a law professor at Harvard Law School and world renowned scholar on terrorism and the law.

[340] HCJ 5100/94 Public Comm. Against Torture in Israel v. Israel, [1999] IsrSC 46(2), ¶ 39, *available at* http://www.derechos.org/human-rights/mena/doc/torture.html.

[341] *See* Golden, *Brutal Details.*

the rule of law? This is the critical question liberal democratic societies face when determining how to combat terrorism. Will such societies be true to their moral ethos even in times of horrific terror attacks or will they place in temporary abeyance those very morals that distinguish them from the terrorist? Liberal democratic societies cannot allow themselves the luxury of disregarding their ethical and moral ethos. In doing so they lose their raison d'être and lower themselves to the level of the terrorist. If they do so, they have lost what they are fighting for.

A careful reading of Professor Mark Danner's book, *Torture and Truth: America, Abu Ghraib and the War on Terror*,[342] suggests that Barak's one-handed approach was not adopted by the Bush administration. In the context of the debate regarding the legality and implementation of torture, the memo drafted by Jay Bybee stands out as most disturbing. Although Danner's book suggests that debate was held regarding the legality of torture, ultimately the policy adopted by the administration reflects the worst in policy-making and legal advice.

The memo's language contributed to the horrific events that transpired at Abu Ghraib, Guantanamo Bay, Bagram, and additional secret facilities. The legalistic hairsplitting and mental gymnastics of the memo is best displayed in the argument regarding "prolonged mental harm."[343] The Bybee memo argues that the harm must be "endured over some period of time." According to the memo, mental strain from an intense interrogation would not be considered prolonged unless it extended for a number of months or years.[344] According to the Bybee memo, for an act to be defined as torture the interrogator must have intended to cause the detainee prolonged harm.[345] Therefore, if an interrogator did not intend to cause harm lasting beyond the interrogation itself, the actions could not be considered torture, regardless of how long the pain actually lasts.

The Role of Policy-Makers

Policy, domestic or foreign, must not only be legal, but will ultimately be judged by its effectiveness. Policy advisors, be they generalists or

---

[342] *See* DANNER.
[343] *See* Bybee Memo.
[344] *Id.* at 120.
[345] *Id.* at 121.

specialists such as a legal counsel, must be confident that their policy recommendations serve not only the short-term political interests of a particular superior but also—and not less importantly—long-term, national strategic goals.

An analysis of the memo in the context of 9/11 shows a national leadership literally scrambling to respond to the terror attacks. Indeed, the United States entered a new age at 8:43 a.m. on September 11, 2001, and has been playing catch-up, trying to make up for lost time in attempting to level the playing field between itself and global terrorism. As has previously occurred in American history, there is a tendency to go overboard under such circumstances.[346] The question as it relates to interrogation was whether the U.S. government was going to throw caution to the wind and adopt a philosophy reflective of "a la guerre comme a la guerre."

Such an approach violates U.S. law[347] under 18 U.S.C. §§ 2340-2340A and international law, particularly the 1984 Convention Against Torture. The Convention states that there are no exceptions that allow torture.[348] In addition, the Convention suggests principles of morality in armed conflict.[349]

---

[346] *See* The Prize Cases, 67 U.S. 635 (1863); Korematsu v. United States, 323 U.S. 214 (1944).

[347] The explicit definition of "severe" given in 18 U.S.C. §2340A is redefined in the Bybee memo to require that the pain not only be prolonged but that a high level of intensity exists. Bybee Memo, *supra* note 46, at 116.

[348] *See* Torture Convention, art. 2. *See also* Geneva I, art. 3; Geneva II, art. 3; Geneva III, art. 3; Geneva IV, art. 3. Universal Declaration of Human Rights, G.A. Res. 217A, at 71, U.N. GAOR, 3d Sess., 1st plen. Mtg., U.N. Doc. A/810 (Dec. 12, 1948). International Covenant on Civil and Political Rights, *supra* note 10. *Siracusa Principles, supra* note 10. Rome Statute of the International Criminal Court, *supra* note 9, art. 7(2)(e). All the aforementioned documents prohibit torture without stating any situation that would allow for the use of torture.

[349] In September, 2003, the Israel Defense Forces, School of Military Law, under my command, produced an interactive training video developed in conjunction with commanders. The video teaches soldiers an 11-point code of conduct based on international law, Israeli law, and the IDF Code. Commanders' and soldiers' personal responsibility to respect international humanitarian law requirements and the dignity of civilians is emphasized. The video's fundamental message is that violations of the principle of morality in armed conflict are not only in violation of international law but ultimately aid only the enemy. The Bybee memo is a classic example not only of a violation of the morality of armed conflict but paradoxically an unintended advantage given to America's enemies in the Middle East.

Implementation of the Bybee Memo

In seeking to define what torture is, Bybee quotes from the 1990 Congressional testimony of Mark Richard, Deputy Assistant Attorney General, Criminal Division, Department of Justice:

> [T]orture is understood to be that barbaric cruelty which lies at the *top of the pyramid* of human rights misconduct.... As applied to physical torture, there appears to be some degree of consensus that the concept involves conduct, the mere mention of which sends chills down one's spine.... [T]he needle under the fingernail, the application of electrical shock to the genital area, the piercing of eyeballs, etc.[350]

As to mental torture, according to Bybee, Richard testified:

> [N]o international consensus had emerged as to what degree of mental suffering is required to constitute torture but ... severe mental pain or suffering "does not encompass the normal legal compulsions which are properly a part of the criminal justice system: interrogation, incarceration, prosecution, compelled testimony against a friend, etc.—notwithstanding the fact that they may have the incidental effect of producing mental strain."[351]

It is not suggested that Richard and Bybee intended for the phrase "top of the pyramid" to be literally understood by Private Graner and his colleagues. However, the picture from Abu Ghraib forever seared into the collective memory of the Arab world will be that of naked Iraqi men forced by U.S. soldiers to form themselves into a human *pyramid* under the enthusiastic eye of American servicemen and women.

The repeated use of certain techniques at Abu Ghraib, such as those that mocked Islamic beliefs, belies the Bush administration's claim that this was the work of a few "bad apples." At least one of the methods used is "an arcane torture method known only to veterans of the interrogation trade."[352] Although any soldier could realize that abuse of the Koran would offend Muslims, the repeated use of methods aimed at detainees'

---

[350] *See* Bybee Memo, at 131 (emphasis added) (citing *Convention Against Torture: Hearing Before the Senate Comm. On Foreign Relations*, 101st Cong. 16 (1990)) (testimony of Mark Richard, Deputy Assistant Attorney General, U.S. Department of Justice).

[351] *Id.*

[352] John Barry et al., *The Roots of Torture*, NEWSWEEK, May 24, 2004, at 26.

religious beliefs suggests that officials in the chain of command have some knowledge of Islamic culture and allow an environment in which such abuses can occur.[353]

One example of military personnel relying on the example set by superiors is that of Army Captain Donald Reese. As the newly installed warden of part of Abu Ghraib, Captain Reese visited it for the first time in October 2003. He was a reservist and window-blinds salesman in civilian life. Captain Reese admits that he was ill-prepared for his posting, as he had never been in a prison, even to visit, and "knew nothing of the Geneva Conventions, which specify conditions for humane treatment of enemy prisoners of war and others."[354] When he arrived and saw many of the prisoners without clothing, Captain Reese was assured by Army intelligence officers that there was nothing "illegal or wrong about it" and that "stripping the prisoners was a tried-and-true intelligence tactic used to make the prisoners uncomfortable."[355]

The litany of the humiliations and degradations inflicted by American soldiers is mind-boggling: building naked human pyramids, staging menstruation, forcing detainees to masturbate, servicewomen fondling themselves in the presence of the detainees, forcing the detainees to walk while leashed to a chain as if they were dogs, and mishandling of the Koran.[356] Bybee and others in the administration argue that the above actions did not cause physical pain. However, mental pain and suffering *is no less severe* than physical pain if it is tantamount to profound violations of Islamic belief.[357]

Graner and others participated in both sadistic and functional torture. By deliberately violating basic Islamic tenets, members of the U.S. military, whose actions were reflective of administration policy, clearly demonstrated to the local population that there was a new sheriff

---

[353] *See generally* Edward T. Pound & Kit R. Roane, *Hell on Earth*, U.S. NEWS & WORLD REP., July 19, 2004, at 10.

[354] *Id.*

[355] *Id.*

[356] Thom Shanker, *Inquiry by U.S. Reveals 5 Cases of Koran Harm*, N.Y. TIMES, May 27, 2005, at A1.

[357] Islam 101, http://www.islam101.com/rights/hrM2.htm (last visited Mar. 3, 2006). Important aspects of the Charter of Human Rights granted by Islam is respect and protection for a woman's chastity, an individual's right to freedom or the right not to be a slave, equality of men, and the right to safety of life. *Id.* Homosexuality and sexual promiscuity are also forbidden. Many of the actions performed by Private Graner et al., showed fundamental and mind-boggling disrespect and disregard for these aspects of the Islamic faith.

in town. The concept of the new sheriff was articulated—advertently or inadvertently—by President Bush' s now famous "bring 'em" statement.

Conclusion

The actions of Graner and others caused great mental anguish, which is defined as torture and therefore banned according to 18 U.S.C. § 2340, the 1984 Convention Against Torture, Rome Statute of the International Criminal Court, and the U.S. Senate's definition when it ratified the Convention Against Torture.

Although Graner and others must be punished,[358] the issue at hand goes far beyond the actions of a "few bad apples." The question that must be addressed is how do policymakers construct policy reflective both of an operational reality (counterterrorism) and the rule of law while balancing between legitimate national security concerns and equally legitimate rights of the individual.

The Bybee memo is an excellent example of how not to develop, articulate, and implement policy. It is wrong legally and creates an environment whereby the actions of Graner and others were inevitable. In the context of the United States attempting to develop a new Middle East, it dramatically fails on the policy front.

The theories such as those postulated both in the Landau Commission and by Dershowitz are conceivably adaptable even though highly problematic legally, morally, and operationally. They are legally problematic because the distinction between harsh, yet permissible, methods of interrogation and torture is tenuous and requires superb training and outstanding command and control mechanisms. However, should a

---

[358] *New Hearing for Soldier over Abu Ghraib Charges*, CNN.com, May 19, 2005, http://www.cnn.com/2005/LAW/05/19/england.courtmartial/. Private Graner was found guilty on nine of the ten major counts, guilty for three photographs and guilty of each charge of abuse and is currently serving a sentence of ten years. A mistrial in Private First Class England's court-martial was declared after Private Graner testified at Private First Class England's sentencing phase. *See also Harmon Gets 6 Months for Abu Ghraib Scandal*, USA Today.com, May 17, 2005, http://www.usatoday.com/news/nation/2005–05–17-harman-convicted_x.htm. Specialist Harmon was sentenced to six months after being convicted on six of seven counts for her role in Abu Ghraib. Specialist Harmon and Private Graner are the only two soldiers to be tried in the scandal as others have arranged plea bargains.

government decide to implement such measures, the potential consequences must be clear to decision and policymakers alike who must not
allow themselves, nor be allowed, to hide behind plausible deniability.
There are few things more demoralizing and debilitating to those in the
front lines. Should decision and policymakers decide to allow the implementation of measures such as those discussed in *Ireland*, *there must be
clearly articulated* guidelines that include limits that err on the side of
caution.

The question will inevitably be asked: if an interrogator is convinced
that the detainee knows on which bus the bomb is placed and when is it
to go off, can harsher measures be implemented? I was professionally
involved for almost two decades in such matters. My involvement was
not in the context of an abstract, intellectual exercise but rather hands-
on legal and policy advice regarding counterterrorism. I ordered the
detention of hundreds of Palestinians suspected of terrorism and
spent literally thousands of hours in detention facilities with suspects and
interrogators alike.

I also had the opportunity to examine the conditions of suspects and
was subjected (like them) to the loud and obnoxious music. I met with
sleep deprived individuals who complained about the temperature in the
detention facility. In addition, I saw detainees sitting for extended periods
in very uncomfortable positions with hoods over their heads. Although
these measures may be difficult and possibly repugnant to some, an
interrogation is not meant to be a pleasant conversation between friends
over coffee and cake.

The interrogation is a vital cog in counterterrorism. Based on the
information the interrogator receives, additional suspects can be detained,
and the bomb may well be neutralized before innocent civilians are killed.
The ultimate question is one of balance. Coercive methods can be implemented provided the interrogator is highly trained and that the head of
the organization has *personally* approved the decision and hands-on
oversight is institutionalized. However, torture as described by Richard[359]
and as performed by Graner and others is prohibited by both law and
morality.

---

[359] *See* Bybee Memo, at 130–32 (emphasis added) (citing *Convention Against Torture:
Hearing Before the Senate Comm. On Foreign Relations*, 101st Cong. 16 (1990)) (testimony
of Mark Richard, Deputy Assistant Attorney General, U.S. Department of Justice).

The Bybee memo has done the United States a great disservice; untrained and unsupervised individuals with their own sadistic agenda acted in its spirit. Ultimately, intelligence that could directly contribute to counterterrorism measures was not received.

One of the significant problems with torture is that a detainee will tell his interrogator *what he thinks the interrogator wants to hear* to stop the pain. From an operational perspective, both are highly problematic. Limited resources can be misdirected (a military force will stop bus number five, rather than bus number seven that actually has the bomb). That, in and of itself, is cause enough to forbid torture.

CHAPTER 8

Interrogation Methods and the Eighth Amendment

Although addressing the Eighth Amendment prohibition against excessive bail and cruel and unusual punishment can seem out of place in a discussion of interrogation, there is an important relationship between the two. Although punishment can initially be understood to only refer to postconviction actions, the concepts of punishment are also relevant to pretrial detention measures.

To discuss this concept, interrogation must be viewed as broadly as possible. That is, not just the actual questioning by an interrogator. From the perspective of the detainee, interrogation incorporates *all* aspects of life inside the detention center from the moment the doors are locked behind him. As such, one must appreciate the reality of the detention center as viewed by the detainee. All individuals with whom the interrogatee comes in with are possible interlocutors, whether directly or indirectly, whether in a questioning context or any other verbal encounter.

Lyndi England did not technically interrogate the Iraqi men whom she subjected to torture. However, she had direct contact with the detainees, which enabled her to torture them. From the detainee's perspective, England's effect on his life in detention was no less significant than the actual interrogator's. By forcing him to participate in a human pyramid, standing naked while photographing him, or "walking" him with a collar around his neck, her actions were a critical aspect of the detainee's interrogation process and experience.

Solitary confinement is an example of how preconviction actions can be viewed as cruel and unusual punishment. To that end, the Eighth Amendment will be analyzed by examining the solitary confinement of the detainees in Guantanamo, Bagram, and elsewhere. The underlying premise is that interrogations must be viewed broadly rather than as a single event.

A discussion of solitary confinement in the coercive interrogation debate requires an examination of the Eighth Amendment's prohibition against cruel and unusual punishment. Such a discussion, with respect to the post-9/11 detainees, is predicated on the granting of non-American citizens constitutional protections *as if* they are American citizens.

There is a wide body of literature available regarding solitary confinement and its effects on the individual detainee or prisoner. Solitary confinement represents, perhaps more than any other aspect of the interrogation process, the Eighth Amendment's prohibition regarding cruel and unusual punishment. Critics will suggest that the difficulty, if not danger, emanating from solitary confinement is exaggerated and that putting someone to the rack is far more evil. Others would suggest that waterboarding is torture, whereas solitary confinement is a legitimate measure. Is forced masturbation worse than solitary confinement? Is the alleged ripping of pages from the Koran in the presence of Arab detainees and then flushing the pages down the toilet worse than solitary confinement?

These are all legitimate questions requiring serious debate. They are also subject to interpretation, cultural relativism, and personal value systems. That is, ripping the pages of the Koran in the presence of a non-Muslim is offensive but does not have the same emotional impact. Similarly, ripping the pages of the New Testament should be offensive to a Muslim but would, in all likelihood, not have the same emotional effect that it would have for a Christian. Forced masturbation, as practiced by Lyndi England, regardless of ethnicity or religious beliefs, in front of a video camera is, no doubt, humiliating, sadistic, and reprehensible.

What, then, sets solitary confinement apart? The Eighth Amendment's language with respect to "excessive bail" articulates the Founding Fathers' concern that an individual's freedom not be denied because of an inability to meet financial demands not commensurate with the charged crime. The word *excessive*, however, is ill-defined and vague, as financial resources vary from individual to individual. In advocating standards for coercive interrogation methods, vague terms such as excessive are problematic as is unlimited discretion in the interrogator's hands, whether in Montgomery,

Alabama or Abu Ghraib, leading to excess and violations of constitutional rights.

Nevertheless, efforts to establish institutionalized limits on coercive interrogation are augmented by the Eighth Amendment's language regarding excessive bail. After all, the Eighth Amendment articulates the Founding Fathers' concern with undue infringement on an individual's rights *prior* to trial. By seeking to ensure that an individual not be imprisoned unnecessarily before trial, the Founding Fathers' intended to maximize an individual's freedom. The Eighth Amendment can be superimposed on coercive interrogation in the following manner—that although interrogations are lawful, excessive interrogations are unlawful. To wit: although bail is lawful, excessive bail is unlawful; punishment is lawful; cruel and unusual punishment is unlawful.

What is the practical benefit of extending Eighth Amendment protections to the interrogation setting? Why are the Fifth and Fourteenth Amendment protections discussed earlier insufficient? Why should an additional right be extended to an otherwise unprotected class who some argue are undeserving of any such protections? The response is directly linked to the fundamental issue this book addresses—the need to develop clearly articulated limits on interrogation that include granting constitutional protections to individuals suspected of involvement in terrorism.

However, it is important to note that the hybrid paradigm does not propose extending full constitutional protections to the detainee. To wit, the Sixth Amendment's right to confront the accuser is extended in part, not in full. Why the bifurcation? Because of a belief that the detainee is most vulnerable in the interrogation setting. That is where the individual most requires institutionalized, rigorous protections. In the courtroom, represented by counsel, the detainee is less vulnerable and exposed even if, as the hybrid paradigm suggests, classified information may be submitted as part of the prosecution's evidence.

What then does protection against cruel and unusual punishment in the coercive interrogation paradigm suggest? Certainly a detainee cannot be subjected to cruel and unusual punishment. The harder test is seeking to define cruel and unusual punishment in the coercive interrogation paradigm. The interrogation is the most complicated and complex aspect of operational counterterrorism and requires granting the detainee rights not granted to him in the courtroom.

It is important that the interrogator obtain the information the detainee poses. However, as the right is not absolute, limits are mandatory. That is why the detainee is granted more rights in the interrogation setting than in the courtroom setting. Furthermore, unlike in the zone of combat where the individual facing the soldier may or may not be a terrorist and may or may not be armed, in the interrogation cell he is no more than an unarmed suspect.

Eighth Amendment Jurisprudence

Eighth Amendment rules apply both to release from detention and post-conviction punishment, including, but not limited to, the imposition of the death penalty. To safeguard the manner in which the state interrogates the detainee, it is vital that the Eighth Amendment's principles be extended to the interrogation setting. What is cruel and unusual postconviction, can also be considered cruel and unusual preconviction. Furthermore, what is considered excessive from the perspective of bail, can also be considered excessive from the perspective of interrogation.

In *Stack v. Boyle*,[360] the Supreme Court held that bail is "excessive" in violation of the Eighth Amendment when it is set at a figure higher than an amount reasonably calculated to ensure the asserted governmental interest.[361] Governmental interest with respect to bail—"that the accused will stand trial and submit to sentence if found guilty"[362]—has been held by the Court in *United States v. Salerno*[363] to mean that "bail must be set by a court at a sum designed to ensure that goal, and no more."[364]

Applying *Salerno* to the coercive interrogation paradigm requires articulating the governmental interest with respect to the limits of interrogation. In other words, what is the primary governmental interest in the interrogation of a detainee in Guantanamo Bay suspected of involvement in terrorism?

How do *Stack* and *Salerno* relate to coercive interrogation? In the following manner—if an interrogation is excessive, then the interrogatee's rights are violated. In addition, if the interrogation is excessive, then compelling government interests are not served. Doubters, skeptics,

---

[360] 342 U.S. 1, 4–6 (1951).
[361] *See* http://www.usconstitution.net/const.html#Am8 (last visited May 2, 2007).
[362] *See* http://supreme.justia.com/constitution/amendment-08/01-excessive-bail.html (last visited May 2, 2007).
[363] United States v. Salerno, 481 U.S., at 754.
[364] *Id.*

and critics[365] will respond with at least two legitimate and important questions: What is excessive, and is the primary government interest not to get information at all costs?

Although the government and the public have a strong interest in receiving information from the detainee, it is not in the government's interest to implement an interrogation regime premised on *all means necessary*. The development of a lawful and moral coercive interrogation regime represents the ultimate in the balancing dilemma that is the essence of counterterrorism. In seeking to determine how to balance the rights of the legitimate rights of the individual with the equally legitimate national security rights of the state, it is critical to apply the test the Supreme Court articulated in *Stack* and *Salerno*.

Finding a balance between national security and the rights of individuals is the most significant issue faced by liberal democratic nations in developing their counterterrorism strategy. Without a balance between these two tensions, democratic societies lose the very ethos for which they fight. As Benjamin Franklin once said, "those who would give up essential liberty, to purchase a little temporary safety, deserve neither liberty nor safety."[366] Yet, the struggle to balance competing interests of the individual freedom and group security is the fundamental dilemma confronting democracies today.

The ultimate test in balancing is to determine whether a policy, however negatively it may impact a particular population group, also contributes to a nation's security. If the policy does not have a proven, positive effect, then the desired balance has not been struck. Without a proven, positive effect, the policy is simultaneously ineffective, problematic, and potentially unconstitutional. A policy that suggests a *lashing out* rather than a calculated response will not—under any circumstance—be considered balanced. In the context of counterterrorism, the question to be addressed is whether the administration's actions contributed to

---

[365] I have presented this thesis at innumerable academic conferences, media appearances, and public forums; the question and answer discussion is invariably lively, replete with fascinating discourse characterized by healthy and spirited debate. Those who disagree with me suggest that my thesis weakens the state in the face of dedicated terrorists and that "tough times require tough actions." Although I intellectually understand the argument, I believe it to be shortsighted, and it ultimately presents a significant threat from within to the state—from ourselves in what I have previously referred to as "panic response."

[366] Benjamin Franklin, *Pennsylvania Assembly: Reply to the Governor, November 11, 1755*, *in* THE PAPERS OF BENJAMIN FRANKLIN 242 (vol. 6, Leonard W. Labaree ed., 1963).

preventing additional attacks. If yes, then the additional query of at what cost, must be examined.

The question with respect to cruel and unusual punishment is what is excessive—in the balancing equation—with respect to interrogations? If setting bail at a level that the particular suspect cannot meet under any circumstances is considered excessive, then is not subjecting the detainee to the harsh methods excessive? If it is unconstitutional to deny the suspect his freedom by imposing excessive bail, are not the interrogation methods imposed on Guantanamo Bay detainees inherently unconstitutional?

In analogizing cruel and unusual punishment to the interrogation setting, it is important to develop a regime that protects the detainee's rights. To do so requires avoiding the vagueness that has characterized case law with respect to the Eighth Amendment. Vagueness, in the context of cruel and unusual punishment allows—deliberately or not is irrelevant—the interrogator and his superiors too much discretion. The requirement to develop an institutionalized interrogation regime, largely devoid of an overabundance of wiggle room is critical in the effort to develop a lawful interrogation regime.[367] In analyzing interrogations in the context of cruel and unusual punishment, an act that would be considered cruel and unusual in the punishment context for someone *convicted* of a crime *must* be impermissible for someone only a suspect. The rub is that the principles although seemingly clear (but necessarily obvious) are imprecise in that they fail the vagueness test.

In *Estelle v. Gamble*, the plaintiff argued inadequate medical treatment was provided in prison. This was the Supreme Court's initial application of the Eighth Amendment to deprivations and conditions not specifically part of a prisoner's postconviction sentence. In *Estelle*,

---

[367] My conviction regarding the need to institutionalize processes for interrogations was largely framed by two separate professional experiences: as a prosecutor in the West Bank Military Court, when I decided to withdraw a charge sheet previously filed against a Palestinian after meeting with the General Security Services interrogator whose testimony, I felt, a mini-trial convened to determine the confession's admissibility predicated on a "free will and volition" standard, would not be deemed reliable by the court and when I served as a Judge in the Gaza Strip Military Court I convened a hearing to determine whether the defendant had voluntarily confessed and concluded that he had not (with respect to a particular interrogator). My decision was premised on sense that the interrogator had exceeded the bounds of the interrogation; my fears were confirmed when, in a later conversation, the same interrogator commented that the GSS "never crosses the bounds." The statement, largely neutralized the particular interrogator's credibility.

the plaintiff claimed that he received inadequate medical treatment from prison personnel after sustaining an injury. Failure to do so "may actually produce physical 'torture or a lingering death,'" which the Eighth Amendment originally prohibited. The Court stated that "[t]he infliction of such unnecessary suffering is inconsistent with contemporary standards of decency as manifested in modern legislation." The Court held that the government owes an obligation to provide proper medical care to those incarcerated, where failing to do so could "actually produce physical torture or lingering death," as prohibited by the Eighth Amendment. In holding such actions toward an individual held in jail, the Court further enunciated that "deliberate indifference to serious medical needs of prisoners constitutes the 'unnecessary and wanton infliction of pain.'"

In *Hutto v. Finney*, the Court held that "conditions of confinement" can be considered to violate the Eighth Amendment. The U.S. Supreme Court agreed with the lower court that conditions of solitary confinement constituted cruel and unusual punishment under the Eighth Amendment. However, this holding is not so broad as to say that solitary confinement is per se violative of the Eighth Amendment. Rather, the Court stated that the unconstitutionality of solitary confinement depends on its duration and conditions. After examining the inmates' diet, the crowding, vandalism, violence, and diseases, the Court found the conditions to be unacceptable.

The morality argument is also, inherently, vague and rife with interpretation. Nevertheless, in the effort to develop a lawful coercive interrogation regime, considerations of morality must be given their due. To what extent is a legitimate question; nevertheless, if we are to apply a *decency* test to cruel and unusual punishment then decency is inherently related to—if not adjoined—to morality. However, there is an inherent problem with decency as a concept relevant to the interrogation setting. Can there be anything decent about subjecting an individual to the rigors of an interrogation? After all, the interrogation setting is fraught with fear and anxiety. Precisely because it is "filled with the sweat of anxiety," it is critical to adopt standards equated with morality, and yes, decency.

Application of the Eighth Amendment prohibition against cruel and unusual punishment with respect to detainee interrogation in Guantanamo Bay requires undertaking the difficult task of clearly articulating do's and don'ts. Otherwise we will be treading water while conceivably subjecting the detainee to water-boarding.[368] How, then, do these standards apply to the discussion of the Eighth Amendment's prohibition of cruel and inhuman punishment? Although such discussion is typically confined only to the postconviction world, a setting basically inapplicable to this book's discussion of interrogation, there is a connection to be made to the times where punishments *prior* to conviction raise the Eighth Amendment.

The primary example of the application of the Eighth Amendment to the preconviction setting is solitary confinement, which is defined as "the confinement of a prisoner in isolation from all other prisoners."[369] The typical focus on such analysis is the psychological effect solitary confinement has on the detainee. It can be used, similar to cumulative mistreatment, as a way to break a detainee's will, leading to a confession that may in fact be coerced and false. The Court in *In re Medley*, through dicta, discussed the particularly horrific conditions historically attributed to solitary confinement:

> The peculiarities of this system were the complete isolation of the prisoner from all human society, and his confinement in a cell of considerable size, so arranged that he had no direct intercourse with or sight of any human being, and no employment or instruction. ... But experience demonstrated that there were serious objections to it. A considerable number of the prisoners fell, after even a short confinement, into a semifatuous condition, from which it was next to impossible to arouse them, and others became violently insane; others still, committed suicide; while those who stood the ordeal better were not generally reformed, and in most cases did not recover sufficient mental activity to be of any subsequent service to the community. It became evident some changes must be made in the system.[370]

---

[368] Water-boarding has been described by Vice President Cheney as "a dunk in the water" and is universally understood by experts to be a form of torture. Sheikh Khalid Muhammad who masterminded 9/11 was, according to his testimony and other reports, subjected to water-boarding. Although he confessed to his involvement in a long series of terrorist acts, it is unclear if he did so because of water-boarding. Accordingly, it is all but impossible to verify its effectiveness.

[369] http://www.answers.com/topic/solitary-confinement (last visited May 5, 2007).

[370] *In re Medley*, 10 S.Ct. 384, 386 (1890)

In *Rhodes v. Chapman*, the Court added a totality of the circumstances test regarding conditions in solitary confinement. The Court announced that "[c]onditions … alone or in combination, may deprive inmates of the minimal civilized measure of life's necessities."[371] The *Rhodes* Court, however, noted that the Constitution does not mandate comfortable prisons. Therefore, the Court showed great deference to the legislature and prison officials in allowing them to determine and implement effective measures of prison reform.

If solitary confinement is held to be psychologically damaging to the inmate, then it can be extrapolated that an interrogator who moves a detainee into solitary confinement is inflicting the same psychological impact on the *preconviction* individual. The interrogation process must be viewed as expansively as possible. To that end, how the detainee is held, in what conditions, subject to what detention regime is as much a part of the interrogation process as is the actual questioning by a particular interrogator. Solitary confinement, then, between interrogation sessions (the length of which is unknown to the detainee) is an inherent part of the expanded interrogation experience. Accordingly, an attempt to artic-ulate the limits of coercive interrogation in the hybrid paradigm must necessarily include a psychological and constitutional analysis of solitary confinement to which post-9/11 detainees are subjected.

Although *Estelle* expanded the scope of the examination to include nonpunishment aspects of the process, holding a detainee in solitary confinement as part of the interrogation process necessarily implies *punishing* the individual. Although the context is not punishment as in, ten years of incarceration, subjecting an individual to solitary confine-ment has the practical effect of inflicting punishment on the detainee.

Punishment is defined as "some pain or penalty warranted by law, inflicted on a person, for the commission of a crime or misdemeanor, or for the omission of the performance of an act required by law, by the judgment and command of some lawful court."[372]

Although this book proffers a number of lawful, specific coercive interrogation measures, solitary confinement is not included precisely because of the documented psychological damage it causes the suspect. Herein lays the tension: What are the limits, how far can the state go, and

---

[371] *Rhodes v. Chapman*. 452 U.S. 337, 347 (1981)
[372] *See* http://www.lectlaw.com/def2/p201.htm (last visited May 5, 2007).

how much damage is too much and what is the best mechanism for determining? In analyzing how to determine, it is equally legitimate to ask who determines and subject to what oversight and control.

In applying the Eighth Amendment to preinterrogation coercive interrogation, the initial step is to define punishment as directly applying to the nonpunishment phase of the process. By expanding the definition of punishment to include pretrial detention, the placing of the detainee in solitary confinement can be viewed as punishment. The next step in the logical progression is ascertaining whether solitary confinement is not only punishment, but *also* cruel and unusual. That is, whether solitary confinement inherently violates the Eighth Amendment or is the analysis predicated on a case by case examination. Can solitary confinement be categorically defined as cruel and unusual or are there degrees and categories of solitary confinement that do not violate the Eighth Amendment in all cases?

To apply these questions to the hybrid paradigm and to therefore facilitate analysis of solitary confinement with respect to the detainees held in Guantanamo Bay requires closely examining these detention conditions. There are a series of questions relative to the administration's detention policies. What goals were established? How was effectiveness to be defined? What was the purpose of imposing solitary confinement on the detainees?

To properly determine whether use of solitary confinement violates the Eighth Amendment, an examination of its psychological impact is appropriate. According to Dr. Stuart Grassian:

> Indeed, by 1890, in *In re Medley*, 10 S. Ct. 384, the United States Supreme Court explicitly recognized the massive psychiatric harm caused by solitary confinement: "This matter of solitary confinement is not ... a mere unimportant regulation as to the safe-keeping of the prisoner. A considerable number of the prisoners fell, after even a short confinement, into a semi-fatuous condition, from which it was next to impossible to arouse them, and others became violently insane; others still, committed suicide; while those who stood the ordeal better were not generally reformed, and in most cases did not recover sufficient mental activity to be of any subsequent service to the community."

The consequences of the Supreme Court's holding were quite dramatic for Mr. Medley. Mr. Medley had been convicted of having murdered his wife. Under the Colorado statute in force at the time of the murder, he would have been executed after about one additional month of incarceration in the county jail. But in the interim between Mr. Medley's crime and his trial, the Colorado legislature had passed a new statute which called for the convicted murderer to be, instead, incarcerated in solitary confinement in the State Prison during the month prior to his execution. Unhappily, simultaneously with the passage of the new law, the legislature rescinded the older law, without allowing for a bridging clause which would have allowed for Mr. Medley's sentencing under the older statute.

Mr. Medley appealed his sentencing under the new statute, arguing that punishment under this new law was so substantially more burdensome than punishment under the old law, as to render its application to him ex post facto. The Supreme Court agreed with him, even though it simultaneously recognized that if Mr. Medley was not sentenced under the new law, he could not be sentenced at all. Despite this, the Court held that this additional punishment of one month of solitary confinement was simply too egregious to ignore; the Court declared Mr. Medley a free man, and ordered his release from prison.[373]

According to Nan Miller:[374]

As early as 1820, when New York decided to eliminate the system of absolute isolation at Auburn Prison, the detrimental psychological effects of solitary confinement were recognized." Because of mental breakdowns, the system was changed to permit prisoners to work together during the day in total silence and return to their cells at night." Moreover, in the 1830s, statistical evidence began indicating severe problems caused by solitary confinement, especially insanity.

In defining the "cruel, inhuman or degrading treatment or punishment" standard, the international community has extended the protection of prisoners to include, not only the physical confinement conditions, but also the psychological effects of

---

[373] See http://humanrights.ucdavis.edu/documents/library/documents-and-reports/Grassian.pdf (last visited May 5, 2007).

[374] Nan Miller, *International Protection of the Rights of Prisoners: Is Solitary Confinement in the US a Violation of International Standards?* 26 Cal. W. Int'l L. J. 139.

the confinement. Generally, international courts, commissions and committees have applied the "totality of conditions" test for ascertaining prisoners' rights violations.

As elucidated by the literature, the psychological impact of solitary confinement amounts to a syndrome which causes severe and possibly permanent mental suffering. Due to its severity, the syndrome would probably "attain the minimum level required" to establish it within the scope of the "cruel, inhuman or degrading" standard. Moreover, the symptoms of RES syndrome are almost certain to occur with any case of prolonged solitary confinement.

The Human Rights Committee has also applied a "totality of conditions"-type test in evaluating possible violations of Articles 7 and 10 of the ICCPR and has found that solitary confinement can be a violation of both articles. The Committee seemed willing to extend the protection against "cruel, inhuman or degrading" treatment to include protection from emotional and psychological harm. Moreover, even if the Committee was unable, or unwilling, to find a violation of the "cruel, inhuman or degrading" standard based solely on the psychological effects of solitary confinement, they would assuredly find a violation of the Article 10 requirement that "all persons deprived of their liberty shall be treated with humanity and respect for the inherent dignity of the human person." As discussed supra, the symptoms of RES syndrome can be so emotionally devastating that they can lead to anger, hostility, violence and even death by suicide.[375]

With this understanding of the effects of solitary confinement, it is clear that the measure can constitute violation of the Eighth Amendment prohibitions against cruel and unusual punishment. The government must guarantee that it does not use such harmful techniques in the interrogation of detainees.

---

[375] *Id.*

CHAPTER 9

International Law Pertaining to Torture and Interrogation

Expanding the discussion to the international sphere is critical to our overall focus: the development of a lawful coercive interrogation regime predicated on the rule of law. In the effort to do so, it is important to examine and analyze existing international standards for interrogation and torture alike. Furthermore, it is important to ask whether international standards are relevant and appropriate for the American experience. That is, does international law have any relevance for the development of a coercive interrogation regime in the post-9/11 world?

Such a discussion requires an analysis of international law principles and comparative case law. Although Justice Scalia has posited the inapplicability of international law to American jurisprudence,[376] Justice Kennedy's approach[377] represents a preferred approach in an increasingly internationalized world. In that spirit, a discussion intended to recommend concrete coercive interrogation measures must include a discussion of torture in the context of international law.

International law is a set of agreements, sometimes called conventions, freely entered into by states to regulate relations between themselves on particular issues or matters such as extradition, trade relations, and mutual defense. In addition, international agreements can establish

---

[376] Atkins v. Virginia, 536 U.S. 304 (2002).
[377] *Id.*

an organization, such as the United Nations (U.N.), whereby like-minded states seek to resolve issues of mutual concern.

When international law was developed, the world was composed largely of nation states. Nonstate actors, such as Al Qaeda, were not a factor in the development of international law. Furthermore customary international law—the manner in which states conduct their affairs—was predicated on nation-states developing and implementing agreed-on rules or codes of conduct.

According to the 1868 St. Petersburg Declaration,[378] the only legitimate object that states should endeavor to accomplish during war is to weaken the military force of the enemy.[379] In examining and analyzing the relationship between international law and counterterrorism, one of the most important issues is defining terrorism, and subsequently "who is the enemy."

In seeking to articulate the relationship between international law and the development of a coercive interrogation regime, the interrogation setting can be perceived as a zone of combat with specifically articulated guidelines. Some readers may perceive this discussion to exaggerate the interrogation context and to dramatize the relationship between the interrogator and the detainee. To those readers, it is recommended to ask whether the means justify the ends in an effort to determine and articulate the limits of interrogation.

In 1837, U.S. Secretary of State Daniel Webster articulated a definition of self-defense, which evolved into customary international law.[380] Webster's definition followed what has come to be known as the Caroline incident. The *Caroline* was a U.S. steamboat attempting to transport supplies to Canadian insurgents. A British force interrupted the *Caroline's* voyage, shot at it, set it on fire, and let it wash over Niagara Falls. Webster said that Britain's act did not qualify as self-defense because self-defense is only justified "if the necessity of that self-defense is instant, overwhelming, and leaving no choice of means, and no moment for deliberation." According to Webster, Britain could have dealt with the *Caroline* in a

---

[378] Declaration Renouncing the Use, in Time of War, of Explosive Projectiles Under 400 Grammes Weight, Saint Petersburg, November 12, 1868, *available at* http://www.icrc. org/ihl.nsf/FULL/130?OpenDocument (last visited Sept. 17, 2006).

[379] *Id.*

[380] Customary international law "derives from 'a general practice accepted as law.'" International Committee of the Red Cross, Customary International Humanitarian Law: Questions & Answers, Aug. 15, 2005, *available at* http://www.icrc.org/Web/eng/ siteeng0.nsf/iwpList133/E02D32D1A4976030C1256FEB005007A1.

more diplomatic manner. He limited the right to self-defense to situations where there is a real threat, the response is essential and proportional, and all peaceful means of resolving the dispute have been exhausted. This principle known as the Caroline doctrine was considered customary international law until a competing definition of self-defense arose in Article 51 of the U.N. Charter[381] which authorizes self-defense only if an armed attack "occurs."[382]

The excerpt below highlights an issue of great significance to the actual implementation of self-defense as authorized by the U.N. Charter. The fundamental question facing decision makers in the context of self-defense is when preemptive measures can be taken. Preemptive self-defense is predicated on intelligence information that must be reliable, viable, valid, and corroborated to be deemed actionable. Furthermore, preemptive action must be proportional to the attack it intends to prevent.[383] In determining proportionality, decision makers must determine both the immediacy of the threat and its severity.

> A second limitation on the self-defense exception is that not all uses of force qualify as "armed" attacks. As the International Court of Justice concluded in *Nicaragua v. United States*, only a substantial military attack, and not isolated armed incidents, rises to the level of an "armed attack...."

Finally, governments cannot lawfully use force to respond to terrorist threats that do not rise to the level of an armed attack, unless those threats are widespread and imminent. The Charter thus seems to preclude any open-ended use of anticipatory self-defense. The unanimous Security Council condemnation of the 1981 Israeli attack on the Iraqi nuclear reactor at Osarik reinforces this proscription.

> Despite this traditional, restrictive scheme designed to narrowly limit a nation's right to use force in self-defense, various scholars have argued for a more expansive view of a nation's military options in fighting terrorism. The driving force behind that argument is the

---

[381] Emanuel Gross, *Thwarting Terrorist Acts by Attacking the Perpetrators or Their Commanders as an Act of Self-defense: Human Rights versus the State's Duty to Protect its Citizens*, 15 TEMPLE INT'L & COMP L. J. 195, 211 (2001).

[382] U.N. Charter art. 51., *available at* http://www.un.org/aboutun/charter/.

[383] *See* Israel Committee Against Torture in Israel v. Government of Israel, HCJ 769/06, citing Guiora, Guiora, *Targeted Killing as Active Self-Defense*, 36 CWRU JIL 319 (2004).

perceived political and military desirability of employing force against terrorists. Former Legal Advisor to the State Department Abraham Sofaer has argued that "self-defense allows a proportionate response to every use of force, not just "armed attacks." Sofaer also claims that any aid given by a state to terrorists—for instance, allowing terrorist groups to use its territory—renders that state complicit and subject to attack. Finally, Sofaer argues that "defensive measures may be taken to preempt attacks, as in Sudan, where necessary for deterrence." Thus, a nation suspecting that a terrorist group is planning future, unspecified attacks against it would be justified in using military force against that group and any country knowingly harboring it.[384]

The intent of Article 51 was to limit the invocation of the right to self-defense. Any limitation, however, still required a discussion regarding the right to engage in anticipatory self-defense. "The United Nations, and the international community, are wary of potential abuses of the rights inherent under Article 51 and has established four standards to prevent nations from abusing those rights."[385] States needed to not only defend themselves against active and ongoing attacks, but also to act preemptively to prevent aggressive acts from being carried out. Customary international law permits a state to respond to a threat and infringe on the territorial sovereignty of another nation when the following four criteria are met: (1) it is acting in self defense; (2) the attack is substantial and military (i.e., not an "isolated armed incident"); (3) the offending nation is complicit, unwilling, or unable to prevent further attacks; and (4) the attack is widespread and imminent.[386] The fourth criteria narrows the Caroline doctrine as the attack must be deemed "imminent."[387]

States, to adequately defend themselves, must be able to take the fight to the terrorist before the terrorist takes the fight to it. The state must act preemptively to either deter terrorists or, at the very least, prevent terrorism. The question that must be answered is: What tools are necessary for the state to combat terrorist bombings? Active self-defense would appear

---

[384] Jules Lobel, *The Use of Force to Respond to Terrorist Attacks: The Bombing of Sudan and Afghanistan*, 24 YALE J. INTL L. 537 (Summer, 1999).

[385] Frank A. Biggio *Neutralizing the Threat: Reconsidering Existing Doctrines in the Emerging War on Terrorism*, 34 CWRJIL 1 (2002).

[386] *Id.*

[387] Amos N. Guiora, *Targeted Killing as Active Self-Defense*, 36 CWRU JIL 319 (2004).

to be the most effective tool; that is, rather than wait for the actual armed attack to "occur" (Article 51), the state must be able to act anticipatorily (Caroline) against the nonstate actor (not considered in Caroline).

The development of a new body of international law providing legal justification for such actions (active self defense against a nonstate actor) must be consistent with existing principles and obligations such as proportionality, military necessity, collateral damage and seeking alternatives. The two concepts—active self-defense and the four fundamental principles are not in conflict; rather, they are critical to formulating international law's response to modern armed conflict, a very different war than previous traditional ones.

What does all this tell us in the context of torture, coercive interrogation, and international law? In the effort to define the limits of interrogation, it is instructive to articulate the limits of self-defense. A practical application of the Caroline doctrine to the interrogation setting strongly suggests that limits are both critical and mandatory. Furthermore, although Article 51 articulates when states can attack another sovereign, it is relevant by extrapolation and analogy to the issue before us for it defines—and limits—state action.

Interrogation pits the agent of the state against an individual who is at that moment no more than a suspect. By an admittedly broad analogy to the Article 51 paradigm, if the individual is no more than a suspect and if the state is no more than a perceived threat, then the fundamental principle is a limitation on possible state response.

Intelligence gathering is one of the most important issues in counterterrorism. Some would argue intelligence is perhaps *the* most critical issue. Otherwise, operational counterterrorism would literally be "groping in the dark." Although the focus of this book is interrogation, the relationship between interrogations and intelligence gathering contributes to the effort to define the limits of interrogation.

The gathering of counterterrorism intelligence fundamentally differs from how criminal evidence is obtained and subsequently submitted to a court of law. To understand the differences between the two, it is necessary to define intelligence and the critical role it plays in counterterrorism. Intelligence gathering best illustrates that counterterrorism exists in the world of dark shadows and back alleys.

Discussions of intelligence gathering and interrogation necessarily includes how a state gathers intelligence, the availability of resources for intelligence gathering, what means can be used for intelligence gathering, and with which sources a state is willing to work. To that end, analyzing how international law defines torture is facilitated by a discussion of intelligence gathering.

Intelligence has been defined as the collection and analysis of information relevant to a government's formulation and implementation of policy designed to further its national security interests and respond to threats from actual or potential adversaries.[388] A source is defined as "a person who provides information."[389] Critical to fully understanding these terms is how governments "translate" intelligence information into operational measures.

As discussed earlier, the most appropriate starting point for understanding torture in the context of international law is the 1984 Convention Against Torture and other Cruel, Inhuman, or Degrading Treatment or Punishment (1984 Convention Against Torture)—which prohibits signatory parties from using any torturous acts against any detainee.

In the immediate aftermath of 9/11, the United States defined the limits of interrogation extremely broadly. The administration based this policy on the assumption that, other than basic rights, the detainees are not entitled to Geneva Convention protections. The result was a policy that directly led to abuse.

International law provisions, particularly the Geneva Conventions, accord detainees certain protections.[390] The administration's initial approach of granting only basic, minimum rights was overwhelmingly discredited by independent observers and subsequently modified by the White House. Although Al Qaeda operatives are not considered prisoners of war (POWs), it is important for any discussion concerning interrogation to note that under Part II, Article 13 of the Geneva Convention relative to the treatment of POWs:

> Prisoners of war must at all times be humanely treated. Any unlawful act or omission by the Detaining Power causing death or seriously endangering the health of a prisoner of war in its custody is prohibited, and will be regarded as a serious breach of the present

---

[388] A. SHULSKY & G. SCHMITT, SILENT WARFARE: UNDERSTANDING THE WORLD OF INTELLIGENCE (3d ed. Brassey's 2002); *See also* Raymond Wannall, *The FBI's Domestic Intelligence Operations: Domestic Security in Limbo*, 4 No. 4 INT'L J. INTELLIG. & COUNTERINTELLIG. 446 (1991).

[389] THE AMERICAN HERITAGE DICTIONARY.

[390] *See* Chapter Three.

Convention. In particular, no prisoner of war may be subjected to physical mutilation or to medical or scientific experiments of any kind which are not justified by the medical, dental or hospital treatment of the prisoner concerned and carried out in his interest.

Likewise, prisoners of war must at all times be protected, particularly against acts of violence or intimidation and against insults and public curiosity.

Measures of reprisal against prisoners of war are prohibited.[391]

Which of these standards should apply to the interrogation of detainees held in Guantanamo Bay? Before we move onto the last chapter—the actual recommendations for the development of a lawful coercive interrogation regime, it is critical to determine whether international law principles and standards are relevant to this effort. If they are relevant, to what extent? Is the United States obligated to respect the 1984 Convention Against Torture? Does 9/11 suggest that the rules of the game have significantly changed and therefore agreements entered into force prior to that Tuesday need be viewed as null and void?

It seems to be a safe assumption, based on the writings and statements of Bush administration spokesmen, that international law was viewed dismissively; "ignorable" would be a more succinct description. Whether Attorney General Gonzales' perspective was specifically related to the Geneva Conventions or to CAT is largely irrelevant. What is critical to understand is that the administration's approach to interrogations was that torture was a legitimate means of interrogating detainees.

Although then Secretary of Defense Rumsfeld referred to the detainees as the "worst of the worst," the numbers speak for themselves: A significant number were released from Guantanamo after officials recognized that their initial detention had been without cause. In other words, a torture regime was established for individuals who had not presented a security threat to the United States. The United States violated international conventions to which it was signatory.

Under both international and domestic law, torture is illegal. The standard that international law posits with respect to torture, then,

---

[391] Geneva Convention (III) Relative to the Treatment of Prisoners of War, *opened for signature* Apr. 12, 1949.

is highly applicable to the central thesis of this book. Similar to the constitutional based argument proposed in previous chapters, international law is clear in articulating a demand for the implementation of an interrogation regime devoid of torture.

To that end, the discussion must necessarily focus on the limits of interrogation. In that sense, we have come full cycle in reaching the conclusion that we are obligated to define the limits of interrogation in an effort to articulate the paradigm this book propounds: coercive interrogation.

CHAPTER 10

Concluding Recommendations

The interrogator's dilemma (Does the detainee know anything, and how much does he or she know?) goes to the heart of the interrogation setting. However, there are additional important questions: if the detainee knows something, is that information still timely or, because of his or her detention, have operational plans been modified, if not cancelled? On a different level, perhaps the detainee is the victim of mistaken identity and is not who the interrogator believes him or her to be. All of this raises the following question—how does the interrogator know who the detainee is and why is the detainee being interrogated?

With the exception of an individual caught in the act (a rarity in counterterrorism and even rarer in the zones of combat that have come to define Iraq and Afghanistan) the individual brought to the detention setting is there because another individual has provided his or her name. And who is that other individual? As discussed elsewhere in this book, the detainee—in the overwhelming majority of cases—is there because a source has given his or her name. The source may have provided his or her handler with the detainee's name not because the latter was involved in terrorism, but because the latter was involved with the former's sister or brother. In other words, grudge factors are more than real possibilities as to why someone finds himself or herself in the interrogation setting.

In that same vein, even if the detainee is rightly suspected of terrorist activity, should we not differentiate between categories of terrorist involvement? After all, not all terrorists are the same and not all acts of terrorism are equal. Just as proportionality is required in the context of operational counterterrorism, the four fundamental principles of international law—collateral damage, proportionality, military necessity, and alternatives are as relevant to the detention context as they are to operational counterterrorism. In that sense, it is suggested that interrogations are as much a part of operational counterterrorism as are decisions whether to conduct a targeted killing or forcibly enter a home.

Interrogations are an example of operational counterterrorism measures subject to the principles listed above. Therefore, for an interrogation regime to be lawful, limits must be both articulated and respected. Those limits must be based on four legs: constitutional law, international law, morality in armed conflict, and operational constraints. To illustrate the point, the following is offered.

In the Israeli operational counterterrorism paradigm, targeted killing reflects a deliberate decision to order the death of a Palestinian terrorist.[392] An individual will only be targeted if he or she presents a serious threat in the future to public order and safety based on criminal evidence or reliable, corroborated intelligence information clearly implicating him or her. Intelligence information is corroborated when confirmed by at least two separate, unrelated sources. There also must be no reasonable alternative to the targeted killing; meaning that the international law requirement of seeking another reasonable means of incapacitating the terrorist prior to a future attack has proved fruitless.[393]

In the aftermath of the Israel Supreme Court decision in December 2006 upholding targeted killings, I wrote the following:

(T)he decision and order to go after a terrorist must be rooted in principles that take into consideration proportionality, collateral damage and alternatives.

The decision, the last in Barak's corpus of rulings on fighting terrorism, is the final piece in a puzzle of judicially mandated rules for

---

[392]   *See* Arieh O'Sullivan, *IDF Kills Two Key Hamas Terrorists,* JERUSALEM POST, Nov. 1, 2001, at 1, *available at* LEXIS, News Library, Jerusalem Post File.

[393]   Robert F. Teplitz, *Taking Assassination Attempts Seriously: Did the United States Violate International Law in Forcefully Responding to the Iraqi Plot to Kill George Bush?*, 28 CORNELL INT'L L.J. 569, 610–613.

how an army should conduct operational counterterrorism. Barak's Supreme Court decisions over the past 15 years reflect a realization that damage to democracy and human rights outweigh whatever operational advantages commanders can gain from judicial ambiguity. Operational success would be enhanced by a strict moral and legal code.

The ruling establishes a checklist of how the state is to proceed in these cases. Harming civilians who "take direct part in hostilities," as defined in the decision, "even if the result is death, is permitted, on the condition that there is no other means which harms them less, and on the condition that innocent civilians nearby are not harmed. Harm to the latter must be proportional. That proportionality is determined according to a values-based test, intended to balance between the military advantage and the civilian damage."

Barak has commented that civil, democratic states must conduct counterterrorism with "one arm tied behind their back." When I used that phrase, military commanders often told me that terrorists fight with two arms in front, implying that Barak's theory will lead to soldiers' deaths.

Barak's one-armed approach is reflected in his opinion on targeted killings: If we fight with both our arms, we not only will be in violation of international law but will have lost the moral high ground.

In holding that targeted killings are lawful, the Israeli Supreme Court established a clear baseline of legally authorized, aggressive, operational counterterrorism.

The Israeli model of active, interventionist judicial review in armed conflict is foreign to American commanders, decisionmakers and jurists. Nevertheless, the decision extends far beyond Israel's borders.

Recently, the U.S. Supreme Court, in *Hamdan v. Rumsfeld*, held that the military tribunals established by President Bush in the aftermath of the Sept. 11 attacks did not pass judicial muster. The presidential order of November 2001 creating the tribunals was not subject to rigorous checks and balances. The Congress was largely somnolent, and then-Chief Justice William H. Rehnquist previously had written that in times of conflict, the court must be "reticent."

Counterterrorism consists of four "legs": the rule of law, moral-ity, operational considerations and intelligence gathering. Successful, aggressive counterterrorism operations reflect a confluence of the four. Balancing the rights of the individual with the equally legiti-mate rights of the state is the essence of counterterrorism. It is also very difficult to develop, implement and articulate.

Nevertheless, decisionmakers in civil, democratic societies have no alternative but to address this extraordinarily complicated principle. A nation's leadership cannot, in the name of "national security," duck the necessity of carefully vetting operational decisions to make sure that they always meet obligations of international law and reflect a firm moral compass. One can argue that the Abu Ghraib prison scandal is an example of what happens when this process is not followed.

By not allowing "national security" as an excuse for not charting a legal and moral path in fighting terrorists, the court grants the executive power to make the most awesome decision—the killing of a human being—while explicitly limiting that power.

This is the essence of checks and balances and of active judicial review, which is the hallmark of civil, democratic society. It also reflects a moral code that makes a society worth fighting for.[394]

How does that translate to the standards required for defining the limits of interrogation? That is, what is the connection between operational counterterrorism and the interrogation? The answer in the aftermath of 9/11 is that the interrogation of a suspected terrorist is to be viewed in the same light as operational counterterrorism. Just as there are limits on operational decisions, there are limits on an interrogation be it in Guantanamo Bay, Bagram, or Abu Ghraib. Furthermore, just as domes-tic and international law is to apply to traditional operational decisions, they are to apply to interrogations.

Before returning to the constitutional law argument at the heart of this book, it is important to address one more issue relevant to interna-tional law: proportionality. Targeted killing cannot be implemented against a Palestinian whose involvement in terrorism is minor and whose

---

[394] BALTIMORE SUN, Dec. 23, 2006.

actions do not endanger public safety. Targeted killing can only be implemented against those terrorists who either directly or indirectly participate in terrorism in a fashion that is equivalent to involvement in armed conflict.

The Israel Defense Force (IDF) does not use this ultimate weapon at will and with impunity. It is more appropriate to consider targeted killing as a weapon of last resort to be implemented only when all other reasonable alternatives have been ruled out as operationally unfeasible.The terrorist in question must present a significant enough threat that the state has determined that there is no other option

This international law principle requires commanders to distinguish between combatants and civilians. The critical dilemma facing commanders is determining who is a legitimate target. To wit: One of the critical questions that must be answered is whether suicide bombers and those involved in terrorist infrastructure are legitimate targets. If the answer is yes, then we must examine how they can be fought. They are not soldiers in the traditional sense of the word. In the present conflict, terrorists who take a direct role are viewed as combatants, albeit illegal combatants not entitled to POW status, but are indeed legitimate targets. Furthermore, the legitimate target is not limited to the potential suicide bomber who, according to corroborated and reliable intelligence is "on his way" to carrying out a suicide bombing. Rather, the legitimate target is identified as a Palestinian that plays a significant role in the suicide bomber infrastructure.

It is important to remember that, in terms of the international law, terrorists who actually attack civilians or send others to commit attacks are not, according to international law, innocent civilians in the traditional context. Rather, they are full-fledged combatants.[395] Unlike soldiers who, as part of a regular army, are obligated to honor international law conventions regulating the conduct of war, terrorists are not bound to these agreements.

The above discussion is relevant to the question of whether all detainees subjected to the interrogation process should actually be held in detention. That is, in seeking to determine the limits of interrogation predicated on constitutional law, it is critical to distinguish between combatants and noncombatants as required by international law. The hybrid

---

[395]   Geneva Convention Relative to the Treatment of Prisoners of War, art. 4., para. (A)(2).

paradigm reflects a confluence between constitutional and international law enabling the state to lawfully and effectively protect itself, while simultaneously protecting the rights of the individual.

The first step in defining the limits of interrogation is to distinguish between who should and should not be in the interrogation setting. It must be noted that this analysis is not intended to be a defense of the detainee.[396] Rather, the fundamental concerns are twofold: (1) protecting the interrogator from his or her own government's refusal—or at least hesitation—to clearly articulate the limits of interrogation and therefore encourage murkiness, and (2) ensuring that constitutional guarantees be respected.

Specifically, unrestrained coercive interrogation and torture comport neither with domestic nor international law. Thus, the United States government must establish clearly delineated rules for coercive interrogation. It must be acknowledged that the establishment of strict standards may in fact limit effective operational counterterrorism. If such standards do result in limiting the executive's ability to act with unfettered discretion, it follows that the recommendations contained herein can lead to the death of innocent people. However, the interests of operating within civil society require that the United States engage in the requisite balance between the interests of national security and the equally valid interests of an individual. Erring wholly on the side of governmental interests with no consideration of the costs all but guarantees a return to the dark pages of American history.

---

[396] Over the course of a nineteen-year career in the Israel Defense Forces, Judge Advocate General Corps I prosecuted, sat in judgment of, recommended the imposition of a wide range of administrative sanction against and was consulted on extraordinarily difficult and complex issues pertaining to Palestinians accused of having committed acts of terrorism against Israelis and Palestinians alike. I add this only to ensure the reader that the basis for a concern regarding the detainee is not a result of "softness" nor misplaced innocence. Not in the least nor could I be accused of that. Rather, the philosophical underpinnings of this concern are based precisely on my highly relevant professional experiences in the West Bank, the Gaza Strip and elsewhere and my well-developed understanding of how the best intentioned, most highly trained "best of the best" can, under stress, commit egregious errors. I write these words out of the deepest respect for those who have committed their professional career, at personal risk, to protect society. I have developed enormous respect for these individuals; many whom society would never recognize for their identities must remain confidential. Therefore, I am so profoundly concerned, both personally and professionally, when policy recommendations are exclusively jurisprudentially based and not reflective of "life on the ground" as I (and others) have seen it.

Despite CAT, existing domestic legislation, and relevant Geneva Convention protections and obligations, the administration established the following guidelines for the harsh interrogation of detainees:

Guidelines for Aggressive Interrogations

Which "harsher methods" have been approved? No documents have yet been declassified that show what techniques are used specifically by the CIA, but one can reasonably assume that the Agency has at least the same range of freedom as that given to the Department of Defense in interrogating unlawful combatants outside the United States. In a Department of Defense memorandum entitled Working Group Report on Detainee Interrogations in the Global War on Terrorism, military officials divided non-routine interrogation techniques into two broad categories. The first category contained 26 techniques, all recommended for approval. These included techniques with names like "Fear Up Harsh," "Rapid Fire," "Dietary Manipulation," "Environmental Manipulation," and "Isolation.

"A second set of eight techniques was recommended for approval only "where there is a good basis to believe that the detainee possesses critical intelligence" and where the detainee has been determined to be medically suitable to withstand the technique. The report also calls for an "appropriate specified senior level approval [to be] given for use with any specific detainee" These eight "exceptional" techniques, advanced in the report as legal, are:

Isolation: Isolating the detainee from other detainees while still complying with basic standards of treatment.

Use of Prolonged Interrogations: The continued use of a series of approaches that extend over a long period of time (e.g. 20 hours per day per interrogation).

Forced Grooming: Forcing a detainee to shave hair or beard. (Force applied with intention to avoid injury. Would not use force that would cause serious injury).

Prolonged Standing: Lengthy standing in a "normal" position (non-stress). This has been successful, but should never make the detainee exhausted to the point of weakness or collapse. Not enforced by physical restraints. Not to exceed four hours in a 24-hour period.

Sleep Deprivation: Keeping the detainee awake for an extended period of time. (Allowing individual to rest briefly and then awakening him, repeatedly.) Not to exceed 4 days in succession.

Physical Training: Requiring detainees to exercise … Assists in generating compliance and fatiguing the detainees. No enforced compliance.

Face slap/Stomach slap: A quick glancing slap to the fleshy part of the cheek or stomach. These techniques are used strictly as shock measures and do not cause pain or injury. They are only effective if used once or twice together. After the second time on a detainee, it will lose the shock effect. Limited to two slaps per application; no more than two applications per interrogation.

Removal of Clothing: Potential removal of all clothing; removal to be done by military police if not agreed to by the subject. Creating a feeling of helplessness and dependence. This technique must be monitored to ensure the environmental conditions are such that this technique does not injure the detainee.

Increasing Anxiety by Use of Aversions: Introducing factors that of themselves create anxiety but do not create terror or mental trauma (e.g., simple presence of dog without directly threatening action). This technique requires the commander to develop specific and detailed safeguards to insure detainee's safety.

In response to the Working Group Report, Defense Secretary Rumsfeld sent a directive to the Commander of the U.S. Southern Command specifically accepting a number of the techniques endorsed in the report, but not the eight exceptional tactics. Rather, the Secretary directed that, in the event that the eight exceptional tactics are warranted, the Commander "should provide [the Secretary], via the Chairman of the Joint Chiefs of Staff, a written request describing the proposed techniques, recommended safeguards, and the rationale for applying it with an identified detainee."

The guidelines just described concern interrogation methods used by the Department of Defense, not necessarily the CIA. One can expect a similar degree of latitude, however, for detainees under the control of the CIA, especially since it appears that the

CIA is expected to manage interrogations of senior terrorist leaders.[397]

Be it slaps and forced grooming (in violation of a detainee's religious practices) or the presence of a dog, the methods are inherently dangerous for two primary reasons: They do not require that their implementation be strictly limited to facilitating an actual interrogation and the presence of a physician is not a requirement. The report below is an all but inevitable result of the measures above. Those measures that are ultimately unrelated to an interrogation also invite excess:

Reports of abuse of detainees in US custody in Afghanistan, Iraq, Guantánamo Bay, and at secret detention facilities continued to mount. Between 2002 and end of 2005, over three hundred specific cases of serious detainee abuse had surfaced. At least eighty-six detainees have died in US custody since 2002, and the US government has admitted that at least twenty-seven of these cases were criminal homicides.

The abuse did not end after Abu Ghraib became public: US military personnel revealed new cases of abuse in 2004 at forward-operating bases in Afghanistan and Iraq, where prisoners were kept temporarily. Detainees at the Guantánamo Bay detention center, scores of whom now have access to legal counsel, have made new allegations of prisoner mistreatment.

An officer and two non-commissioned officers of the US Army's 82nd Airborne Division who served at FOB Mercury told HRW that detainees were mistreated on the instruction of military intelligence personnel as part of the interrogation process or simply because some soldiers were seeking "stress relief." One of the interviewees said the commonly used methods included keeping arrestees in stress positions for up to two days, depriving them of food and water, giving blows to the head, chest, legs, and stomach, and making arrestees kneel on each other in a human pyramid, etc.

---

[397] *See* Kenneth J. Levit, *The CIA and the Torture Controversy: Interrogation Authorities and Practices in the War on Terror,* http://www.mcgeorge.edu/jnslp/media/01–02/05% 20Levit%20Master%20c.pdf (last visited Dec. 18, 2006).

He also noted that After Abu Ghraib things toned down but continued.[398]

In response, the United States government issued a new Army Field Manual in 2006 to address growing concerns regarding the abuse of detained individuals. Concurrent with the new manual, the Department of Defense released directive number 2310.01E, regarding the detainee program:

E4.1.1 All persons captured, detained, interned, or otherwise in control of DoD personnel during the course of military operations will be given humane care and treatment from the moment they fall into the hands of the DoD personnel until release, transfer out of DoD control, or repatriation, including:

E4.1.1.1. Adequate food, drinking water, shelter, clothing, and medical treatment;

E4.1.1.2. Free exercise of religion, consistent with the requirements of detention;

E41.1.3. All detainees will be respected as human beings. They will be protected against threats or acts of violence, including rape, forced prostitution, assault and theft, public curiosity, bodily injuries, and reprisals. They will not be subjected to medical or scientific experiments. They will not be subjected to sensory deprivation. This list is not exclusive.

E41.4. The inhumane treatment of detainees is prohibited and is not justified by the stress of combat or deep provocation.[399]

The government has many different places to look for lessons on how to respond to the need to establish standards and guidelines for interrogations. From a domestic standpoint, the government can apply procedures appropriate for interrogations in the criminal law paradigm. The treatment of African Americans in the Deep South is not a period in

---

[398] Human Rights Watch, *Leadership Failure: Firsthand Accounts of Torture by the U.S. Army's 82nd Airborne Division*, Sept. 2005, *at* http://hrw.org/reports/2005/us0905/2. htm#_Toc115161401. See also IHF, open letter to U.S. President George W. Bush on the ban of torture, Dec. 15, 2005, *at* http://www.ihf-hr.org/documents/doc_summary. php?sec_id=3&d_id=4167.

[399] *Available at* http://news.findlaw.com/hdocs/docs/dod/detainee90506directive11.html (last visited Dec. 21, 2006).

American history society wishes to repeat. Precisely because it must not be repeated, we can draw on its lessons. Those lessons clearly illustrate the results of an unfettered government not encumbered by legislative or judicial oversight. The sheriff in the back woods and the back seat was the most powerful and frightening manifestation of such a government figure. The lessons of that period are clear: Unlimited governmental power is an evil and must be an anathema to society.

Lawful coercive interrogation seeks to strike a balance predicated on the state's obligation to protect its citizens. To do so requires detaining those who endanger public safety and subsequently interrogating them. In the post-9/11 world, characterized by the absolute determination of terrorists to kill innocent civilians and to cause enormous damage to society, the traditional criminal law interrogation regime is inappropriate.

Interrogators must be granted sufficient means to receive vitally needed information. However, the need for that information cannot be used as a pretext for torturing the detainee. It can, however, be used to justify lawful coercive interrogation measures. Those measures, to be constitutional, must be subject to control and restraint. Furthermore, coercive interrogation does not suggest an anything goes situation.

"Anything goes" is nothing but a justification for torture. A constitutional coercive interrogation regime is based on the Fifth, Eighth, and Fourteenth Amendments. The particular interrogation measures recommended for adopting by policymakers are in harmony with constitutional limits on the executive.

The specific measures are premised on preserving the interrogatees Fifth Amendment right against self-incrimination, respecting the Eighth Amendment prohibition on cruel and unusual punishment, and granting the detainee Fourteenth Amendment due process rights. In addition, the hybrid paradigm unequivocally calls for an interrogation regime in accordance with America's international law obligations.

So, what is the difference between interrogation and coercive interrogation? Coercive interrogation is methods that cause interrogatees discomfort in controlled circumstances. They are not to be implemented in every interrogation, but only when the interrogator so recommends to the Head of the intelligence service.

That is, coercive interrogation measures are available if necessary for limited time periods. They are not a carte blanche for *torture lite* or a washed-over version of the Bybee memos. Rather, they are a reflection of operational reality tempered by constitutional restraint. That operational reality has been imposed on the state by those dedicated to attacking the state. However, that imposition in the aftermath of 9/11 does not justify excess.

In a spectrum-predicated analysis, coercive interrogation is the most appropriate, effective, and legal interrogation regime. It is neither torture nor the traditional interrogation regime. It represents a balanced approach that is fully implemented in conjunction with the hybrid paradigm.

This hybrid model comprised of melding aspects from both the criminal law and POW paradigms and applying it to the current detainees, based on a historical analogy, provides a unique opportunity to formulate concrete policy recommendations—rooted in the law—to decision makers.

The twelve recommendations outlined below—*for all branches of the U.S. government, civilian and military alike*—are premised on the assumptions articulated throughout this book:

Recommendation 1: Coercive interrogation measures may be used **only** to facilitate a specific interrogation provided that less coercive measures have proven unsuccessful and that they be directly related to the questioning of the individual in direct contrast to what transpired at Abu Ghraib and that their effectiveness be measured on that criteria.

Recommendation 2: Detainees, even if not American citizens, are entitled to basic constitutional protections.

Recommendation 3: Torture as an interrogation method is illegal, and the so-called *ticking time bomb* exception is not to be condoned or adopted.

Recommendation 4: The *void for vagueness* doctrine is applicable in determining the limits of coercive interrogation, because the instructions must be clear to the interrogator.

Recommendation 5: Both the spirit and the law of *Hamdan*, holding that the military commissions are illegal, are to be applied when determining the limits of interrogation.

Recommendation 6: The *Bram-Brown* progeny, as developed in this book, articulates clear guidelines with respect to the limits of interrogation where neither threats nor cumulative mistreatment can be permitted to exist.

Recommendation 7: The process of extending constitutional guarantees to the detainees should draw from the Supreme Court's response to the African American experience in the Deep South and the ensuing extension of constitutional rights.

Recommendation 8: Coercive interrogation parameters must be *clearly* established to specifically articulate the five acceptable measures, which are:

(A) The use of uncomfortable chairs (what is referred to as the *stress position*)

(B) Room temperature modification

(C) Sleep deprivation (according to the Geneva Conventions, detainees are to be ensured eight hours sleep in a twenty-four hour period; however there is no obligation that the eight hours be continuous)

(D) Loud music

(E) The placing of hoods (odor free) over the detainees head

Recommendation 9: Interrogation of detainees without protecting the detainees' rights with respect to self-incrimination and due process violates the Constitution.

Recommendation 10: The United States Supreme Court must engage in active judicial review of an otherwise unfettered executive regarding the interrogation methods used.

Recommendation 11: The decision to implement the five measures described in Recommendation 8 require the written authorization of the Head of the relevant security agency. This ensures both responsibility and accountability on the part of senior command and also removes discretionary powers from the interrogator, under enormous pressure from senior command to *deliver the goods*. Senior command will be held liable if harm befalls the detainee if the interrogator acted in accordance with written instructions authorizing implementation of these measures. Similarly, the interrogator will be held liable if harm befalls the detainee if he acted in violation of written instructions

Recommendation 12: The decision to implement the five measures described in Recommendation 8 must be accompanied by written authorization by an on-site physician who is not in the chain of command either of the specific interrogator or senior operational command. The physician will be held liable to the principles both of the Hippocratic Oath and the licensing requirements of the relevant state medical board. The physician will be held liable in the event harm befalls the detainee.

To avoid the mistakes of the past, we need to learn the relevant lessons that history provides, for the interrogation cells of the Deep South are applicable to the interrogation cells of Guantanamo Bay. The coercive interrogation regime effectively strikes a balance between competing interests. In conjunction with the hybrid paradigm it enables the state to conduct lawful and moral interrogations. However, in contrast to traditional criminal law interrogation methods, the measures advocated in this book reflect the reality of the post 9/11 world. Those additional measures, however are tempered by law and morality. The mistakes of history must not be repeated.

INDEX

Abu Ghraib, 3, 50, 60, 80, 99–100
  Arab memory, effect on, 124
  events discussed, 124–26
  and hybrid paradigm, 11, 12
  and policymakers, 102
  publication of abuses, lack of impact,
    157–58
  scandal as example, 152
"Actionable intelligence," 17n20
Active judicial review, 2–3
  Israeli model, 2
Afghanistan
  detainees in, 13, 27
  slippery-slope interpretations, 109
African Americans
  Deep South. See also Deep South,
    African American interrogations
    accusations by white women, 48
    jails, history, 49–50
    lynchings, 47, 50
    Scottsboro Case, 48n109
Aggressive interrogations, guidelines,
  155–56
Alabama, 1930s, 11–12
Aliens
  constitutional rights of, 73n198
  due process, 71
  interrogation standards, 65
    See also Fifth Amendment;
    Fourteenth Amendment
  legal v. illegal, 68
Al Qaeda
  contact with members of, 27

detainees having no connection with,
  48n108
impact of American actions on, 6
and international law, 142
operatives as POWs, 146
and "round up" of suspects, 12
search for members of, 15
American Deep South, 1930s
    See Deep South, African American
    interrogations
Anderson v. United States, 96
Arab Americans, detention of, 6
Arafat, Yasser, 39n90, 40n93
Army. *See* U.S. Army
Ashcraft v. Tennessee, 59–60
Auburn Prison, 139
Aversions, increasing anxiety by use
  of (aggressive interrogations,
  guidelines), 156
Aweis, Nasser, 39n90

Bagram Detention Center (Afghanistan),
  12, 100n258, 130
Banality of evil, 62
Barak, Ehud, 121, 122, 150–51
Barghouti, Ahmed, 39n90
Barghouti, Marwan, 39–42
bin Laden, Osama, 13, 15
"The Black hole," 106
Bram-Brown progeny, 45–62, 104, 160
  Ashcraft v. Tennessee, 59–60
  bright-line test, 53, 55
  Brown v. Mississippi, 55–57, 61

Bram-Brown progeny (*cont.*)
  case law of, 52–60
  detainees, meaning for, 61–62
  and Fifth Amendment, 72
  and Fourteenth Amendment, 73
  and hybrid paradigm, 60–61
  self-incrimination, right against, 69
  Ward v. Texas, 58–59
  White v. Texas, 57
Bram v. United States, 47n105
      See also Bram-Brown progeny
  bright-line test, 53, 55
Bright-line test, 53, 55
Britain
  and international law, 142–43
  torture, definition, 113–14
Brown, Ed, 55–57
Brown v. Mississippi, 55–57, 61, 76
Bush administration. *See also*
      Bush, George W.
  on Article III, 21–22
  coercive techniques authorized by, 108–9
  current combatant paradigm, 29
  Geneva Convention and rights of
      detainees in "War on Terrorism," 25
  legal and moral dilemmas, 121–22
  military commissions,
      establishment of, 27
  "new day of excessive detentions," 70
  9/11, immediate response to, 4, 6
  on treatment of prisoners, 91
Bush, George W. *See also* Bush
      administration
  "bring 'em" statement, 126
  Executive Order (November 2001), 15,
      18–19, 36, 79
  on harboring of terrorists, 15
  military tribunals, 151
  "new day of excessive detentions," 70
  "war on terrorism"
      declaration of, 4, 12
      use of phrase, 14
      use of term "war," 48n110
Bybee, Jay, 19, 99, 106, 124
      See also Bybee memos
Bybee memos, 6–7, 61, 99–100, 112, 128, 159
  analysis in context of 9/11, 123
  disturbing nature of, 122
  implementation of, 124–26

Caroline doctrine, 142–45
Caroline (steamboat), 142–43
Case Western School of Law, 107n272
CAT. *See* 1984 Convention Against Torture
      and Other Cruel, Inhuman or
      Degrading Treatment or Punishment
The Center for Victims of Torture, 108
Central Intelligence Agency (CIA), 7, 156–57
Cheney, Richard B., 6, 136n368
CIA. *See* Central Intelligence Agency (CIA)
Citizens and persons, demarcation, 74
Civil War, military commissions, 17–18
Cleveland Principles, 107
Coercive interrogation. *See also specific topic*
  aversions, increasing anxiety by use of, 156
  defining, 98–102
  dog, presence of, 157
  face slap, 156
  food and drink deprivation, 119
  forced grooming, 155
  isolation, 155
  lawful methods, 85
  loud, cacaphonous music, 85, 119, 161
  modern day, 102–3
  modulation of room temperature, 85, 161
  overview, 85–87
  parameters, establishing, 161
  physical training, 156
  placing sack over head (hooding), 85,
      118–20, 161
  prolonged interrogations, 155
  prolonged standing, 155
  removal of clothing, 156
  slaps, 156, 157
  sleep deprivation, 85, 119, 161
      aggressive interrogations,
      guidelines, 156
  spectrum-predicted analysis, 160
  stomach slap, 156
  stress position, 85, 161
  as torture, 98
  void for vagueness doctrine, 160
  wall standing, 119
Combat zone, interrogations, 101
Congress
  and *Hamdan v. Rumsfeld,* 102, 103
  Military Commissions Act of 2006
      See Military Commissions
      Act of 2006

Constitution. *See also specific amendments*
 Article III, 9, 17, 21–22
Constitutional Center for Rights Report, 106
Constitutional rights
 aliens, 73n198
 detainees, 33
 in hybrid paradigm, 75–77
Convention Against Torture (1984)
  See 1984 Convention Against
  Torture and Other Cruel, Inhuman
  or Degrading Treatment or
  Punishment
Counterterrorism, 99, 127
 "four legs" of, 152
 and human intelligence, 10
 and intelligence gathering, 145
 international law, 142
 operational counterterrorism,
  150, 152
Criminal law paradigm, 23–24, 86–87,
 104, 160
Criminal law principles, application
  regarding threats, 90, 92
Criminal procedure laws, failure of law
  enforcement to comply, 95–96
Cruel and unusual punishment, 131,
 135–36, 139, 159
Cumulative mistreatment
 defined, 85, 92–93
 violative nature of, 97–98
Current combatant paradigm, 29–30

Decency test, 135
Deep South, African American
  interrogations, 45–63, 91, 158–59
 Bram-Brown progeny, 45–62, 104, 160
  Ashcraft v. Tennessee, 59–60
  Bram v. United States, 52–55
  Brown v. Mississippi, 55–57, 61, 76
  case law of, 52–60
  and Fifth Amendment, 72
  and Fourteenth Amendment, 73
  and hybrid paradigm, 60–61
  Ward v. Texas, 58–59
  White v. Texas, 57
 1930s, 11–12
 normative behavior, 61
 "rounding up" of African Americans,
  47–48

torture, 46
and voluntariness, 93–94
Wickersham Commission Report on
  Lawlessness in Law Enforcement, 49
Defense Emergency Regulations Act
 (1945), 36, 38n88
Department of Defense. *See* U.S.
  Department of Defense
Department of Homeland Security
  See U.S. Department of Homeland
  Security and Transportation Safety
  Authority
Dershowitz, Alan, 121, 126
Detainees, 14–21. *See also*
  Guantanamo Bay
 administrative hearings for, 37–38
 assumption of guilt of, 13
 Bram-Brown progeny, meaning for, 61–62
 and command structure, 99–100
 constitutional rights of, 33
 definitions lacking, 26–27
 McNabb, applicability to, 94–97
 "new day of excessive detentions," 70
 "round up" of suspects, 12
 trials of, 37, 91n233
 violations of human rights of, 50–51
Diria, Muhaned, 39n90
Dog, presence of in interrogations, 157
Dred Scott, 65
Due process
 aliens, 71
 in hybrid paradigm, 75–77
 right to, citizens and noncitizens,
  73–74, 159
 voluntariness test. *See* Due process
  voluntariness test
Due Process Clause, 71
Due Process voluntariness test, 54n133,
 62, 75, 87
 articulation by Supreme Court, 94
 as standard, 93–94
 threat, testing impact of, 88–90

Eighth Amendment
 and interrogation methods
  See Interrogation methods, Eighth
  Amendment and
Eisentrager, 67–68
England, Lyndi, 99, 100, 130

Estelle v. Gamble, 134–35, 137
European Commission of Human
        Rights, 111
European Court of Human Rights, 119
Evidence, tainted, 94
Exceptions, 95
Executive Order (November 2001)
    definitions lacking, 26–27
    Military Commissions, establishment
        of, 21–22, 36
    on terror suspects, 15, 18–19, 79
    transfers of detainees, 28
    violations of, 27
Exigency, 95
Ex Parte Quirin, 18–19, 21

Face slap (aggressive interrogations,
        guidelines), 156
Federal Bureau of Investigation (FBI), 5
"Field Commanders," 39n90
Fifth Amendment, 17
    African Americans, Deep South, 46, 51,
        55, 57, 59
    and cumulative mistreatment, 98
    insufficiency of protection, 131
    interrogation standards, applicability
        to both citizens and noncitizens,
        65–81
    self-incrimination, right against,
        69–72
    noncitizens outside the U.S., 71
    self-incrimination, right against, 69–72,
        86, 159
FOB Military, 157
Food and drink deprivation, 119
Forced grooming (aggressive
        interrogations, guidelines), 155
Forced masturbation, 130
Foreign Intelligence Surveillance Act
        (FISA), 9
Fourteenth Amendment
    African Americans, Deep South, 46, 51,
        55, 57
    and cumulative mistreatment, 98
    due process, right to, 73–74, 159
    insufficiency of protection, 131
    interrogation standards, applicability
        to both citizens and noncitizens,
        65–81
    due process, right to, 73–74

Fourth Amendment
    noncitizens outside the U.S., 71
    protection of the people, 67
Franklin, Benjamin, 133

Gaza Strip, 34–35
    aftermath of Six Day War (June 1967), 114
Gaza Strip Military Court, 108n277
General Security Service (GSS), 35–38,
        114–16
    *Public Committee Against Torture in
        Israel v. State of Israel and General
        Security Service,* 117–19
Geneva Convention for the Amelioration
        of the Wounded and Sick and
        Shipwrecked Members of the
        Armed Forces, 111n288
Geneva Convention for the Amelioration
        of the Wounded and Sick in
        Armed Forces in the Field,
        111n288
Geneva Convention Relative to the
        Protection of Civilian Persons in
        Time of War, 34n74
Geneva Conventions, 5
    application to detainees in "War on
        Terrorism," 25–26, 146
    Common Article III, 30, 51, 103, 111
    prisoners of war, 146–47, 153
    on terrorists, 10, 125
German saboteurs, capture of during
        World War II, 18–19
Gonzales, Alberto R., 108, 147
Graner, Charles Jr., 100, 124–27
Grassian, Stuart, 138–39
GSS. *See* General Security Service (GSS)
Guantanamo Bay
    detainees, 12–14, 60
        Category III techniques of
            interrogation, 120
        constitutional rights of, 33
        cruel and unusual punishment,
            135–36
        due process, 79
        In re Guantanamo Bay Detainees, 42
        reports of abuse, 157
        solitary confinement, 130, 138
        transfers of, 27–28
    as territory of U.S., 66
In re Guantanamo Bay Detainees, 42, 67–68

Hamdan v. Rumsfeld
 and Geneva Convention protection,
   51–52, 95
 and interrogation standards, 102
 military issues and enemy combatants
   addresses, 19–20, 30
 and military tribunals, 151, 160
 as modern version of *Youngstown Sheet
   & Tube Co. v. Sawyer,* 2
 response by Congress, 103
 rules, failure to articulate, 42
 self-incrimination, right against, 69–70
Hamdi v. Rumsfeld, 24, 28, 74n198, 75n202
Hamdi, Yaser Esam, 13, 14, 20–21
   See also Hamdi v. Rumsfeld
 and Mobbs Declaration, 24–25
Hamid, Nasser Abu, 39n90
Harman, Sabrina, 100
Haupht, Herbert Hans, 18
HCJ (High Court of Justice, Israel)
   See Israel
Herbert Fuller (ship), 52
High Court of Justice, Israel. *See* Israel
Hippocratic Oath, 161
Hooding, 85, 118–20, 161
Hoover, Herbert, 46n101
 Wickersham Commission Report on
   Lawlessness in Law Enforcement, 49
Hovey, Brevet Major General, 17
HRW. *See* Human Rights Watch (HRW)
Human pyramid, 124, 129
Human Rights Committee, 140
Human Rights Watch (HRW), 157–58
HUMINT. *See* Intelligence information
   based on human sources
   (HUMINT)
Hussein, Saddam, 6
Hutto v. Finney, 135
Hybrid paradigm, 9–31, 153–54
 American Deep South, 1930s, 11–12
   and *Bram-Brown* progeny, 60–61
 application of, 33–43
   to interrogations, 42–43
 and *Bram-Brown* progeny, 60–61
 constitutional rights in, 75–77
 criminal law paradigm, 23–24, 86–87, 104
 and cumulative mistreatment, 98
 current combatant paradigm, 29–30
 defining terrorism, 12–14

 described, 10
 due process in, 75–77
 practical advantages, 11
 self-incrimination, right against, 86

ICCPR, 140
IDF. *See* Israel Defense Force (IDF)
Immigration debates, 67n167
Inbau, Fred, 89, 90
Indifference, deliberate, 135
Insular Cases, 66
Intelligence gathering, 2, 145–46
Intelligence information based on
   human sources (HUMINT),
   10, 15
International Court of Justice, 143
International Criminal Court
 Rome Statute, 126
 torture, definition, 112
International law pertaining to torture and
   interrogation, 141–48
 and counterterrorism, 142
 illegality of torture, 147–48
 intelligence gathering, 145–46
 prisoners of war (POWs),
   146–47, 153
 self-defense exception, 143–45
Interrogation methods, Eighth
   Amendment and, 129–40, 159
 cruel and unusual punishment, 131,
   135–36, 139
 decency test, 135
 indifference, deliberate, 135
 jurisprudence, 132–40
 morality argument, 135
 preconviction individual, 137
 punishment, defined, 137
 solitary confinement, 130, 136–38
 vagueness, 134
Interrogations
 aggressive interrogations, guidelines,
   155–56
 American Deep South. *See* Deep South,
   African American interrogations
 Category III techniques, 120
 coercive. *See specific topic*
 combat zone, 101
 controls on methods, 121
 hybrid paradigm, application, 42–43

Interrogations (*cont.*)
   international law. *See* International
      law pertaining to torture and
      interrogation
   limits, articulating, 84–85, 91, 154, 161
   methods. *See* Interrogation methods,
      Eighth Amendment and
   race-based, 12
   specific methods, 83–104
   standards, applicability. *See* Fifth
      Amendment; Fourteenth
      Amendment
   "ticking time bomb" interrogation,
      115–17, 121, 160
   torture, interrogation-based, 114–15
   U.S. methods, 120
Iraqi nuclear reactor at Osrig, attack on, 143
Ireland, torture, 127
Ireland v. United Kingdom, 107, 119
Isolation (aggressive interrogations,
   guidelines), 155
Israel
   active judicial review, 2
   Barghouti, Marwan case, 39–42
   detainees, death of, 116–17
   General Security Service (GSS), 35–38,
      114–16
      Public Committee Against Torture in
      Israel v. State of Israel and General
      Security Service, 117–19
   High Court of Justice, 38
      5100/94, 117–19
      on torture, 107, 116–19
   Iraqi nuclear reactor at Osrig,
      attack on, 143
   judicial review, generally, 42
   June 1967 Six Day War, 34, 114
   Military Court of Appeals, 35
   National Committee of Inquiry, 114–16
   operational counterterrorism, 150
   Public Committee Against Torture in
      Israel v. State of Israel and General
      Security Service, 117–19
   Supreme Court, 117–19, 150–51
   targeted killings, 150–53
   torture, State of Israel definition, 113
Israel Commission of Inquiry, 107, 121
Israel Defense Force (IDF), 34, 36, 37, 105,
   154n396

aftermath of Six Day War (June 1967), 114
Barghouti, Marwan, arrest of, 39–40
killing of terrorist by GSS member,
   114n304
School of Military Law, 123n349
targeted killing, 153
training video, 123n349

Jails, African Americans in Deep South,
   49–50
Japanese Americans, internment of, 10
Johnson, Douglas A., 108–9
Judge Advocate Generals, 6
June 1967 Six Day War, 34, 114
Jurisprudence
   interrogation methods, Eighth
      Amendment and, 132–40

Karmi, Ra'ad, 39n90
Kennedy, Justice Anthony M., 71, 141
Khalid v. Bush, 67
Koran, ripping of pages from, 124, 130
Korematsu v. United States, 10

Landau Commission, 114n304, 126
Landau, Moshe, 114n304
Loud, cacaphonous music, 85, 119, 161
Lynchings
   African Americans, Deep South, 47, 50

Mackey, Chris, 109
Magid, Laurie, 76–77
Masturbation, forced, 130
McNabb v. United States, 93
   detainees, applicability to, 94–97
In re Medley, 136, 138–39
Military Commissions
   establishment of, 21–22, 27
   mechanism, 36
Military Commissions Act of 2006, 19–20,
   102, 109
   passage of, 30–31
   sufficiency of, 103–4
Military Order of November 13, 23
Miller, Nan, 139
Milligan, Lambden, 17–18
Miranda protection, 9, 42, 86
Mistreatment. *See* Cumulative
   mistreatment

Mobbs Declaration, 24–25
Mobbs, Michael, 24–25
Morality, 135
  teaching, 80–81
Moran v. Burbine, 77
Mowhoush, Abed Hamed, 50
Muhammad, Sheikh Khalid, 136n368
Musalah, Muhammad, 39n90
Muslims, 124, 130

National Commission on Terrorist Attacks
  Upon the United States, 16
National Committee of Inquiry (Israel),
  114–16
New York Times, 99–100
Nicaragua v. United States, 143
9/11
  armed conflict resulting from
    attacks, 23
  Bush administration response, 4, 6
  and Bybee memos analysis, 123
  damaging nature of response, 100
  immediate aftermath, 106, 146, 151
  responsibility for, 7
  "war on terrorism," declaration of, 4,
    12, 15
9/11 Commission. *See* National
  Commission on Terrorist Attacks
  Upon the United States
1984 Convention Against Torture
  and Other Cruel, Inhuman
  or Degrading Treatment or
  Punishment, 80, 146, 147
  definition of torture, 111–13, 123, 126
Normative behavior
  Deep South, African American
    interrogations, 61
Nuclear reactor
  Iraqi nuclear reactor at Osrig, attack
    on, 143

O'Connor, Justice Sandra Day, 28
Office of Legal Counsel, 113
Operational counterterrorism, 150, 152

Padilla, 28, 42
Palestinians, terrorism, 34–35
  killing of terrorist by GSS member,
    114–15n304

trials of detainees, 37, 91n233
Pentagon, report on ethics and military, 80
Pfifer, Jerald, 120
Philippines, planned terrorist attack, 116
Physical training (aggressive
    interrogations, guidelines), 156
Placing sack over head (hooding), 85,
    118–20, 161
Policy makers, role of, 122–23
Political intimidation, means of, 99
Posner, Eric A., 98–100, 102–3
POWs. *See* Prisoners of war (POWs)
Preconviction individual, 137
Prisoners of war (POWs), 146–47, 153
  POW paradigm, 160
Prolonged interrogations (aggressive
    interrogations, guidelines), 155
Prolonged standing (aggressive
    interrogations, guidelines), 155
Protected classes, 33–34
*Public Committee Against Torture in
    Israel v. State of Israel and General
    Security Service,* 117–19
Punishment, defined, 137

Quirin, 18–19, 21

Race-based interrogation, 12
Ramallah, 39–42
Rasul v. Bush, 42, 67
Recommendations, 149–62
  list of, 160–62
Reed, Justice, 95
Reese, Donald, 125
Rehnquist, Justice William H., 61,
    87, 151
Reid, John, 89, 90
Removal of clothing (aggressive
    interrogations, guidelines), 156
Rhodes v. Chapman, 137
Richard, Mark, 124, 127
Rolston, Attorney, 58
Rome Statute International Criminal
    Court, 126
Room temperature, modulation of, 85, 161
Roosevelt, Franklin D., 18
In re Ross, 66n165
Rumsfeld, Donald. *See also Hamdan v.
    Rumsfeld; Hamdi v. Rumsfeld*

Rumsfeld, Donald. *See also Hamdan v. Rumsfeld; Hamdi v. Rumsfeld (cont.)*
    detainees, assumption of guilt of, 13, 147
    and Guantanamo Bay, 12–13
    techniques authorized by, 49n111
    torture, authorization of, 7, 63
    water-boarding, 120, 136n368
    and Working Group Report on Detainee Interrogations in the Global War on Terrorism, 156

Sadistic torture, 121–22
Scalia, Justice Antonin, 141
Scottsboro Case, 48n109
Self-defense exception, 143–45
Self-incrimination, right against, 69–72, 86, 159
September 11, 2001. *See* 9/11
Shaking, torture, 115–17
Shamgar, Meir, 116n311
Shamir, Yitzhak, 114n304
"Shocks the conscience" test, 76–77
Shrim, Mansour, 39n90
SIGINT. *See* Signal Intelligence
Signal Intelligence, 17
Six Day War (June 1967), 34, 114
Sixth Amendment, 17
    noncitizens outside the U.S., 71
    right to confront accuser, 131
Slaps (aggressive interrogations, guidelines), 156, 157
Sleep deprivation, 85, 119, 161
    aggressive interrogations, guidelines, 156
Slippery-slope interpretations, 101, 109
Sofaer, Abraham, 144
Solitary confinement, 130, 136–38
Special circumstances, 95
Stack v. Boyle, 132, 133
Star Chamber, 45, 51
State Department, 144
Stevens, Justice John Paul, 28
Stewart, Justice Potter, 18
Stewart, Raymond, 55
Stomach slap (aggressive interrogations, guidelines), 156
St. Petersburg Declaration (1868), 142
Stress position, 161
Stress relief, 157
Suicide, 140

Suicide bombers as targets, 153
Supreme Court (Israel). *See* Israel
Supreme Court (U.S.)
    aliens, due process, 71
    cases. *See specific case*
    Constitutional protections to citizens, applicability, 66
    Deep South, African American interrogations, 160–61
    and Hamdi, Yaser Esam, 20–21
    limits of interrogation, articulation, 84–85, 91
    1920s and 1930s, 61. *See also* Deep South, African American interrogations
    and voluntariness test, 94

Taguba, Antonio, 50
Taliban, demand made to, 15
Tanzim, 39
Targeted killings, 150–53
Tel Aviv District Court, 39–42
Terrorism
    counterterrorism, 99, 127
        "four legs" of, 152
        and intelligence gathering, 145
        international law, 142
        operational counterterrorism, 150, 152
    defining, 1, 12–14
    and hybrid paradigm, 12–14
    "war on." *See* "War on terrorism"
Terrorists
    harboring of, statement by Bush, 15
    Palestinians, 34–35
        killing of terrorist by GSS member, 114–15n304
        trials of detainees, 37, 91n233
"Third degree," 49
Threats
    application regarding, 89–92
    criminal law principles, 90, 92
    defined, 85
    forms of, 87–88
    lawful threats, delineating, 90
    and voluntariness test, 88–90
"Ticking time bomb" interrogation, 115–17, 121, 160
Titi, Mahmoud, 39n90

"Top of the Pyramid," 124
Torture, 105–28
    authorization of, 27, 63
    British government definition, 113–14
    Bybee memos. *See* Bybee memos
    Cleveland Principles, 107
    coercive interrogation as, 98
    Deep South, African American
        interrogations, 46
    definitions, 110–14
    European Commission of Human
        Rights definition, 111
    functional torture, 121–22
    generally, 83
    human pyramid, 124, 129
    intentions of, 86
    International Criminal Court
        definition, 112
        Rome Statute, 126
    international judicial precedent, 119–20
    international law. *See* International
        law pertaining to torture and
        interrogation
    interrogation-based, 114–15
    Israel High Court of Justice
        on torture, 107, 116–19
    justification for, 106
    nature of, 2
    "necessity" defense, 118
    1984 Convention Against Torture
        and Other Cruel, Inhuman
        or Degrading Treatment or
        Punishment, 111–13, 123, 126,
        146, 147
    policy makers, role of, 122–23
    political intimidation, means of, 99
    sadistic torture, 121–22
    shaking, 115–17
    State of Israel definition, 113
    "ticking time bomb" interrogation,
        115–17, 121, 160
    "top of the pyramid" phrase, 124
    torture lite model, 91, 159
    U.S. Code definition, 110,
        112–13, 123, 126
    U.S. interrogation methods, 120
    water-boarding, 120, 136
Totality of conditions test, 140
Totality of the circumstances test, 75–77

"Troops at Odds with Ethics
    Standards," 80

United Nations, 142
    Article 51 of U.N. Charter, 143–45
    Security Council, 143
United States v. Salerno, 132, 133
United States v. Verdugo-Urquidez, 67, 71
Upshaw v. United States, 95–97
U.S. Army
    82nd Airborne Division, 157
    Field Manual, 101, 158
    Regulation 190-8, 101
U.S. Code
    torture, definition, 110, 112–13,
        123, 126
U.S. Department of Defense, 22, 156
    directive number 2310.01E, 158
    and Mobbs Declaration, 24
    Working Group Report on Detainee
        Interrogations in the Global War
        on Terrorism, 155, 156
U.S. Department of Homeland Security
    and Transportation Safety
    Authority, 6
U.S. Senate's Armed Services and Judiciary
    Committees, 21
U.S. Supreme Court. *See* Supreme
    Court (U.S.)

Vermeule, Adrian, 98–100, 102–3
Void for vagueness doctrine, 160
Voluntariness test, 54n133, 62, 75, 87
    articulation by Supreme Court, 94
    as standard, 93–94
    threat, testing impact of, 88–90

Wall standing, 119
Ward v. Texas, 58–59
"War on terrorism"
    declaration of, 4, 12
    forcing of United States into, 15
    significance of, 13
Washington Post, 106
    "Troops at Odds with Ethics
        Standards," 80
Water-boarding, 120, 136
Webster, Daniel, 142
Welshofer, Lewis Jr., 50

West Bank, 34–35, 36n82
  aftermath of Six Day War
    (June 1967), 114
  trials of detainees, 37, 91n233
West Bank Military Court, 40, 108n277
White v. Texas, 57
Wickersham Commission, 46, 47, 102
  Report on Lawlessness in Law
    Enforcement, 49
Working Group Report on Detainee
  Interrogations in the Global War
  on Terrorism, 155, 156

World Trade Center
  1993 bombing, 116
  2001 terrorist attacks. *See* 9/11
World War II
  German saboteurs, capture
    of, 18–19

Yoo, John, 19, 99, 106
Youngstown Sheet & Tube Ctto. v. Sawyer, 2
Yousef, Ramzi, 116

Zadvydas v. Davis, 71